Literacy and Language Diversity in the United States

Terrence G. Wiley
College of Education and College of Liberal Arts
California State University, Long Beach

Center for Applied Linguistics and Delta Systems

Printed in the United States of America

10 9 8 7 6 5 4 3 2 1

Language in Education: Theory and Practice 87

Editorial/production supervision: Fran Keenan, Joy Peyton
Editorial assistance: Lucinda Branaman, Amy Fitch
Copyediting: Fran Keenan, Elizabeth Rangel
Proofreading: Amy Fitch
Indexing: Lys Ann Shore
Interior design/production: Julie Booth
Cover design/production: Vincent Sagart

ISBN 0-937354-86-4

This publication was prepared with funding from the Office of Educational Research and
Improvement, U.S. Department of Education, under contract No. RI 93002010. The opinions
expressed in this report do not necessarily reflect the positions or policies of OERI or ED.

Library of Congress Cataloging-in-Publication Data

Wiley, Terrence G.

    Literacy and language diversity in the United States / Terrence G. Wiley.

        p.   cm. — (Language in education ; 87)

    Includes bibliographical references (p.) and index.

    ISBN 0-937354-86-4

    1. Literacy—United States. 2. Sociolinguistics—United States.
3. Multilingualism—United States. 4. Language policy—United States. 5. Education,
Bilingual—United States. I. Title. II. Series.

LC151.W45   1996   96-17991

302.2'244—dc20   CIP

DEDICATION:
For Reynaldo Macías

CONTENTS

ACKNOWLEDGMENTS   i

CHAPTER 1
Introduction and Overview   1

CHAPTER 2
**Common Myths and Stereotypes about Literacy
and Language Diversity in the United States**   7

CHAPTER 3
Literacy and the Great Divide: Cognitive or Social?   29

CHAPTER 4
Defining and Measuring Literacy: Uses and Abuses   57

CHAPTER 5
Literacy, Schooling, and the Socioeconomic Divide   98

CHAPTER 6
Language, Diversity, and the Ascription of Status   119

CHAPTER 7
Literacy and Language Diversity in Sociocultural Contexts   135

CHAPTER 8
**Contemporary Bilingual Education Theory
and the Great Divide**   152

CHAPTER 9
**The Impact of Literacy Policies and Practices
on Language Minority Learners**   188

REFERENCES   **199**

INDEX   **225**

TABLES, FIGURES, AND ILLUSTRATIONS

*Table 1. Estimates of People Who Speak a Language
Other than English at Home*   *8*

*Table 2. Relative English-Speaking Ability
of Home Speakers of Non-English Languages*   *9*

Table 3. Estimated Numbers of Non-English Speakers   *10*

*Table 4. Speakers of American Indian and Alaska Native Lan-
guages and Numbers Who Do Not Speak English*   *11*

Table 5. Decennial Flows of Immigration to the United States *13*

*Table 6. European Migration Between the United States and
Europe, 1908-23*   *16*

*Table 7. Which Language Should Individuals
of Mexican Descent Speak in the United States?*   *17*

*Table 8. What Are the Advantages of Being Bilingual
in the United States?*   *19*

Photo of Ellis Island Bible Passages Used in Literacy Tests *59*

Photo of Ellis Island Immigrants Marked with Xs   *62*

NALS Headlines   *83*

*Figure 1. Average Literacy Proficiencies of Young Adults,
1985 and 1992*   *86-87*

*Figure 2. Literacy Levels and Average Literacy
Proficiencies, by Race/Ethnicity*   *88*

*Figure 3. Average Literacy Proficiencies, by Highest Level
of Education Completed and Race/Ethnicity*   *89*

*Figure 4. Differences Between Adults in Various
Racial/Ethnic Groups in Average Literacy Proficiencies
and Average Years of Schooling*   *90-91*

Table 9. Frequencies for Biliteracy in Four Values   *93*

Table 10. Frequencies for Grade-Level Achievement   *93*

Table 11. Literacy by Selected Characteristics   *94*

Figure 5. Percentages of Adults in Poverty, by Literacy Level   *104*

Figure 6. Percentages of Adults Who Received Certain Types
of Nonwage Income or Support   *104*

Figure 7. Chicano Literacy by Family Income 1979   *105*

Table 12. Race/Ethnicity, Language Spoken at Home,
and Progress Through School   *110*

Table 13. Progress Through School   *111*

Figure 8. Surface and Deep Levels of Language Proficiency   *160*

Figure 9. Communicative Quadrant: Range of Contextual
Support and Degree of Cognitive Involvement   *161*

Figure 10. Iceberg Representing a Common Underlying
Language Proficiency   *162*

Figure 11. The Contextual Interaction Model
for Language Minority Students   *163*

Figure 12. The Communicative Quadrant Operationalized   *177*

ACKNOWLEDGMENTS

As my dear friend Meyer Weinberg often reminds me, "One thing leads to another." Many of the ideas for this work took shape after I agreed to join my doctoral adviser, Reynaldo Macías (now Director of the Language Minority Research Center at the University of California at Santa Barbara), for a quick lunch across the street from the University of Southern California in 1986. Reynaldo convinced an otherwise skeptical erstwhile student of comparative intellectual history to assist him in a study on biliteracy. A growing interest in the subject and a dissertation followed. I later realized that, for a time, Reynaldo and a very small number of scholars had carried this issue. Since the late 1980s, a growing chorus has begun to lend their voices to biliteracy studies and is helping to define the field. Particularly noteworthy are Nancy Hornberger and David Spener, whose works are cited in this volume.

In preparing this text I owe a debt to many people, including members of my family (my wife, Eileen, and my sons, Aaron, Kris, and Kevin) who have had to endure the burden that comes with living with someone who attempts to write a book while being employed in the California State University system.

My principal editor, Dr. Joy Peyton of the Center for Applied Linguistics (CAL), deserves special thanks both for convincing me to agree to this project at the 1992 Vancouver TESOL convention and for keeping me on task ever since. Thanks also to Fran Keenan of CAL who coordinated the final editing and production of the book and to Lucinda Branaman and Amy Fitch of CAL for invaluable editorial assistance and proofreading.

Comments and criticisms from a number of colleagues have been very helpful in revising and reconsidering the original draft. These include Professor Reynaldo Macías of the University California of Santa Barbara (to whom this work is dedicated); Professor Gail Weinstein-Shr of San Francisco State University; Professor Magaly Lavadenz of Loyola Marymount University; Professor Natalie Khulman of San Diego State University; Elizabeth Rangel of the Learning Research and Development Center, University of Pittsburgh; and LeAnn Putney of the University of California at Santa Barbara. I am also fortunate to have been part of the Southport Institute for Policy Analysis working group on adult ESL policy issues in 1993-1994 that was headed by Dr. Heide Spruck Wrigley and Dr. Forrest Chisman and included Dr. JoAnn Crandall of the University of Maryland, Baltimore County.

In the process of studying issues related to language, literacy, and diversity in the United States, I am indebted to the work of many scholars; a small number are acknowledged here: again, Reynaldo Macías and Meyer Weinberg, Professor Emeritus, W.E.B. Dubois Department of African American Studies, University of Massachusetts, Amherst (whose two-year tenure at California State University, Long Beach provided the ultimate role model of a productive scholar whose sole agenda is the promotion of equal human worth), Professors James Paul Gee, Nancy Hornberger, Thomas Ricento, Brian Street, James Tollefson, Sandra McKay, Carol Edelsky, Elsa Auerbach, and Katherine Walsh.

Also, I am perpetually indebted to my friend and colleague, Robert Berdan, Joint Professor of Linguistics and Educational Psychology at California State University, Long Beach, whose collegial support, sparring, and second-guessing are much appreciated. I am also appreciative of the ongoing intellectual support of my colleagues, Professors Elaine Haglund, Alice Harris, Yoko Pusavat, J. David Ramírez, Stephen Ross, and Ronald Schmit.

Several individuals provided valuable assistance in preparing drafts of this manuscript. Special thanks are due to Gloria Inzuza-Franco, Molly Dúron-Gómez, and Evelyn Haralson of California State University, Long Beach, and Michael and Trish Lande. Lastly, I would like to thank my current and former students for helping me consider, reconsider, and critique the issues addressed here in my literacy and linguistics seminar and bilingualism seminar.

CHAPTER 1
Introduction and Overview

The development of a schooled literacy that grew up around the development of Western patterns of schooling gradually privileged one kind of literacy. Literacy was not tied exclusively to just one sense of grammatical correctness, as the term grammar school usually suggests to us. Rather the original sense of a common literate discourse was based on a notion of social democracy in the making—a community discourse available to all....We need continually to remind ourselves that other voices need to be heard and not disenfranchised by a single view of a correct language of literacy. (Cook-Gumperz & Keller-Cohen, 1993, p. 286)

In the United States, as in many other countries where the majority of the population is literate and where free public schooling has been available for about a century, illiteracy[1] is portrayed as a social disease. Concerns about illiteracy and low levels of literacy in the United States are not new; they have long been stressed by the popular media and have captured the attention of generations of policymakers and educators. Historically, when the topic is illiteracy, the spotlight is often aimed at non-English-speaking immigrants and ethnic and linguistic minorities. For example, a recent magazine article's title declares: "Dumber than We Thought" and follows with the subheading: "Literacy: A new study shows why we can't cope with everyday life" (Kaplan, *Newsweek*, September 20, 1993). Taking up half of the first page of the article is a picture of an early twentieth-century classroom populated with adult immigrants from various national origins. The connection between the picture and the article's content is not explained. However, its not-so-subliminal message is clear: The "we" who are "dumber" are more likely to be immigrants and minorities, especially language minorities.

In describing literacy problems in this country, both the media and scholars tend to make cross-group comparisons on the basis of race,[2] immigration status, or language background. The achievements of

1

ethnic and linguistic minority groups[3] seem low when compared with "mainstream"[4] Whites. Findings from two national young adult English literacy surveys conducted in 1985 and 1992 (see Chapter Four) indicate that Whites, as a group, consistently score higher than other groups even when adjustments are made for comparable years of schooling. Native speakers of English, those who grew up in an English language environment, generally outperform nonnative speakers of English who grew up speaking another language. In addition, according to recent United States Census data, individuals age 16-24 who speak languages other than English are three times more likely than native English speakers to have not completed, or not to be enrolled in, high school (McArthur, 1993).

Given these and similar findings, one purpose of this book is to probe the underlying issues related to the differences between the literacy performance and educational achievement of language minorities and native speakers of English; these differences constitute the "great divide" discussed in Chapter Three. It is necessary, therefore, to scrutinize the dominant popular and scholarly views governing much of the social and educational policy debates that surround literacy. To do this one must analyze literacy in its traditional context of rhetoric and education, as well as its evolving relationship with the fields of psychology, anthropology, linguistics, sociology, social theory, history, economy, and policy. It is also necessary to consider literacy in terms of other dimensions, particularly race, ethnicity, and social class. Finally, the major popular and scholarly beliefs about literacy and language diversity must be considered.

According to Scribner (1988), three basic metaphors underlie most beliefs about literacy: literacy as adaptation, literacy as power, and literacy as state of grace. Literacy as adaptation holds that literacy is the key to social and economic access and provides a solution to functional English problems of individuals. Measuring and defining English functional literacy, however, are problematic. For example, who defines what it is? How is it to be measured? Does literacy in the native language count? Nonetheless, literacy as adaptation has tended to be the dominant metaphor in debates about adult literacy policy.

In recent years, however, the metaphor of literacy as power has become more visible in the literature (Scribner, 1988). In this sense, literacy is seen as a critical and transformative tool for changing existing social relations. Literacy as power differs from literacy as adaptation in that literacy as power becomes an instrument for *praxis* to promote a more just society (Walsh, 1991). This position has been most notably pursued by Paulo Freire (1970a; 1970b). Valadez (1981), drawing on the work of Freire (1970b), argues that literacy generally, and writing specifically, "empowers" students by breaking the "culture of silence" (see also Edelsky, 1991).

Literacy as power recognizes languages other than English as valuable literacy resources (see Ruíz, 1984). Native language literacy is increasingly seen as a means of breaking cultures of silence for those language minorities who are not literate in English. For those who are biliterate (literate in more than one language), each additional language of literacy provides another channel for voice (see Spener, 1994).

Traditionally, literacy as state of grace represents literacy as a kind of salvation in which the literate person or the *literati* are considered to have special virtues. According to Scribner (1988, p. 77), literacy as state of grace is a metaphor that helps perpetuate the belief that there is an intellectual or "cognitive great divide" between literates and nonliterates. A major focus of this book involves a critique of views derived from this metaphor as it appears in both the general literacy literature (Chapter Three) and as it is reproduced in some of the dominant theoretical constructs in bilingual education theory (Chapter Eight).

Chapter Two introduces and critiques commonly held myths and assumptions about literacy and language diversity in the United States. Because literacy is often confused with English literacy, it is necessary to acknowledge the extent of language diversity in the United States in order to address literacy issues. The second part of the chapter looks at scholarly assumptions about literacy and English literacy that influence the ways in which research questions are framed. The chapter ends with implications for policy and practice.

Chapter Three reviews and critiques major scholarly orientations toward the study of literacy and probes the notion of a great divide between literates and nonliterates, and between those who have acquired literacy through formal schooling and those who have developed vernacular or restricted literacies without formal schooling. The great divide view of literacy is based on the premise that literates have cognitive advantages over nonliterates and that these cognitive benefits result in social and technological advantages for both literate individuals and literate societies. Because literacy is often associated with schooling, it is also necessary to explore this relationship, to determine whether those who are schooled have cognitive advantages over those who are not. After exploring these issues, attention is shifted to the social consequences of literacy wherein the great divide between literates and nonliterates, schooled and nonschooled, becomes more an issue of differences in social practices and social consequences than cognitive consequences.

Chapter Four is divided into four sections: (1) historical motivations for measuring literacy and intelligence; (2) a review of definitions of literacy and of the problems with such definitions for the measurement of literacy, especially for language minorities; (3) an analysis of the strengths and weaknesses of the three common approaches to national literacy assessment, self-reported measures, surrogate measures, and direct measures; and (4) a review of two literacy surveys, the 1992 National Adult Literacy Survey (NALS) and the 1979 National Chicano Survey (NCS). The chapter ends with recommendations for national literacy assessments that are more reflective of this nation's language diversity and biliteracy.

Chapter Five concerns the purported socioeconomic consequences of illiteracy. I argue that the focus on illiteracy as a problem of underskilled individuals lends itself to a blame-the-victim psychology that perpetuates rather than addresses the problem. Assumptions about the relationship between literacy and economic mobility are probed, and the commonly held view that illiteracy is the cause of individual economic problems is linked to an ideological climate in which a perpetual literacy crisis accompanied by an expectation of failure of particular groups is maintained.

Chapter Six considers issues related to the ways in which a lower language and literacy status is ascribed to speakers of so-called "non-standard" varieties of English. It opens with a discussion of status ascription based on language background, the kinds of labels that are routinely used in education programs, and the attitudes often associated with those labels. A discussion follows regarding the status of nonstandard varieties of language and the promotion of literacy. The chapter includes a discussion of African American language and the debate regarding its status and use in schools.

Chapter Seven presents a discussion of the importance of ethnographic studies that focus on literacy in the community, home, and school. It notes the usefulness of studies that reflect the social practices orientation (discussed in Chapter Three). The chapter also under-scores the importance of analyses that include an ideological perspec-tive. Such analysis is needed to demonstrate how the literacy practices and expectations of dominant groups can affect other groups. The chapter ends with a review of three education strategies: assimilation, accommodation, and adaptation.

Chapter Eight revisits issues related to the purported cognitive great divide (Chapter Three) within the context of contemporary bilingual education theory, which has largely been directed toward children. A focus on grade-school education is included because when we look to the future, this population represents the next potential adult educa-tion population, especially if their grade-school education is inad-equate. The central issue addressed is the extent to which notions of an oral/literate dichotomy influence, intentionally or not, some of the popularly accepted notions and assumptions in bilingual education theory.

The final chapter briefly addresses the impact of societal attitudes, education policies, and pedagogical practices on the language and literacy development of language minority adults and children. It revisits the three major orientations to literacy studies and their influence on pedagogical practices. The chapter concludes with sev-eral recommendations.

Further Reading

Crandall, J.A. (1991). Adult literacy development. *Review of Applied Linguistics, 12*, 86-104.

Provides an accessible introduction to many of the issues in the area of adult literacy including definitions, goals of literacy instruction, choice of language of instruction, and assessment and evaluation.

McKay, S. (1993). *Agendas for second language literacy*. Cambridge: Cambridge University Press.

Provides an overview of the various agendas associated with the acquisition of English literacy; incorporates both domestic and international perspectives.

Scribner, S. (1988). Literacy in three metaphors. In E.R. Kintgen, B.M. Kroll, & M. Rose (Eds.), *Perspectives on literacy* (pp. 71-81). Carbondale, IL: Southern Illinois University Press. (Reprinted from *American Journal of Education*, 1984, *93*, 6-21.)

Locates some of the conflicting assumptions within the field by focusing on metaphors that underlie much of the literature on literacy.

Notes

[1] "Illiteracy" (for reasons to be elaborated) is a status-ascribing, stigmatizing term. It is used in this book only in reference to its common usage, not as an endorsement of its status-ascribing function.

[2] For the purposes of this book, "race" refers to an arbitrary social (as opposed to biological) classification of individuals based on relatively superficial physical characteristics such as skin color.

[3] The expression "linguistic minority" refers to a "social subgroup (e.g., a conquered indigenous people, or an immigrant group) the identity of which is defined in terms of language" (Bright, 1992, p. 313). "Language minority" is used as an equivalent expression in this text. In the United States, I would add to this group African Americans, most of whose ancestors were involuntary immigrants (see Gibson & Ogbu, 1991; Ogbu & Matute-Bianchi, 1986), who developed a distinct language variety variously called Ebonics, Black English, or African American language (see Chapter Six).

[4] The notion of "mainstream" needs scrutiny and explication because it often masks the ethnic and linguistic identity and gender of those whose behaviors are implicitly being taken as normative. Sometimes the word "majority" is used synonymously with "mainstream." Because in some regions of the country, White, middle-class, old immigrant background individuals are in the minority, the notion of mainstream more accurately can be seen as carrying a connotation of dominance rather than of simple majority.

CHAPTER 2

Common Myths and Stereotypes about Literacy and Language Diversity in the United States

It may seem rather indelicate...to stress...that biliteracy—the mastery of reading in particular, and at times also writing, in two (or more) languages—is not at all a rare skill among that portion of mankind that has successfully won the battle for literacy. (Fishman, 1980a, p. 49)

A number of popular myths surround discussions of literacy and language diversity in the United States. To adequately discuss literacy, it is necessary to look also at dominant attitudes and beliefs about language diversity. Taken as a whole, these attitudes and beliefs are part of the dominant ideology about language and literacy in the United States, characterized by English monolingualism. Ideology refers to beliefs and convictions that dictate, direct, or influence policy and behavior. English monolingualism reflects an ideology that languages other than English must be aberrant and bilingualism must be unnatural (see Skutnabb-Kangas & Phillipson, 1989). These assumptions underlie much of the public discussion about literacy and language diversity and shed light on much of the education research, policy, and practice directed at language and literacy issues.

The first part of this chapter critiques six common myths or misconceptions about literacy and language diversity in the United States by drawing on both historical evidence and contemporary data. The latter part of the chapter looks at the impact of the ideology of English monolingualism on the way that scholarly issues and research are framed with respect to language, literacy, and diversity. The chapter concludes with implications for policy and practice.

Common Myths

Myth 1: The United States is most appropriately described as an English-speaking, monolingual nation.

Lamenting the cultural isolation and lack of interest by the English-speaking majority in foreign languages in the United States, Senator Paul Simon (1988) has said, "We should erect a sign at each point of entry into the United States [saying]: Welcome to the United States—we cannot speak your language" (p. 1). Although the "we" in this case refers to the majority of monolingual English speakers, the 1990 U.S. Census data indicate that, in that year, there were approximately 32 million speakers of languages other than English (see Table 1). The U.S. Census and the 1989 Current Population Survey (CPS) provide the major sources of information about language diversity at the national level.[1]

Table 1. Estimates of People (Aged 5+) Who Speak a Language Other than English at Home		
	1979	*1989*
Current Population Survey	17.6 million (9%)	23.1 million (12%)
	1980	*1990*
United States Census	23.1 million (11%)	31.8 million (13.8%)

Source: McArthur, 1993, p. 43. Reprinted by permission.

According to U.S. Census data, only 1.8 million (less than 6%) of the 31.8 million persons age five or older who speak a language other than English at home do not speak any English (see Table 3). Seventy-nine percent of those who reported that they spoke no English were speakers of Spanish. About four out of five of the 31.8 million report speaking English well or very well. However, the overall English-speaking ability index, based on an average of a six-point scale (with six indicating speaks "very well") dropped slightly from 4.645 in 1980 to 4.587 in 1990 (Waggoner, 1993, p. 3; see Table 2).

According to 1989 CPS estimates, persons who reported speaking no English were more likely to be elderly and born in Puerto Rico or

Table 2.
Relative English-Speaking Ability of Home Speakers of Non-English Languages

Language	Number	IRESA*	% non-English speaking
Total, all languages	31,845,000	4.587	5.8
Dutch and Afrikaans	148,200	5.449	0.3
Hebrew	144,300	5.422	0.5
German	1,547,100	5.365	0.3
French	1,702,200	5.246	0.5
Yiddish	213,100	5.238	1.0
Asian Indian languages	644,400	5.188	1.9
Filipino languages	898,700	5.121	0.6
Greek	388,300	5.117	1.3
Hungarian	147,900	5.099	0.8
Arabic	355,100	5.082	1.7
Italian	1,308,600	5.078	1.3
Ukrainian	96,600	4.965	1.3
Polish	723,500	4.9051	1.8
Amer. Indian/Alaskan Native languages	331,600	4.943	2.7
Farsi	201,900	4.936	2.7
Turkish	41,900	4.907	2.4
Aramaic	35,100	4.784	4.1
Romanian	65,300	4.604	3.8
Portuguese	429,900	4.511	6.3
Japanese	427,700	4.488	1.8
Haitian Creole	187,700	4.437	3.3
Spanish	17,339,200	4.354	8.4
Armenian	149,700	4.302	8.9
Russian	242,700	4.302	8.9
Thai and Laotian	206,300	4.096	5.1
Vietnamese	507,100	4.071	4.9
Korean	626,500	4.066	5.4
Chinese languages	1,319,500	4.045	8.5
Mon-Khmer (Cambodian)	127,400	3.460	10.8
Hmong	91,600	3.215	14.3

*The IRESA (Index of Relative English-Speaking Ability) is an average of responses to the Census question "How well does this person speak English?" with 6 for "very well," 4 for "well," 2 for "not well," and 0 for "not at all."

Source: Data from the 1990 Census of Population as reported in Numbers and Needs, September 1993. Reprinted by permission.

Table 3.
Estimated Numbers of Non-English-Speakers, (Aged 5+) by Language or Language Group

Language Group	Number	Percent*
Total, all languages	1,845,200	100.0
Spanish	1,460,200	79.1
Chinese languages	111,800	6.1
Korean	33,800	1.8
Portuguese	27,000	1.5
Vietnamese	25,000	1.4
Italian	17,100	0.9
Russian	14,900	0.8
Mon-Khmer (Cambodian)	13,700	0.7
Armenian	13,300	7.0
Polish	13,100	0.7
Hmong	13,100	0.7
Asian Indian languages	12,000	0.7
Thai and Laotian	10,500	0.6
Amer. Indian/Alaskan Native languages	9,100	0.5
French	8,200	0.4
Japanese	7,800	0.4
Haitian Creole	6,200	0.3
Arabic	5,900	0.3
Filipino languages	5,800	0.3
Farsi	5,500	0.3
Greek	5,200	0.3
German	4,400	0.2
Romanian	2,500	0.1
Yiddish	2,000	0.1
Serbo-Croatian	1,800	0.1
Aramaic	1,400	0.1
Ukrainian	1,200	0.1
Hungarian	1,100	0.1
Turkish	1,000	0.1

* Percentages calculated on unrounded numbers.

Source: Data from the 1990 Census of Population as reported in Numbers and Needs, September 1993. Reprinted by permission.

Table 4.
Speakers of American Indian and Alaska Native Languages (Aged 5+) and Numbers Who Do Not Speak English

Language Group	Total #	Total %	non-English speakers #	non-English speakers %
Total, all languages	331,600	100.0	9,100	100.0
Navajo	148,500	44.8	7,600	84.0
Eskimo languages	23,200	7.0	500	5.0
Dakota	15,500	4.7	*	0.3
Apache languages	13,800	4.2	*	0.6
Cherokee	11,900	3.6	*	1.4
Pima and Papago	11,800	3.6	*	2.0
Choctaw and Chickasaw	9,200	2.8	*	0.9
Keresan	8,700	2.6	*	0.5
Tewa, Tiwa, and Towa	7,400	2.2	*	0.3
Zuñi	6,400	1.9	*	0.5
Hopi	5,400	1.6	*	0.4
Ojibwa	5,100	1.5	*	0.1
Crow	4,300	1.3	*	0.2
Shoshoni	2,300	0.7	*	0.1
Ute	2,000	0.6	*	0.2
Tlingit and Haida	1,400	0.4	*	+
Mohawk	1,700	0.5	*	0.1
Cheyenne	1,700	0.5	*	+
Paiute	1,600	0.5	*	0.1
Athabascan	1,600	0.5	*	+
Aleut	1,100	0.3	*	+
Kiowa	1,100	0.3	*	+
Cree	1,100	0.3	*	+
Blackfoot	1,100	0.3	*	+
Arapaho	1,000	0.3	*	+

(*) Fewer than 500 persons (est.)   (+)Less than 0.1 percent (est.)

Source: Data from the 1990 Census of Population as reported in Numbers and Needs, September 1993. Reprinted by permission.

other U.S. territories, or outside the United States (McArthur, 1993). Nevertheless, based on 1990 Census data, slightly over half of those persons (age five or older) who speak languages other than English (the majority of whom also speak English) were born inside the United States (Waggoner, 1993). Many of these were Native Americans (see Table 4).

Based on both current U.S. Census data and CPS data, it is clear that English is overwhelmingly the majority language; however, the presence of nearly 32 million individuals who speak other languages indicates that the United States is more appropriately described as a multilingual nation in which English is the dominant language.

Myth 2: The predominance of English and English literacy is threatened.

English has been the dominant language of the United States since its founding, and there is no reason to assume that it is in any danger of being eclipsed in the near or foreseeable future. Nevertheless, it is equally true that this country has always been linguistically diverse.

Although the dominance of English was established at the time of the first census in 1790, estimates of the ethnic origins of the population can be taken as indirect indicators of language diversity. According to Pitt (1976), roughly 49 percent of the population was of English origin; nearly 19 percent was of African origin; 12 percent was Scotch or Scotch Irish; and Irish accounted for about 3 percent of the total. Dutch, French, and Spanish origin peoples represented an aggregate 14 percent; Native Americans were largely ignored by the U.S. Census.

Through the mid-nineteenth century, a high percentage of immigrants were from predominantly English-speaking areas; however, by the end of the twentieth century, the majority of immigrants spoke languages other than English. Native language instruction and bilingual education were not uncommon in areas where language minority groups comprised a major portion of the local population until the early twentieth century, when legislation was passed mandating English as the official language of instruction (Kloss, 1977; Leibowitz, 1971). By 1909, the United States Immigration Commission reported that among the nation's 37 largest cities, 57.8 percent of children in the schools were of foreign-born parentage. In New York, 71.5 percent of the parents of school children were foreign born; in Chicago, 67.5 percent; and in San Francisco, 57.8 percent (Weiss, 1982, p. xiii). In 1910, there were 92 million people in the United States. Some 13 million people age ten or older were foreign born, 23 percent of whom did not speak English (Luebke, 1980, p. 2).

Contemporary immigration restrictionists point with alarm to the fact that recent immigration has reached historic highs. Although this claim is true in terms of raw numbers, it presents a distorted view of the impact of recent immigration in comparison to that of prior decades. When the total numbers of immigrants per decade are presented as a percentage of the total population, it is apparent that the recent impact of immigration (from 1980 to 1990) is rather moderate in comparison to that of past decades. In the seventeen decades in which immigrant Census counts have been taken, the average immigrant population as a percentage of total population per decade has been 4.4 percent. Immigration rates of the past two decades (at 3.1 percent and 3.6

Table 5. Decennial Flows of Immigration to the United States 1830 - 1990			
Census Count		**Immigration During Prior Decade**	
Year	*Millions*	*Millions*	*Percent of Census Count*
1830	12.9	0.1	0.8
1840	17.1	0.6	3.5
1850	23.2	1.7	7.3
1860	31.4	2.6	8.3
1870	38.6	2.3	6.0
1880	50.2	2.8	5.6
1890	63.0	5.2	8.3
1900	76.2	3.7	4.9
1910	92.2	8.9	9.7
1920	106.0	5.8	5.5
1930	123.2	4.1	3.3
1940	132.2	0.5	0.4
1950	151.3	1.0	0.7
1960	179.3	2.5	1.4
1970	203.3	3.8	1.9
1980	226.5	7.0	3.1
1990	248.7	9.0	3.6

Source: McArthur, 1993, p. 43. Reprinted by permission.

percent) have been below average and are substantially lower than the 9.7 percent high of the 1901-1910 decade, even though the 9 million figure for the decade ending in 1990 is slightly higher than the 1910 figure of 8.9 million figure of the decade ending in 1910 (see Table 5).

Current statistics on immigration and language diversity in the United States, despite these increases, indicate that English is in no danger of being eclipsed by other languages; however, recent fears that the dominance of English is in danger echo concerns that have been raised periodically for more than 200 years (see Crawford, 1991, 1992a, 1992b; Simpson, 1986).

Myth 3: English literacy is the only literacy worth noting.

Just as there is a failure to acknowledge the extent of language diversity in the United States, there is also a general failure to acknowledge literacy in languages other than English. This omission adds to much of the confusion about literacy. Although millions of people are literate in languages other than English, their abilities are ignored. By ignoring literacy in other languages, literacy becomes confused with English literacy. This confusion is reflected in most surveys and measures of literacy, which fail to accurately describe literacy characteristics among language minority groups because they focus only on English (Macías, 1994; Vargas, 1986; Wiley, 1991; see also Chapter Four). According to Macías (1990), there are three patterns of literacy among language minority groups in the United States: (1) native language literacy, which is literacy in one's native language; (2) second language literacy (usually in English), which implies no native language literacy; and (3) biliteracy, literacy in two languages (typically in one's native language and in English) (p. 18). Nonliteracy (i.e., no literacy in any language) is also a possibility.

Although English is the dominant language of the United States and it is important that speakers of other languages learn to speak, read, and write it, it is not the case that English literacy can or should fulfill all of the needs of language minority groups (Fishman, 1980a). When all literacy is reduced to English literacy, the myth that the United States is a monolingual nation is promoted (see Bhatia, 1984; Simon, 1988).

Limited English oral proficiency is commonly confused with illiteracy. Some language minority individuals read and write in English but may not speak the language well; conversely, some who are fluent orally in English are not English literate. The problems of becoming literate in a second language need to be differentiated (1) from the challenges of learning to speak a second language and (2) from initial literacy in a first or second language (Vargas, 1986).

Myth 4: English illiteracy is high because language minorities are not as eager to learn English and assimilate as prior generations were.

A common criticism aimed at recent immigrants and language minority groups is that they are disinclined to learn English or acquire literacy in English because of their loyalty to their native languages and cultures. This myth is based partly on the assumption of the English-speaking majority that languages other than English should be surrendered as a kind of rite-of-passage (see Kloss, 1971). It is also based on the erroneous assumption that all non-English languages are "immigrant" languages (Macías, 1984). However, as indicated above, because approximately 50 percent of the language minority population was born in the United States (Waggoner, 1993), these assumptions are specious. American Indian languages and languages such as Hawaiian are not foreign, but indigenous languages. Thus, it is inappropriate to view all language minorities as if they were immigrants—even if one could accept the assimilationist rite-of-passage point of view. Historically, indigenous languages antedate European and English colonization and the formation of the United States as an independent county. English—in addition to being the dominant national language—is also accurately characterized as an "old colonial language" (as is Spanish; see Molesky, 1988).

It is also argued that recent non-English-speaking immigrants are different from those of a century ago who, it is believed, readily surrendered their languages and cultures. However, a study by Wyman (1993) of late nineteenth- and early twentieth-century European immigrants concludes that a high percentage of European immigrants emigrated back to their homelands (see Table 6). As now, millions of immigrants returned to their homelands while millions more remained here. Then as now, the image of opportunistic, disloyal immigrants fostered resentment among restrictionists, who, in turn, created a past in which former immigrants were somehow more loyal and willing to be Americanized and Anglicized than those of the present.

Table 6.
European Migration Between
the United States and Europe, 1908-23

Race or Nationality	Immigration into U.S.	Emigration from U.S.	Net gain	Percent Emigrating
Bohemian, Moravian (Czech)	77,737	14,951	62,786	19%
Bulgarian, Serbian, Montenegrin	104,808	92,886	11,922	89%
Croat, Slovene	225,914	114,766	111,148	51%
Dalmatian, Bosnian Herzegovinian	30,690	8,904	21,786	29%
Dutch, Flemish	141,064	24,903	116,161	18%
English	706,681	146,301	560,380	21%
Finnish	105,342	30,890	74,452	29%
French	304,240	62,538	241,702	21%
German	669,546	119,554	550,010	18%
Greek	366,454	168,847	197,607	46%
Hebrew	958,642	52,034	906,608	05%
Irish	432,668	46,211	386,457	11%
Italian (north)	401,921	147,334	254,587	37%
Italian (south)	1,624,353	969,754	654,599	60%
Lithuanian	137,716	34,605	103,111	25%
Magyar	226,818	149,319	77,499	66%
Polish	788,957	318;210	470,747	40%
Portuguese	128,527	39,527	89,000	31%
Romanian	95,689	63,126	32,563	66%
Russian	210,321	110,282	100,039	52%
Ruthenian (Russniak)	171,823	23,996	142,827	17%
Scandinavians (Norwegian, Danish, Swedish)	448,846	97,920	350,926	22%
Scottish	301,075	38,600	262,475	13%
Slovak	225,033	127,593	97,440	57%
Spanish	153,218	61,086	92,132	40%
Welsh	26,152	3,376	22,776	13%

Source: Wyman, 1993, p. 11. Reprinted by permission.

What, then, of the current situation? Are individuals who speak languages other than English really reluctant to learn English? Crawford (1992a) notes that in California on the day that Proposition 63 (a proposal to make English the official language of California) passed, "more than 40,000 adults were on waiting lists for ESL [English as a second language] instruction in Los Angeles alone" (p. 17).

Myth 5: Many language minority adults favor English Only policies

Ironically, while language minority populations are sometimes blamed for not wanting to learn English, supporters of "English Only" and official English initiatives boast of support for their positions among language minority groups. Opinion surveys citing support for learning English often focus *only* on English and fail to either ask for or report information regarding language minority persons' desire to maintain their native languages. To probe this issue, it is useful to consider data on attitudes within multilingual communities toward maintenance of languages other than English. Attitudes toward bilingualism and biliteracy are also of particular interest. To date, the 1979 National Chicano Survey (discussed further in Chapter Four) is one of the few national surveys that has provided comprehensive data on such questions. The survey is particularly interesting because it provides data on one of the largest Spanish-speaking subpopulations in the United States. In one question on the survey, respondents were asked which language individuals of Mexican descent should speak in the United States. The results are indicated in Table 7:

Table 7. "Which Language Should Individuals of Mexican Descent Speak in the United States?"	
Only English	3.6%
Mostly English	13.4%
Both English & Spanish	70.6%
Mostly Spanish	9.6%
Only Spanish	2.9%

Source: Wiley, 1988, p. 197.

From these data one could claim that 97 percent of Chicanos surveyed favored use of English. However, English Only advocates could hardly be encouraged that less than 4 percent indicated that exclusively English should be spoken. The great majority, about 93 percent, favored some degree of dual language use. These data illustrate the importance of framing language preference questions in such a way that the middle is not excluded (i.e., that dual language use is presented as an option).

Similarly, in response to the question, "Should children of Mexican descent learn to read and write in both Spanish and English?" the results were solidly affirmative with nearly 96 percent agreeing that their children should learn both languages (Wiley, 1988, p. 205). Another question asked whether parents should discourage their children from speaking Spanish. Only one percent agreed (1988, p. 203). When asked whether children of Mexican descent should learn to speak Spanish, 99 percent agreed (1988, p. 202). These data indicate that the nearly all Chicano parents surveyed supported the goals of bilingualism and biliteracy for their children.

Given the difficulties in acquiring two languages and becoming literate in them, it is reasonable to ask why there should have been such strong support for bilingualism and biliteracy among Chicanos. Responses to a related question help to explain. Respondents were asked whether there were advantages to being bilingual in the United States. Ninety-three percent felt there were (Wiley, 1988, p. 198). There were ten response choices regarding the types of advantages bilingualism offered. Six related to perceived "personal benefits" of bilingualism (pride, self-esteem, and improved communication skills), and the other four concentrated on "practical benefits" (social communication, improved employment, and educational opportunities). Practical benefits were chosen more frequently than personal benefits as the respondents' first choice. Improved employment opportunities was ranked first, selected by 45 percent of the respondents. Improved personal communication was second; more than 26 percent selected this option. Improved social communication was third with more than 10 percent of the sample choosing it (see Table 8).

Table 8.
"What Are the Advantages of Being Bilingual in the United States?"

Personal Benefits	
a. Improves self esteem, personal satisfaction	0.6%
b. Broadens cross-cultural understanding generally	2.9%
c. Increases communication skills	26.4%
d. Improves one's image	1.0%
e. Home/family advantages	0.5%
Practical Benefits	
f. Societal/community benefits	10.4%
g. Improves employment opportunities	45.1%
h. Improves education opportunities or success	5.8%
i. General approval, improves opportunities generally	6.6%

Source: Adapted from Wiley, 1988, pp. 199-200.

Other results from this study confirmed the practicality of these selections. Biliterates, for example, were slightly more likely to be employed (see Chapter Five). In multilingual communities, bilinguals and biliterates have valued skills as translators and as cultural brokers that monolinguals often lack. Thus, the fact that practical benefits were selected so frequently is significant because it is often argued that only English has practical relevance.

Myth 6: The best way to promote English literacy is to immerse language minority children and adults in English-only instruction

One of the more enduring misconceptions is that raising children bilingually confuses them and inhibits their cognitive development. This misconception was bolstered by several generations of biased and flawed research (see Hakuta, 1986, and Chapter Four in this volume). It continues to underlie much of the opposition to bilingual education. It has resulted in generations of language minority parents being admonished not to speak to children in their native language at home, even when parents have little facility in English. Hakuta (1986) contends that this issue involves two key assumptions:

[The first is] the effect of bilingualism—indeed, the human mind—can be reduced to a single dimension [ranging from "good" to "bad"], and that the treatment [bilingualism] moves the individual child's standing up or down the dimension. The second assumption is that choosing whether the child is to be raised bilingually or not is like choosing a brand of diaper, that it is relatively free of the social circumstances surrounding the choice. (pp. 43-44)

It is not particularly helpful to offer linguistic or educational advice to language minority parents when their social and cultural circumstances are not adequately understood.

It is also often argued that the best way to promote literacy is to push people into English-only immersion (i.e., sink-or-swim) programs.[2] However, again, neither the historical record nor the research support this view. The most extreme attempt to implement an English-only education program began after the Civil War when the U.S. government began to pursue an aggressive Indian deculturation and domestication program. According to Spring (1994), deculturation involved "replacing the use of native languages with English, destroying Indian customs, and teaching allegiance to the U.S. government" (p. 18). Education programs were seen as the principal means by which this could be accomplished. Central to this "educational policy was the boarding school, which was designed to remove children from their families at an early age and, thereby, isolate them from the language and customs of their parents and tribes" (p. 18). The schools vigorously taught the Indian children to "'despise every custom of their forefathers, including religion, language, song, dress, ideas, and methods of living'" (p. 206). Among the tactics used "was an absolute prohibition on Native American children speaking their own languages, and those that did were humiliated, beaten, and had their mouths washed with lye soap" (Norgren & Nanda, 1988, p. 186). In spite of these practices, Weinberg (1995) notes that "Indian children were notoriously slow learners of the English language [not because English was difficult to learn, but because] they had been taught from earliest childhood to despise their conquerors, their language, dress, customs—in fact everything that pertained to them" (p. 206). Such tactics were not particularly useful in promoting English literacy. According to Weinberg (1995), these lessons of deculturation were learned more readily than those related to instruction in reading (p. 206).

The impact of English-only policies on Cherokee literacy is particularly noteworthy. In 1822, the Cherokee had developed a syllabary to promote literacy in their own language. Sequoyah, the syllabary named after its inventor, had been enthusiastically embraced and widely used among the Cherokee. It provided the basis for a Cherokee financed and governed school system that allowed instruction through high school. Missionaries working with the Cherokee in 1833 estimated that "three-fifths of the Cherokee were literate in their own language and one-fifth in English" (Weinberg, 1995, p. 184). Cherokee educational progress, based largely on the development of native language literacy, was so dramatic that one observer noted in 1852, "the Cherokee Nation had a better common school system than either Arkansas or Missouri, the two neighboring states" (Weinberg, 1995, p. 185). Crawford (1991) contends the literacy rate was 91 percent during the 1850s. However, by 1906, in the aftermath of deculturation policies carried out by the U.S. government, the Cherokee Nation, its reservations, and school system had been destroyed. According to Weinberg (1995):

> The loss of tribal [Cherokee language] schools spelled the end of the widespread bilingual literacy that had distinguished Cherokees in the nineteenth century. In the [English-only] public schools of northeastern Oklahoma the Cherokee children were served poorly. During the thirty-five years or so after 1932 the percentage of Cherokees who could read English well increased only from 38 to 58. The median school grade completed among Cherokees over eighteen years of age rose from third grade in 1933 to fifth grade in 1952 to the second half of the fifth grade in 1963. "Should a Cherokee move to one of the cities in Oklahoma...he [or she] would encounter a population whose median level of school completion was six or more years beyond his." (pp. 222-223)

The attack on Cherokee language and literacy was not motivated by a desire to promote their literacy or their educational achievement. Similarly, Crawford (1992a) maintains that the attack on languages other than English and on bilingual education today is motivated solely by agendas unrelated to effective literacy instruction.

Current research on the effectiveness of bilingual education[3] indicates that it is generally more effective than the old sink-or-swim approach if students are put into comparable programs with comparable resources. Federally and state-assisted bilingual education programs, however, reach a fraction of the students who meet the eligibility criteria for such programs. Thus, although it is often assumed that lower rates of academic performance can be blamed on bilingual programs, the burden appears to reside more with the English-only programs that do not provide for native language development.

Assumptions Underlying Scholarly Work

Scholars are not immune to the impact of the ideology of English monolingualism. Even in academic discussions about literacy, a number of tenuous assumptions have been made about language diversity. Bhatia (1984) has analyzed these and contends that there are four dominant assumptions about societies that are predominantly monolingual: "(1) in comparison to multilingual societies, linguistic diversity is negligible in ML [monolingual] societies; (2) the phenomenon of monolingualism has a feeding relationship with literacy, whereas multilingualism induces a bleeding relationship...; (3) communication problems are more severe and complex in multilingual than in ML societies..., and (4) the linguistic situation is too obvious to warrant any serious language planning in ML societies."(pp. 23-24)

These assumptions have important implications for literacy policy. An underlying theme is that language diversity is a problem rather than a resource (see Ruíz, 1984). Most disturbing is the assumption that given the dominance of one language, such as English, that the linguistic situation does not require any thoughtful language planning—other than perhaps simply transitioning language minorities into the dominant language. Bhatia (1984) contends that the linguistic situation in so-called monolingual societies is always more complex than is commonly assumed, because monolingualism in any speech community is a myth and because no speech community "is either linguistically homogeneous or free from variation" (p. 24; see also Fishman, 1967). The persistence of the myth of monolingualism reflects the dominant relationship of one language over others. It is also perpetuated by attitudes toward dialect and register (i.e., the appropriate level of discourse), whereby one variety of language, the school-taught standard, is seen as being inherently superior to other varieties. Thus, attitudes toward non-English literacy are often tied to negative predispositions toward nonstandard varieties of English (see Chapter Six).

The emphasis on English monolingualism influences the way in which research questions are formulated by scholars in other ways. For example, if researchers assume that an intergenerational shift from other languages to English is desirable and inevitable, they narrow the range of their research findings by excluding bilingualism. By so doing, they also narrow their research task to one of merely documenting the rate of shift from other languages to English. Veltman (1983), for example, has made a strong empirical case for the unidirectional shift from other languages toward English. Significantly, he contends that not only is there a general language shift toward English, but also that any movement away from English is so negligible that it is equal to zero. This argument is worth presenting in detail.

> There is almost no in-migration into language groups from the English language group. We are not here referring to the numbers of people from English language backgrounds who learn a minority language. Rather, when we speak of linguistic migration into a language group, we require that a person of English language origin adopt the minority language as his principal language of use. This is a rather stringent test....What is important to understand, however, is that in terms of this definition, there is virtually no linguistic in-migration into minority language groups. *A high degree of bilingualism in a minority language does not constitute linguistic immigration.* A linguistic immigrant to the Spanish group is someone who becomes Spanish-speaking in the full sense of the term. He is an active participant in the daily life of the Spanish language group, not someone who simply speaks Spanish, however well. (pp. 12-13, emphasis added)

Veltman's definition of language shift is so intentionally "stringent" that the *bi* of bilingualism does not count; determining the extent of bilingualism in society is excluded. As a result, language shift is presented as an either/or phenomenon in which one is either an English-speaking person or a speaker of another language. By virtue of facility in English, one becomes a statistic in the world of English speakers, regardless of his or her facility in other languages. In other words, the research is designed in such a way that bilinguals are treated as if they were English-speaking monolinguals. In reality, however, some bilinguals, despite their facility in English, drift more toward the world of other languages when their spouses, friends, families, and co-workers use these languages more than English.

Despite general shifts toward English from minority languages, language loyalty and maintenance persist (Fishman, 1966, 1980b). Many factors contribute to language loyalty and maintenance, including economic, political, and personal factors, such as a desire to use language as a means of maintaining one's cultural identity. A monolingual English ideology would seem to support the notion that one can change his or her linguistic membership for whatever reason (e.g., to improve one's economic and social position or to meet the expectations of the majority, dominant, or "host" [from an immigrant perspective] society).

To the extent that language is changeable, the issue becomes one of language choice. However, many factors affect language loyalty. Fishman argues that "[e]thnic newspapers, radio programs, schools, organizations, and churches are not the chief nurturers of language maintenance in the United States; all these institutions may even decrease in number without greatly influencing American non-English-language maintenance..." (1980b, p. 634). More important are "certain central role relationships within the narrower circles (for example, parent-child, cleric-lay) are preserved in the original...language alone. These may be (and usually are) the most intimate or emotional relationships" (1980b, p. 634). Many factors also need to be considered to explain why languages are maintained, not the least of which are physiological factors related to advanced age[4] or to aphasia that cause some individuals to lose facility in English or cease identifying with and using the language (Wiley, 1986).

Some writers (e.g., Gardner, 1985; Lambert, 1974; Schumann, 1978; and Taylor, 1987; see also Baker, 1993, for a review of major second language acquisition theories) have emphasized attitudes (along with other factors) of the language minority groups toward the dominant language as a major factor in language acquisition. What is frequently ignored, however, is the dynamic interaction between language minorities and members of the receiving or dominant society. It is not unusual, for example, for language minority individuals to encounter the irritation of some members of the monolingual English-speaking majority if they are perceived as imperfect speakers and writers of English. This is especially true for adults, because adults are not given the same license as children for deviation from the expected norm. Such encounters with the receiving/dominant society have been found to negatively affect the desire of adults to continue attempting to learn a new language (see Perdue, 1984). This indicates that attitudinal studies on second language and literacy acquisition need to concentrate on the interaction between language minorities and the dominant society rather than only on the attitudes of the language minorities, as is typically the case.

Beyond the issues related to the motivation to learn a new language or to maintain one's native language is the issue of language rights. To mandate that speakers of languages other than English should not use or maintain their native languages is in violation of what the United Nations has seen as a basic human right, that is, the right to use and maintain one's mother tongue. Thus, more is involved than merely whether one *can* change his or her language (see Macías, 1979). Based on the evidence available, most language minority groups in the United States favor both learning English *and* retaining their ancestral languages. These attitudes tend to promote expanding the language resources of the United States.

Implications for Policy and Practice

To determine the full extent of literacy in the United States, it is necessary to make explicit which language or languages are being discussed (e.g., by referring to *English literacy* as opposed to *literacy*, if only English literacy is in question). Most national literacy estimates in the United States are based solely on English, and this tends to inflate the magnitude of the "literacy crisis." They also stigmatize those who are literate in languages other than English (Wiley, 1991). Biliteracy, literacy in two languages, likewise has been largely overlooked in most policy discussions. There is, however, a growing body of literature that deals explicitly with this issue (e.g., Hornberger, 1989, 1990; Hornberger & Hardman, 1994; Kalmar, 1994; Macías, 1988, 1994; Ramírez, 1992; Spener, 1994; and Wiley, 1988, 1990, 1990-1991, 1991). Although biliteracy arguably relates to equal abilities in two (or more) languages, it is unlikely that most biliterates have perfectly "balanced" abilities, because their language experiences and contexts for learning would have to be parallel across languages.

Again, even though literacy in languages other than English is rarely surveyed, it is not uncommon. Thus, claims made regarding the extent of "illiteracy" (meaning English nonliteracy) among language minorities must be re-evaluated, and the assumption that English literacy is the only literacy that counts must be seen as reflective of the dominant ideology of English monolingualism. Whereas English may be the dominant language in the United States, it does not necessarily follow that English literacy can or does fulfill all the literacy needs of language minority groups (see Klassen & Burnaby, 1993). For the elderly, for recent immigrants, and for those who have lacked opportunities to study English, being able to use their native language provides their most immediate means for social participation. For indigenous peoples, native language literacy provides a means of preserving languages and cultures and reversing language shift (see Fishman, 1991). The development of literacy in languages other than English has positive benefits to the majority, monolingual English-speaking population. Senator Paul Simon (1988), for example, is among those who contend that the United States is at a disadvantage internationally in trade, diplomacy, and national security because it has not further developed its linguistic resources.

Further Reading

Crawford, J. (1991). *Bilingual education: History, politics, theory, and practice* (2nd ed.). Los Angeles: Bilingual Education Services.

Details the political history leading to the implementation of bilingual education legislation and its developments since enactment. It also provides an introduction into the research issues related to bilingual instruction.

Crawford, J. (1992a). *Hold your tongue: Bilingualism and the politics of "English Only."* Reading, MA: Addison-Wesley.

Provides an insider's view of local Official English conflicts in California, Florida, and Massachusetts and exposes agendas of the English Only movement while outlining some of the nation's multilingual heritage.

Crawford, J. (Ed.). (1992b). *Language loyalties: A source book on the Official English controversy.* Chicago: Chicago University Press.

A scholarly companion to *Hold Your Tongue*, this work is rich in primary-source documentation.

Simon, P. (1988). *The tongue-tied American* (2nd ed.). New York: Continuum.

Senator Simon helps to explain why the monolingual English-speaking majority needs to be more concerned about developing its linguistic resources in order to promote international trade, diplomacy, and national security.

Spener, D. (Ed.). (1994). *Adult biliteracy in the United States*. Washington, DC and McHenry, IL: Center for Applied Linguistics and Delta Systems.

Includes contributions by a number of important scholars whose research underscores the educational importance of biliteracy and bidialecticism.

Notes

[1] The CPS estimates are lower than the Census counts (by about 22-24%) because they are drawn from an older sampling frame, but they are referred to here since they provide some data that is not yet available through analyses of the Census (see McArthur, 1993, p. 43). Based upon CPS estimates, between 1979 and 1989 the number of persons who speak a language other than English increased by about 40%. There was a 98% increase in the number of speakers of Asian languages and a 65% increase in the number of Spanish-speaking persons (McArthur, 1993).

[2] See Crawford (1991) and Krashen (1981) for a discussion of the limitations of historical and contemporary approaches.

[3] See, for example, Edelsky (1986); Krashen and Biber (1988); Merino and Lyons (1990); Ramírez (1992); and Troike (1978) for research related to children; and Burtoff (1985); Meléndez (1990); and Robson (1982) for studies on adults.

[4] The role of age in language and literacy acquisition is complex. See Singleton (1989) for a survey and critique of the major theoretical views and research on the age factor.

CHAPTER 3
Literacy and the Great Divide: Cognitive or Social?

[If] we believe that literacy is a precondition for abstract thinking, how do we evaluate the intellectual skills of nonliterate people? Do we consider them incapable of participating in modern society because they are limited to the particularistic and concrete? (Scribner & Cole, 1978, p. 449)

This chapter provides an overview of scholarly orientations (or perspectives) toward the study of literacy. Much of the literature discussed here is not specific to language minority literacy issues. Nevertheless, this discussion presents the assumptions that underlie the general field of literacy that are often reflected in the specialized literatures related to second language acquisition, developing literacy in a second language, and bilingual education.

Since the early decades of the twentieth century, literacy researchers have attempted to determine the cognitive effects of literacy. Some scholars (Goody & Watt, 1963; Olson, 1977; Ong, 1982), have contended that literacy produces cognitive effects that make literates and literate societies more logical and analytical. Their conclusions reflect a *cognitive great divide* between literates and nonliterates, which results from the former having mastered the technology of print. The assumption of positive cognitive effects associated with literacy would help explain why highly literate societies and highly literate people appear to have economic, political, and social advantages over those who are not literate or not as literate. In other words, it would help explain the *socioeconomic great divide*. Although a cognitive great divide hypothesis has been the dominant view historically, in recent years a growing body of work has begun to offer alternative views. These alternative views represent a shift in focus from *literacy* (as an autonomous construct) to *literacies* (as socially and culturally embedded practices) (see Cook-Gumperz, 1986; Cook-Gumperz & Keller-Cohen, 1993; Gee, 1986, 1990; Langer, 1987; Street, 1984, 1993; Weinstein-Shr, 1993b).

When cognitive psychologists and anthropologists sought evidence of the cognitive great divide, they encountered a number of methodological and conceptual problems. One particularly troublesome problem was the relationship between literacy and schooling. In contemporary societies, with a few notable exceptions, reading and writing are usually acquired in schools. In most studies on the cognitive effects of literacy, the literate subjects had been to school. In a landmark study, reviewed here, Scribner and Cole (1978, 1981, 1988) tried to disentangle literacy and schooling by studying people who acquired literacy without going to school. The issue is whether the substance of literacy (i.e., the cognitively demanding effects) results from that which is taught in schools, or whether equating literacy with schooling unnecessarily restricts the range of literacy practices and ignores the possibilities of alternative literacies.

Three Scholarly Orientations Toward Literacy

The dispute among literacy experts concerning a cognitive great divide results in part from the different scholarly approaches that researchers have toward literacy. In an effort to analyze and simplify some of these differences, Street (1984, 1993) reduces them to two: the *autonomous* model and the *ideological* model. Street's schema is roughly parallel to what Tollefson (1991) has called the *neoclassical* and *historical structural* orientations in the broader domain of language policy. The work of these authors, along with that of Cook-Gumperz (1986), Gee (1986, 1990), and others, has been instrumental in identifying a major paradigm shift from the autonomous/neoclassical approaches toward the ideological/historical structural approaches.

Three approaches toward literacy are identified in this chapter: (1) the autonomous approach; (2) the social practices approach; and (3) the ideological approach. This schema largely follows Street's; however, the social practices orientation is added to underscore the differences within his ideological model. The differences in these approaches reflect the following: (1) different units of analysis (individual factors versus group factors); (2) different emphases on intergroup power relations; and (3) the role of the social scientist in research and the role of the teacher in education (Tollefson, 1991). In fairness to those authors whose work is positioned in this framework, it is necessary to emphasize that its categories are analytic for the purposes of this discussion. They do not necessarily represent how the authors under discussion would locate their own work.

The Autonomous Approach

The autonomous approach to literacy tends to focus on formal mental properties of decoding and encoding text, excluding analyses of how these processes are used within social contexts. The success of the learner in acquiring literacy is seen as correlating with individual psychological processes. Focus on psychosocial factors is largely limited to studying individual motivation (i.e., one's desire or eagerness to assimilate into the dominant society) (Tollefson, 1991). Those operating within the autonomous approach see literacy as having "cognitive consequences" at both the individual and the societal level, giving literates a mental edge over nonliterates. Cognitive consequences are considered to result from the ability to use print rather than from the social practices in which it is used. An autonomous perspective largely ignores the historical and sociopolitical contexts in which individuals live and differences in power and resources among groups. Significantly, it also neglects the attitudes of dominant groups toward subordinate groups and the way in which the dominant groups treat subordinate groups in school. In other words, it ignores social factors that affect individual motivation to succeed at becoming literate (see also Auerbach, 1992).

The Social Practices Approach

According to Scribner and Cole (1981), this approach differs from the autonomous orientation by approaching literacy as a set of socially organized practices that involve "not simply knowing how to read and write a particular script but applying this knowledge for specific purposes in specific contexts of use" (p. 236). Rather than focusing on the technology of a writing system and its purported consequences, the social practices approach concentrates on the nature of the social practices and technological aspects that determine the kinds of skills associated with literacy. Heath's (1980; 1983) work exemplifies this approach. In particular, her studies of *literacy events* (see Chapter Seven) have helped illuminate literate practices *within* various ethnic/linguistic communities. Tannen's (1982, 1987) analyses of *oral/literate language styles* has also helped confront the paradox of cognitive differences between orality and literacy, and Cook-Gumperz's (1986) emphasis on the *social construction of literacy* has been valuable in schooling practices.[1]

The Ideological Approach

This orientation subsumes the social practices orientation and adds to it a more overt focus on the differential power relations between groups and social class differences in literacy practices. In the ideological approach, literacy is viewed as a set of practices that are "inextricably linked to cultural and power structures in society" (Street, 1993, p. 7). The term ideological is used "because it signals quite explicitly that literacy practices are aspects not only of 'culture' but also of power structures" (Street, 1993, p. 7). Levine (1982), for example, approaches literacy as social practice within a historical context and against which prevailing political and structural realities are reflected. He sees these literacy practices as including activities in which an individual both wishes to engage and may be *compelled* to engage (p. 264). Again, central to both the ideological and social practices perspectives is the notion of *literacy as practice.* The distinction between the two views centers largely on the degree of emphasis each places on how literacy relates to ideology and power relations *between* groups. Freire's work (1970a, 1970b) has helped to inspire both practical and scholarly work involving the ideological perspective and the work of critical pedagogy writers (e.g., Aronowitz & Giroux, 1985; Darder, 1991; Giroux, 1983a, 1983b, 1988; and McLaren, 1989). Many more recent works are also relevant for the ideological perspective—to identify just a few: Auerbach (1989, 1991, 1992), deCastell & Luke (1983, 1986), Delgado-Gaitán (1990), Edelsky (1991), Freire and Macedo (1987), Lankshear (1987), Shannon (1989, 1990), Shor (1987), Stuckey (1991), and Walsh (1991). The perspective of these writers is far from monolithic. However, their work largely reflects concern for the major components of the ideological approach, which Grillo (1989) identifies as including the following:

1. The social practices in which literacy products are composed and communicated;

2. The ways in which these practices are embedded in institutions, settings, or domains and are connected to other, wider social, economic, political, and cultural practices;

3. The organization and labeling of the practices themselves;

4. The ideologies, which may be linguistic or other, that guide the processes of communicative production;

5. The outcomes of utterances and texts produced in these practices. (p. 15)

By taking these factors into consideration, the acquisition and use of literacy is viewed as neither a neutral process nor as an end in itself. Rather, literacy practices are seen as influenced by the dominant social, economic, and political institutions in which they are embedded. Similarly, literacy problems are viewed as related to social stratification and to the gaps in power and resources between groups. Because schools are the principal institutions responsible for developing literacy, they are seen as embedded within larger sociopolitical contexts. Because some groups succeed in school while others fail, the ideological approach scrutinizes the way in which literacy development is carried out. It looks at implicit biases in schools that can privilege some groups to the exclusion of others. Finally, the social practices approach values literacy programs and policies that are built on the knowledge and resources people already have.

The autonomous perspective frames literacy as an individual attribute or ability. Thus, the inability to acquire or demonstrate literacy skills is seen as an individual's failure (see Chapter Five). In contrast, the social practices perspective locates literacy within various social, cultural, and linguistic networks. Different literacy practices are analyzed within the context of these networks, and individual problems are not separated from them (see Chapter Seven). Building on the social practices perspective, the ideological perspective sees failure to develop literacy skills as resulting from unequal social and educational resources, inappropriate educational policies, and culturally and linguistically inadequate curriculum models.

Thus, from the ideological perspective, it is important to explore how differences in literacy and educational attainment function across diverse groups. It also views literacy as more than an individual achievement—it is a social achievement acquired by individuals through social participation, as Scribner & Cole (1978, 1981) and Heath (1983, 1988b) have indicated. As markers of social achievement, however, literacy and educational credentials can be manipulated as gatekeeping devices controlled by those in power (Erickson, 1984; Leibowitz, 1969; McKay, 1993; McKay & Weinstein-Shr, 1993).

The "Great Divide" Hypothesis

This section introduces and critiques some of the major claims supporting the *cognitive great divide* hypothesis. Major proponents of this view are Goody and Watt (1963), Havelock (1963), Olson (1977, 1984), and Ong (1982). According to this hypothesis, there are qualitative differences between oral and literate modes of communication that result in cognitive differences between nonliterates and literates.

Next, Scribner and Cole's West African study (1978, 1981) is reviewed. This study attempted to test the claims regarding the purported cognitive consequences of literacy. It focused on the social practices of those who are not literate, those who are literate but have not been to school, and those who are literate and have been to school. Their trifold focus allowed for analysis of the alleged cognitive effects of literacy across two domains: (1) literacy versus orality and (2) literacy acquired outside school versus that acquired within school.

Background to the Cognitive Great Divide Hypothesis

In human evolution, the development of tools and language are often considered the critical achievements that separate the species from the rest of the animal kingdom. Just as technology has had its impact on human societies, it is commonly assumed that writing, as a technology, has had its impact as well. The development and widespread use of writing systems are often seen as qualitatively separating those societies that use writing from those that do not. A number of claims have been advanced about the cognitive divide between literate and nonliterate societies and between literate and nonliterate people, especially by those scholars who subscribe to the autonomous perspective. Much of the frustration of those interested in proving these claims results from the fact that comparisons of literates and nonliterates have been confounded by schooling; most literates have been to school. Consequently, it is difficult to determine whether alleged cognitive consequences of literacy are actually the result of literacy or of school literacy practices. In other words, do literates have different cognitive abilities because they are literate or because they have been to school? Do the schooled have cognitive advantages, or do they have social advantages?

Orality Versus Literacy from the Autonomous Perspective

Goody and Watt (1963) argued that the development of an easy-to-use writing system (i.e., an alphabetic system) led to major intellectual changes in ancient Greek society, which set the stage for cognitive differences between nonliterate and literate societies. According to Goody and Watt, oral societies were living in mythic time, outside history, which enabled them to maintain an equilibrium; therefore, they could easily transform and forget those elements of tradition that were nonessential. Literate societies, on the other hand, must confront their past beliefs because they are maintained in written records. Goody and Watt assert that when a previously oral society begins storing its records, a schism develops whereby mythic time gives way to historical time. Then, because these societies are unable to readjust the past easily to fit present needs, historical consciousness gives rise to skepticism regarding the authenticity of the legendary past, which, in turn, gives rise to skepticism more generally.

Goody and Watt (1963) contend that, with the rise of skepticism, the desire to test alternative explanations arises. Moreover, they argue that the process of writing is itself more analytic than the process of speaking, because the habitual use of separate, isolated, formal units must be properly applied to convey thought. Consequently, they feel that formal logic probably could not have arisen without the development of writing. In Goody and Watt's portrayal of the rise of literacy, the Greeks are given singular credit for being the inventors of logic. The ancient achievements in logic by the Egyptians, Indians, Chinese, and others are not acknowledged. Thus, a disturbing characteristic of much of the literature related to the historical great divide notion is its Eurocentric focus.

Moreover, Goody and Watt (1963) maintain that oral and literate traditions exist side by side in the modern world in a state of constant tension. According to this view, a residue of the conventions of the oral tradition is seen in texts from cultures where that tradition is more dominant than the literate tradition. Conversely, a literate residue is also posited by David Olson (1977, 1984), who contends that literate parents are more "literate" in their speech and thought processes than less literate parents. He maintains that literacy increases the metalinguistic awareness of literate parents and that this metalinguistic awareness is reflected in their speech and oral interactions with their children. Olson concludes that this literate metalinguistic awareness then helps facilitate the acquisition of literacy among their children.

Goody and Watt (1963) contend that the influence of the literate tradition can be minimized by an undercurrent of nostalgic yearning for the mythic unity of past oral traditions. Oral thinking from this perspective, then, represents the antithesis of literate, logical thinking.

Moreover, good thinking has been often associated with good writing. At least since the 1890s, educators have viewed nonstandard language as a less than logical means for conveying rational thought than standard language. The model for the standard has largely been academic written language (Street, 1984; Stubbs, 1980). As a result, many have assumed that until students have mastered the correct forms of standard academic English, they should not advance their opinions. This emphasis has put speakers of nonstandard varieties of English and speakers of other languages at a considerable disadvantage because more attention is placed on the form of their language than on its content.

Ong (1982) has advanced some of the strongest arguments in support of a cognitive divide. Like Goody and Watt (1963), he contends that the origin of various cognitive differences between literate and oral cultures lies in the inherent differences between communication mediated by print and that which is mediated by speech. His argument proceeds as follows: Speech relies on sound, and sound is transitory. Unlike print, speech cannot be stopped and frozen for observation; it is impermanent. Few would argue that speech and writing are the same, but Ong concludes that the impermanence of sound in oral systems of communication produces qualitatively different cognitive effects from those effects produced by written systems. He sees the restriction of words to sounds as determining both the mode of expression and the mode of thought in oral cultures (Ong, 1982, p. 33).

Following Havelock (1963), Ong contends that thought is intertwined with memory systems to such an extent that mnemonic processing even determines syntax. He argues that thought in oral societies must become heavily rhythmic, requiring "balanced patterns, in repetitions or antitheses, in alliterations and assonances, in epithetic and other formulaic expressions, in standard thematic settings...in proverbs which are constantly heard by everyone" (1982, p. 34). Ong sees the oral mode of thought as depending heavily on conjunctive or additive devices, while the literate mode of thought involves more logical subordination of ideas (p. 37). Following Lévi-Strauss (1966), Ong argues that the oral "savage mind" totalizes.

These purported cognitive differences between oral and literate societies are also believed to have sociopolitical consequences. Extending Goody and Watt's (1963) position, Ong sees oral societies as having a relatively easy time maintaining an equilibrium because they can rid themselves of memories that no longer have relevance for the present or readjust genealogies or other historical accounts to match present purposes. In other words, they have the flexibility to invent or alter the rules as they go along. Literate societies, on the other hand, are bound by written records and dictionaries that allow deeds and meanings to become fixed and be scrutinized critically. This argument seems particularly weak because literate societies are not immune from rewriting their pasts, ignoring their histories, or having information regarding negative or distressful elements of the past censored or suppressed from their histories. Moreover, remembrance of past events tends to vary among cultures. In some oral societies, there is a remarkable emphasis on, and skill in, recalling past events (see Hall, 1959).

According to Ong, oral expression carries a heavy cognitive load of cumbersome, redundant, formulaic baggage that is generally rejected by so-called "high literacy" cultures (1982, p. 38). Gee (1986), however, sees the use of fewer descriptive adjectives in formal (English) writing as indicating its more analytic nature. Gee argues that Ong's assertion that oral devices (such as the overuse of adjectives) are characteristics of the "savage mind" is unfounded. Gee sees this attitude as similar to that of many English teachers who argue that such stylistic devises are inappropriate, or outright illogical, when they are in writing. Whether Ong's views are culture-specific considerations of style (such as the 17th-century British essayist tradition, as Street, 1984, argues), or whether they are more universally held across literate cultures, is a topic worthy of further investigation.

Ong maintains that oral cultures are more intellectually conservative than literate cultures and less open to intellectual experimentation (1982, p. 41). He contends that knowledge in oral societies is difficult to preserve because much energy must be expended to preserve; therefore, tradition and preservation outweigh experimentation. Writing is seen as less taxing because the context of thought can be "stored" outside the mind. The technology of writing is seen as freeing the mind's energies for analysis rather than memory. A significant contention of Ong and other great divide scholars is that oral cultures are more *concretely* grounded in the immediate world of human interaction than are literate cultures, which are more able to deal with *abstraction*. He argues that, unable to store knowledge outside the mind, individuals in oral cultures must ground or contextualize their knowledge in the immediate world of concrete and familiar experience. He maintains that oral cultures are "little concerned with preserving knowledge of skills as an abstract, self-subsistent corpus" (1982, p. 43). Conversely, writing is seen as allowing for more detachment and for more abstract thought. (Olson, 1977, also argues that literacy lends itself to more abstract thought than does orality and that oral language is more context embedded or context dependent than written.) Ong bases much of his position on Luria's (1976) studies of the ability of nonliterates and literates to classify objects. Luria found that those subjects in the study who had been to school for even a short period of time could perform on a much more abstract level than the ones who had not been to school. This tendency toward abstraction is seen as somehow allowing for a greater degree of objectivity through a disengagement of personal identification. According to Ong, distancing oneself is possible for literates, because writing separates the knower from the known. Conversely, he sees communication in oral cultures as being more personal and, thereby, more participatory and less objective.[2]

The Social Practices Critique of the Oral Versus Literate Great Divide

Wright (1980) cautions against the common view that proper form in writing is an indication of logical thinking. Rather, she suggests that this view reflects the "literate" distrust of oral conventions in writing and social class biases concerning propriety rather than clarity of thought. Similarly, the distancing and impersonalization that are manifested in certain types of writing may also be interpreted as stylistic, class-based, or cultural preferences rather than cognitive consequences of writing. From a social practices perspective, Labov (1970) notes that the tendency to distance oneself from a topic through stylistic devices does not necessarily improve the logic of the presentation. Thus, while these authors do not deny that differences between oral and literate discourse exist, they note that differences in style need not necessarily be equated with labels of cognitive "superiority" and "inferiority."

Other aspects of the great divide hypothesis have been questioned by a number of scholars operating within the social practices perspective (e.g., Edwards & Sienkewicz, 1990; Heath, 1980, 1983, 1988a, 1988b; Labov, 1970, 1973; Leacock, 1972; Scribner & Cole, 1978, 1981; and Tannen, 1982, 1987). Scribner and Cole (1978), for example, raise the following concern:

If we believe that writing and logical thinking are always mutually dependent, what do we conclude about the reasoning abilities of a college student who writes an incoherent essay? Is this an automatic sign of defective logic? (p. 449)

This question has strong relevance for practice because it is apparent that the great divide hypothesis is also reflected in the assumptions made by some teachers about their students. Some English teachers and some bilingual educators (see Chapter Eight) tend to hierarchically dichotomize their students based on their purported concrete versus abstract speech, their embedded versus disembedded thought, or their field dependent/field independent cognitive styles. All these dichotomies support the assumption that oral communication is somehow necessarily less abstract than written communication, a conclusion that has been challenged by Leacock (1972) and Edwards and Sienkewicz (1990). These authors cite a number of examples of logical, abstract practices of oral communication, including examples in which non-standard language is used.

The Social Practices View: An Alternative to the Cognitive Great Divide Hypothesis

The paradigm shift away from the autonomous model and the cognitive great divide to the social practice perspective has its roots in studies involving the oral and literate practices of culturally and linguistically diverse groups. Though not overtly ideological in intent, the work of Scribner and Cole (1978, 1981) was significant in pointing to the weakness of the prior autonomous orientation. Their work focused on a multilingual group, the Vai of Liberia. Scribner and Cole's research was motivated by a desire to understand "how socially organized activities come to have consequences for human thought" (1981, p. 235). They were adamant in emphasizing that their framework was neither a grand theory nor a formal model but rather "a practice account of literacy" (1981, p. 235). Despite their modest disclaimers, their approach and conclusions have been instrumental in leading to the paradigm shift in the field of literacy studies toward the social practices perspective, and Gee (1986) and Street (1984) astutely acknowledged the implications of their work for the ideological perspective.

Scribner and Cole (1981) defined *practice* as "a recurrent, goal-directed sequence of activities using a particular technology and a particular system of knowledge." *Skills,* as distinct from practice, are "coordinated sets of actions involved in applying this knowledge in particular settings." *Practices* relate both to whole domains (e.g., law) and to specific endeavors within a domain (e.g., cross-examination), which are "socially developed and patterned ways of using technology, knowledge" and skills "to accomplish tasks" (p. 236).

The key point that Scribner and Cole make is "cognitive skills, no less than...linguistic skills are intimately bound within the nature of the practices that require them" (p. 237).

> In order to identify the consequences of literacy, we need to consider the specific characteristics of specific practices. And, ...we need to understand the larger social system that generates certain kinds of practices (and not others). From this perspective, inquiries into the cognitive consequences of literacy are inquiries into the impact of socially organized practices in other domains (trade and agriculture) on practices involving writing (keeping lists of sales, exchanging goods by letters). (p. 237)

It is necessary to note that some of the scholars whose work has been seen as supporting the great divide have not been satisfied with the way in which their positions have been portrayed. In response to the work of Scribner and Cole, several scholars of the autonomous orientation have attempted to clarify, defend, and expand their position. Goody (1987; see also Olson, 1994), for example, in a critique of Scribner and Cole's research, suggests that their cognitive tests to determine the effects of literacy on individuals are inadequate indicators of the consequences of literacy, which are seen as involving both individual literacy and a society's literate tradition of accumulated knowledge over time.

Orality Versus Literacy

Scribner and Cole (1978) observe that in several important studies (Greenfield, 1972; Olson, 1977) and debates on the alleged differences between oral and literate cultures, schooling became a confounding variable. According to Scribner and Cole (1978), global claims for alleged cognitive differences are based on research that involves the analysis of specific tasks:

> A defining characteristic of the developmental perspective is that *it specifies literacy's effects as the emergence of general mental capacities, abstract thinking, for example, or logical operations rather than specific skills. These abilities are presumed to*

characterize the individual's abilities across a wide range of tasks. Thus, based upon a limited sample of performance in experimental contexts, the conclusion has been drawn that there is a great-divide between the intellectual competencies of people living in oral cultures and those in literate cultures. (p. 451; emphasis added)

Scribner and Cole argued that the great divide debate parallels an old dispute in education regarding whether learning is specific or strengthens the mind in a general way. They conclude that learning is largely skill-specific, embedded within specific contexts. Consequently, literacy instruction (defined as reading and writing skills) and subject matter instruction in general have been taught as discrete skills that can be identified in behavioral objectives and tested. Most of the empirical evidence in support of claims regarding literacy's cognitive effects have been based on specific tasks (as measured by standardized tests). Ironically, then, claims for global qualitative differences between the literate and nonliterate (regarding competence and proficiency) are based on tests that measure rather limited or specific tasks.

School Literacy Versus Literacy Acquired Without Schooling

Again, if there were a cognitive great divide, it would also be desirable to know whether it is a result of schooling (i.e., of specific literacy practices in school) or of literacy in general (i.e., of the global effects of using print technology regardless of context). In order to separate the effects of school-based literacy tasks from literacy tasks that occur outside school, Scribner and Cole (1981) proposed a framework that defines literacy as a practice that is both task- and context-specific. They looked for a society with individuals who were literate but had not been to school, and found such individuals among the Vai. The Vai are a multilingual, rural people. The language of schooling is English. However, Arabic is learned by some Vai to facilitate religious text reading. In addition, some Vai men are able to read and write a syllabic Vai vernacular in a script not taught in school.

Scribner and Cole set up a number of literacy tasks designed to test various cognitive functions associated with literacy. Broadly these were tests of (1) categorization, (2) memory, (3) logical reasoning, (4) encoding/decoding, (5) semantic integration, and (6) verbal explanation. They compared results between those Vai who were literate and had attended English schooling, those who were literate in Qua'ranic Arabic, those who were literate in Arabic, and those who were literate in vernacular Vai but were unschooled. They found that literacy apart from schooling did not substantiate the high expectations held by scholars who subscribe to the great divide view of literacy. Neither literacy in syllabic Vai nor in alphabetic Arabic was found to produce the expected cognitive effects. The expected effects were an increased ability in categorization tasks, a shift to syllogistic reasoning, improved verbal explanations about tasks performed, and facility in the use of categorical labels.

What then of the effects of schooling? Here the results were mixed. Scribner and Cole found that Vai who had attended school generally had an increased ability to produce verbal explanations about the principles involved in performing various literacy tasks. Although these results are consistent with those of previous researchers, this was the first time that schooling effects on verbal performance have been demonstrated apart from the effects on the tasks themselves. The fact that the official language of schooling was English rather than Vai might cause some to speculate on a kind of Whorfian influence of the language itself. Apart from schooling, however, Scribner and Cole found that knowledge of English did not contribute to increased scores on verbalization.

Most significantly, schooling did *not* account for cognitively demonstrated abilities in a number of areas. For example, schooled people were not more adept at solving tasks involving an abstract attitude, such as geometric sorting tasks (confounding factors appeared to affect the findings). Rather, positive cognitive effects appeared to be associated with urbanization, multilingualism, and biliteracy. In summary, attempts to find a correlation with amount of schooling yielded only a partial explanation for cognitive differences and prompted Scribner and Cole (1981) to come to these conclusions:

> Our results raise a specter:...even if we were to accept as a working proposition that school produces general changes in certain intellectual operations, we might have to qualify the conclusion to refer only to students, recent ex-students, or those continuing in school-like occupations. (p. 131)

Moreover, Scribner and Cole concluded that schooling does not appear to be a determinant of performance in tasks involving highly specialized skills. As tasks became less specifically related to either Vai or Arabic scripts, the influences of literacy on task performances became more and more remote (p. 254). As for the alleged cognitive consequences of literacy, they tentatively concluded that school literacy may be somewhat more important as a factor in producing some cognitive effects than nonschooled literacy, but this may be more a result of the school bias toward assessing cognitive skills in the first place. The message would seem to be that one is usually better at what one has practiced.

In a response to and critique of the social practices view, Olson (1994) concludes:

> My own view is that Western literacy can no more be separated from schooling than Vai literacy can be separated from letter writing. Literacy in Western cultures is not just learning the abc's; it is learning to use the resources of writing for a culturally defined set of tasks and procedures. All writers agree on this point. It is the competence to exploit a particular set of cultural resources. It is the evolution of those resources in conjunction with the knowledge and skill to exploit those resources for particular purpose that makes up literacy. That is why literacy competence can have a history. But it does mean that we cannot grasp the full implications of literacy by means of research which simply compares readers and nonreaders. We require a richer, more diversified notion of literacy. (p. 43)

On the face of it, Olson appears to endorse a view of literacy that is more encompassing than that of the social practices scholars. However, literacy retains its centrality and autonomy to such a degree that in "Western" societies it is *indistinguishable from schooling*. In keeping with the autonomous view, it is literacy, not the social uses to which it is put, that remains the primary concern. By equating literacy with schooling, what are we to make of alternative literacies— including those in Western societies—that emerge outside of school contexts?

The Ideological Perspective's Response to the Great Divide Hypothesis

The great divide has also been strongly challenged by those scholars whose views more explicitly reflect the ideological perspective (e.g., Gee, 1986, 1990; Street, 1984, 1993). These scholars tend to see differences between oral versus written styles of communication as cultural and class differences that have unequal social status and authority. Gee (1986), for example, contends that more recent versions of the great divide hypothesis:

> represent a new, more subtle version of the savage-versus-civilized dichotomy: Societies labeled primitive were usually small, homogeneous, nonliterate, highly personal, regulated by face-to-face encounters rather than by abstract rules, had a strong sense of group solidarity. They were sometimes said to be "mystical and prelogical"...incapable of abstract thought, irrational, child-like, ...and inferior.... (pp. 720-721)

Gee (1986) notes the similarity between Ong's (1982) contemporary version of this dichotomy and the positions taken by linguists and educators. He charges that Ong should have been aware that many of his claims regarding the cognitive limitations of nonliterates are applicable to individuals of lower socioeconomic status who are less influenced by school-based literacy than are members of the dominant middle-class. He adds that,

> It is striking how similar Ong's features are to characterizations that linguists have offered of the differences between speech and writing, educators of the differences between "good" and "bad" writers, and sociolinguists of the differences between the way black children of lower socioeconomic status and the way white middle-class children tell stories. (p. 726)

Gee further notes that claims regarding the cognitive effects of literacy tacitly seek to "privilege one social group's ways of doing things as if they were natural and universal" (p. 731). Street (1984) makes a similar point regarding the alleged objective superiority of the essay. In this regard Street and Street (1991) observe,

> We hypothesize that the mechanism through which meanings and uses of literacy take on this role is the "pedagogizaton" of literacy. By this we mean that literacy has become associated with educational notions of Teaching and Learning and with what teachers and pupils do in schools, at the expense of many other uses and meanings of literacy evident from the comparative ethnographic literature. (p. 143)

Street and Street (1991) make a distinction between the notion of pedagogy "in the narrow sense of specific skills and tricks of the trade used by teachers" and its "broader sense of institutionalized processes of teaching and learning, usually associated with the school but increasingly identified in home practices associated with reading and writing" (p. 144). Recently, however, the notion of *alternative literacies* (i.e., as alternatives to school-defined literacies) is receiving increased attention (see Cook-Gumperz & Keller-Cohen, 1993).

In summary, from the ideological perspective, the cognitive great divide hypothesis is largely based on implicit assumptions that mask its cultural and class biases. To make this assertion is not to refute the idea that there are differences in abilities of literates and nonliterates or schooled and nonschooled. Luria (1976), Scribner and Cole (1978, 1981), Vygotsky (1978), and others have found differences. However, the key, from the ideological perspective, is to underscore the necessity to look at differences within the contexts in which they emerge. Again, from the ideological perspective, these contexts are social, economic, and political. The criteria for evaluating purported cognitive consequences are subject to scrutiny because they emerge from particular sociopolitical contexts. Attention is also focused on language and literacy practices both *within* groups and *between* groups, because the norms, standards, and expectations of dominant groups are often imposed—either explicitly or implicitly—on less influential, or less powerful, groups.

Social Consequences of Literacy: Defective Schooling and Biased Practices

From ideological perspective, a major concern involves looking at the historical and contemporary role that schools have played in promoting literacy. The more ideologically focused scholars (among them, Carter & Segura, 1979; Leibowitz, 1969, 1971; Spring, 1994; Weinberg, 1995) are concerned with the social, economic, and political effects of schooling. Literacy and schooling "problems" are not located solely with the student. For example, the real problem is not that language minority groups come from "literacy-deprived" oral cultures or that they lack appropriate home environments to do well in school. Rather, in the process of failing to educate them, schools have become a socially sanctioned mechanism that ascribes a lower status to them (see McDermott, 1987a, 1987b).

Weinberg (1995) maintains that, despite persistent efforts to educate themselves, language minority groups have historically been victims of overt segregation and cultural control through a variety of devices including language suppression, such as that directed at Native Americans (discussed in Chapter Two), and denial of languages other than English for instruction.

Language suppression in the United States reached its peak during the World War I era, when English was mandated as the official language of instruction and bans and restrictions were placed on German and other languages. In many states and U.S. territories, schools prohibited the use of Spanish, Japanese, and Chinese, not only as a means of instruction but even as a means of informal social communication among students during break times (see Crawford, 1991, 1992a, 1992b; Leibowitz, 1969, 1971, 1974). Restrictive practices were continued well into the 1960s and persist in some places. Most importantly, as Leibowitz (1971) contends, the motivation to impose English language and literacy policies on language and other minorities has all too frequently been based on the hostility of the majority toward the minority group "usually because of race, color, or religion" (p. 4; see also Crawford, 1992a).

What have been the consequences of such educational policies? Unfortunately for a disproportionate number of language minority groups, they have been oppressive. For example, the impact on many Chicanos has been particularly harsh. Weinberg (1995), citing the findings of a 1970 memorandum of the Commission on Civil Rights, characterizes the educational experience of Chicanos as demonstrating the following:

> (1) a high degree of segregation, (2) an extremely low academic achievement, (3) a predominance of exclusionary practices by schools, and (4) a discriminatory use of public finance. The pattern is similar to that imposed upon black children, who were regarded by the dominant white society as inferior. Denial of an equal education was a powerful instrument of continued oppression. Those who were not permitted to learn were deemed incapable of learning and could, logically, therefore be confined to a lower status in society. (p.177)

Given the historical context of language minority experience in the United States, underachievement in education by a substantial number of adults is predictable. Consequently, the role of the schools in promoting the general rise of literacy cannot be seen in isolation from sociopolitical ideologies that seek to promote social control (Illich, 1979; Leibowitz, 1971; Street, 1984). Moreover, Collins (1979) argues that the widespread administration of standardized tests of reading and writing have accentuated differences between groups and have thereby reinforced social stratification. Thus, schooling does more than promote literacy or cognitive abilities—it reflects differences in social practices and ascribes different worth to those practices because literacy practices associated with schooling and formal education are typically held to have higher social value than those not promoted by schools.

Erickson (1984) maintains that literacy, defined by school achievement, symbolizes the attainment of culture and civilization. It represents an elite view wherein the literati, well versed in the classics, knowledgeable of philosophy, the humanities, and fine arts, are held in high status. Being literate in this sense carries the connotation of being well educated, and being illiterate, the stigma of being uneducated. In a critique of this status-ascribing function of the schools, he argues that literacy, meaning being lettered, not only promotes prestige of the literate but also promotes strategic power for them because it involves mastery of a communication system. Erickson sees the prestige factor as masking power. It masks the distinction between schooling and literacy such that being lettered implies that one not only has skills, but that one has been to school. Consequently, this elitist view of literacy may also be characterized as a justification for power. Erickson goes on to raise a number of important questions:

> In current public discourse about literacy, are we talking about knowledge and skill in decoding letters, or are we talking about being "lettered" as a marker of social class status and cultural capital? Do we see the school diploma mainly as evidence of mastery of knowledge and skill in literacy? I don't think so. I think that the high school diploma functions, for low SES [socioeconomic status] students, primarily as a docility certificate....This would especially make good sense if ordinary work in most of the company's jobs does not really require literacy as schools define it. (p. 527)

Erickson's analysis has much in common with the social practices perspective. As do Scribner and Cole (1978, 1981), he makes a distinction between literacy and schooling. He also accepts their view that cognitive operations associated with literacy should be seen as "practices" within "task domains." However, Erickson extends his analysis and probes the sociopolitical significance of these differences, which makes his work more representative of the ideological approach. Literacy tasks at work and in everyday life are seen as different from literacy tasks at school; each are defined by a different social context. School tasks are often seen as more cognitively demanding than out-of-school tasks, which are often defined as "context independent" (or as Cummins, 1981, says, "context reduced," see Chapter Eight). From this perspective, fewer cues are available from the environment to aid the learner in negotiating meaning. Erickson (1984) argues that the notion of "literacy practices" requires a careful analysis of the relationship between intellectual capabilities and the social situations in which they are put to use. Despite the attempt to make school exercises about the real world authentic, simulations have limitations. Erickson offers the following example: Mathematical computations performed *in* a grocery store are not the same as pedagogical simulations about what one would do in a hypothetical grocery store. Although the computation skills would appear to be the same in both cases, there is a difference in the social context in which the computation tasks are performed that affects the attitudinal disposition of the learner (p. 529). In the workbook-oriented and skills-based environment of most schools, the learner is not free to negotiate his or her own choices regarding the computation (p. 533). It is not just that a school computational problem is out of context (or in a reduced context); rather, the school exercise occurs "in a context in which the power relations between the student and teacher are such that the student has no influence on problem formulation" (p. 533). Erickson concludes that disproportionate school failure among some groups is related partly to a "schismogenesis," a conflict that is both caused by, and results from, sociocultural and linguistic differences (p. 536; see also Giroux 1983a, 1983b). The differences themselves are not the cause of school failure; rather, failure is "achieved" by a learner's "self-defeating" resistance to being labeled by the school as an individual of less worth than others (p. 538).

> [This] view is at once both pessimistic and affirming. It proposes that children failing in school are working at achieving that failure. The view does not wash its hands of the problem at that point. It maintains, however, that intervention to break the cycle of school failure must start by locating the problem jointly in the processes of society at large and in the interactions of specific individuals. (Erickson, 1984, p. 539)

Given the constraints of their socially defined roles, Erickson portrays both teacher and learner as trapped in an inflexible school culture. More supportive alternative modes of social interaction are possible, but Erickson concludes that, "From a sociocultural point of view, literacy, reasoning, and civility as daily school practices cannot be associated and reordered apart from the fabric of society in which those practices take place" (1984, pp. 543-544).[3]

Erickson calls attention to the work of Scollon and Scollon (1981), who studied the underachievement of Athabaskan Alaskan Natives in written literacy. Scollon and Scollon found that to become literate in the terms of the Western-style school was to lose one's sense of cultural identity (see also Reder & Wikelund, 1993). Thus, the Athabaskan Alaskan Natives resisted school-defined literacy and suffered the consequences of only marginal performance. Most importantly, Erickson's reliance on Scribner and Cole's (1981) definition of literacy as practice helps correct the cognitive great divide notion that school-like literacy tasks inherently involve higher order thinking over nonschool literacy tasks. Debates over language minority groups' disproportionate failure in schools often degenerate either into blaming the victim (i.e., the student and parents) or blaming the schools (see Chapter Five). By locating failure in a complex interrelationship of societal and educational interactions, Erickson (1984) concludes that both "cognitive deficits" and "discriminatory school practices"[4] are insufficient to explain the persistence of failure and lower levels of literacy among some minority groups.

Implications for Policy and Practice

The autonomous perspective offers little in the way of practical advice on how to remedy the cognitive great divide. Olson (1984), for example, contends that literate parents privilege their children with literate speech. Because these parents are competent at using language to describe language (metalanguage), their children's awareness of language is heightened, which in turn is seen as facilitating their children's literacy development. Stated differently, the progeny of highly literate parents have a cognitive head start over those children who must endure a less cognitively embellished heritage. According to Olson (1984),

My conclusion about the role of the metalanguage in literacy is not significantly different from the traditional assumption that the antecedents of literacy lie in the knowledge of the language and that children from more literate homes have larger vocabularies than those from less literate ones, both because their parents have larger vocabularies and because they are exposed to books.... The link, then, between the structures of society and the structures of the individual are to be found in their sharing a common language which, in this case, is the metalanguage for referring to language. It is in this common language that we may find an identity between what is taught and what is learned. (p. 192)

In recent years, such conclusions have been widely advocated and expanded by E.D. Hirsch (Hirsch, 1987; Hirsch, Kett, & Trefil, 1988) and advocates of "cultural literacy" (see Walters, 1992, for a critique). Publications promoting English as the common language and cultural literacy have been widely endorsed and marketed. Their popularity is proof of the dominance of and persistence of the autonomous approach.

However, if educators and schools are to be more responsive to the needs of language minority students, more functional analyses are needed of literacy activities as they relate to social practices, especially in education, including analyses of what people actually do with literacy. It is important to note that Scribner and Cole (1978, 1981) do not question that there is a relationship between specific literacy practices in specific social contexts and cognitive abilities. They do, however, question the assumptions about alleged general, or global, cognitive consequences of literacy apart from a particular context. Following Vygotsky (1978), they caution that the debate over the status of specific skills versus generally transferable, developed abilities "cannot be dealt with by a single formula" (Scribner & Cole, 1978, p. 460).

Along similar lines, Heath (1980) argues that the extent to which all normal people can become literate depends on the functions literacy plays in their lives, a context or setting in which there is a need to be literate, and the presence of literate helpers in the environment. She contends that becoming literate does not necessarily require formal instruction or a sequential hierarchy of skills to be mastered. Heath warns that common instructional practices impose a curriculum that slows down opportunities for actual reading experiences by fragmenting the process into skills and activities alien to the parents' and community's experience. Literacy instruction, when construed and implemented as technical pedagogical skills, requires a level of expertise that leaves parents with a sense of inadequacy and results in their seeing little role for themselves in the process of promoting their children's literacy. Heath (1980) concludes that effective instruction needs to be presented in a more natural and functional context than it has been. She contends that if such changes are made in schools, truly functional literacy instruction could "alter not only methods and goals of reading instruction but also assessments of the accountability of schools in meeting society's needs" (p. 131).

From the ideological perspective, educational practices aimed at promoting literacy always exist within a sociopolitical and sociohistorical context. From this perspective, de Castell and Luke (1983) assert that literacy instruction has been *imposed on society* rather than *derived from it*. This distinction is an important one because the autonomous position assumes that the product of literacy is somehow distinct from the process of acquisition. They conclude:

> Unless the instructional process itself is educational, the product cannot be an educated individual. The context within which we acquire language significantly mediates meaning and understanding in any subsequent context of use. Our analysis has indicated that the processes and materials of literacy instruction have been based historically on ideological codes....We argue that *the whole-sale importation of a literacy model imposed and not locally derived counts as cultural imperialism.* (p. 388; emphasis added)

If literacy practices are not to appear alien to many from language minority backgrounds, then education policy formation and curriculum design must be made meaningful and functional to learners and to the community. Otherwise, literacy skills in the curriculum will be seen as imposed on the community by a school system whose values and motives are alien to it. As the social practices scholars contend, schools need to become more aware of literacy practices within their communities so these practices can be incorporated into the school curriculum. Such inclusion does not preclude teaching those skills valued by dominant groups; rather, it provides a link between the school and the community that imposed, standardized curriculum models are often unable to make. In the words of Erickson (1984),

> Human learning as well as human teaching needs to be seen as a social transaction, a collective enterprise. Society, culture, teacher, and student interpenetrate in the definition and enactment of

learning tasks.... The curricular reform attempts of the recent past attempted to change the academic content of instruction without institutionalizing the fundamental changes in social relations between teachers and students that would enable the kind of learning environment necessary for teaching higher order cognition.... It may be that teachers need more control over their ways of teaching, not less. For classroom teachers to have more authority...would be a change in the allocation of power—social change in the schools as institutions and in society that maintains those schools. From a sociocultural point of view, literacy, reasoning and civility as daily school practices cannot be associated and reordered apart from the fabric of society in which those practices take place. (pp. 543-544)

Whether or not there are cognitive differences between literate and nonliterate people, there are definitely social consequences resulting from the social stigma attached to illiteracy. Language minority populations, whose communication abilities (oral or written) in languages other than English may not be recognized at all, are often unduly stigmatized by a focus on cognitive deficiencies. Although lack of literacy may prevent individuals from achieving their ends, it is important to note also that notions of superiority and inferiority are easily manipulated as instruments of social control.

Further Reading

Auerbach, E.R. (1992a). Literacy and ideology. In W. Grabe & R.B. Kaplan (Eds.), *Annual Review of Applied Linguistics* (pp. 71-86). New York: Cambridge University Press.

Reviews the work of a number of authors who have contributed to the social practices and the ideological views and considers implications for practice.

Cook-Gumperz, J., & Keller-Cohen, D. (Eds.). (1993). Alternative literacies: In school and beyond [Theme issue]. *Anthropology and Education Quarterly, 24* (4).

Confronts explanations for disproportionate educational failure across groups and contains important articles from sociocultural and ideological perspectives.

Edwards, V., & Sienkewicz, T.J. (1990). *Oral cultures past and present: Rappin' and Homer.* Oxford: Blackwell.

This collaboration of a classical scholar and sociolinguist debunks denigrating myths associated with orality. The richness of oral discourse is explored in both classical and contemporary contexts.

Ernst, G., Statzner, E., & Trueba, H.T. (Eds.). (1994). Alternative visions of schooling: Success stories in minority settings. *Anthropology & Education Quarterly 25*(3).

Attempts to transcend the seemingly endless association between minority status and educational failure by validating those examples where students, teachers, parents, and community—in spite of their marginality—have been able to build successful educational endeavors thereby achieving a balance between what Giroux (1988) has called the language of critique and the language of hope.

Gee, J.P. (1990). *Social linguistics and literacies: Ideologies in discourses.* New York: Falmer.

Explores the relationship between orality and literacy. Forwards a sociocultural orientation that links literacies to ideologies (see especially Chapter Three, "Background to the New Literacy Studies").

Gibson, M.A., & Ogbu, J.U. (Eds.). (1991). *Minority status and schooling: A comparative study of immigrant and involuntary minorities.* New York: Garland.

Presents a number of case studies in an attempt to validate the hypothesis that voluntary and involuntary language minority groups respond differently to schooling based on whether it is seen as a positive factor in their folk theory of success.

Ong, W.J. (1982). *Orality and literacy: The technologizing of the word.* London: Methuen.

Provides one of the most articulate *prima facie* cases for the cognitive great divide.

Scribner, S., & Cole, M. (1981). *The psychology of literacy.* Cambridge, MA: Harvard University Press.

A remarkably frank work that reveals many of its initial flaws and false starts. This project was instrumental in debunking many of the assumptions about the alleged cognitive great divide.

Street, B.V. (1984). *Literacy in theory and practice.* Cambridge, England: Cambridge University Press.

Synthesizes common assumptions underlying a variety of disciplines and maps the paradigm shift from autonomous notions of language and literacy to more socially and ideologically based views.

Weinberg, M. (1995). *A chance to learn: A history of race and education in the United States* (2nd ed.). Long Beach, CA: University Press, California State University Long Beach.

Chronicles the historical struggles for equal education and equal access to literacy by African Americans, Chicanos, Puerto Rican Americans, and Native Americans.

Notes

[1] Whereas Street (1984) locates Scribner and Cole's and Heath's work within the ideological approach, I find their work and conclusions less self-consciously ideological and more related to social practice concerns. However, it is largely through the work of Gee (1986), Street (1984), and others that the relevance of this research has come to be appreciated for those operating from an ideological perspective.

[2] Interestingly, distancing is a stylistic characteristic of much scientific writing and academic writing generally, where it is often considered inappropriate to use a personal pronoun. But is it really more objective to write: "The conclusions are...," or "It is concluded...," rather than "I think that..."? Those working from the social practices orientation think not.

[3] Erickson's use of resistance theory to explain self-defeating failure retains some sense that individuals—even if subordinated—still exercise some degree of choice in determining their fate. Such choice appears lost in more deterministic reproduction theory explanations (e.g., Bowles & Gintis, 1976, critiqued by Giroux, 1983a). Erickson's position bears some resemblance to what Ogbu and Matute-Bianchi (1986) have called the "expressive response" of minorities to their "perceived ascribed status." See also Gibson and Ogbu (1991).

[4] Erickson would seem to be referring to overt and intentional discrimination here more than to systematic institutional bias. Prior to the Civil Rights movement and basic changes in the law, it is supportable that discrimination was a sufficient cause of poor educational

performance among groups who were its victims. Because African Americans are more segregated in education today than they were 25 years ago (Kozol, 1991), it is arguable that discrimination, at least in terms of implicit institutional practices, is still a necessary factor—if not a sufficient one—in explaining the persistent disproportionate failure among some groups.

CHAPTER 4
Defining and Measuring Literacy: Uses and Abuses

Who but the person or group involved can really describe what "effective functioning in one's own cultural group" really means? How is a "life of dignity and pride" measured? The basic question may be: Whose needs are served by generalized statistics about the population? (Hunter & Harman, 1979, p. 19)

There has long been an interest in the United States in estimating the nation's literacy, identifying illiteracy in the population as a whole, and locating deficiencies in certain segments of the population. Literacy surveys have been intended as barometers of national well being and as indicators of the capacity of the country to compete with other nations. Employers have looked at literacy assessment as a means of determining the competency of workers. Similarly, the military have relied on literacy and intelligence testing to ascertain the preparedness of recruits. Education policymakers have looked to literacy data for feedback on how well schools are teaching skills considered requisite for participation in the social, economic, and political arenas. There has also been a fascination with measuring intelligence and making cross-group comparisons of IQ based on race, ethnicity, and language background, and it was once thought that bilingualism had a negative impact on intelligence. Unfortunately, results from literacy surveys and intelligence tests are sometimes used more as scorecards of the great divide than as tools to promote an equitable and responsive education system.

Measures of literacy and intelligence are limited by their implicit assumptions about what it means to be literate or intelligent. In national literacy surveys, with few exceptions, there has been a failure to collect data on literacy in languages other than English, and intelligence tests have long been criticized for implicit language and cultural biases. Moreover, standards upon which both functional literacy and academic achievement are based typically reflect the norms of middle-class, monolingual, English-speaking populations. These norms then become imposed on the population as a whole with the result, too often, that those who fail to meet these levels are stigmatized.

This chapter is divided into four sections. The first begins with a discussion of historical motivations for measuring literacy and intelligence. Attention is drawn to how language diversity has been dealt with by surveyors and researchers—some of whom are still revered in introductory testing and measurement texts as "pioneers" in their fields. Many of the earlier measurement efforts were mired in racism. Today, test and survey results sometimes continue to be used to manipulate social and education policies aimed at various groups. A discussion follows of some of the more positive uses of measurement in which language and literacy data have been used to redress past discriminatory practices.

The second section deals with the problem of defining literacy and establishing levels of illiteracy, because literacy measures must have operational definitions. The implications of these definitions for language minority populations are noted. The third section contains an analysis of the strengths and weaknesses of the three major approaches to national literacy assessment—self-reported measures, surrogate measures, and direct measures of literacy. This subtopic is not specifically focused on literacy and language diversity, but it has general relevance to understanding how literacy is measured in any language.

The final section reviews two contemporary literacy surveys: the 1992 National Adult Literacy Survey (NALS) and the 1979 National Chicano Survey (NCS). The NALS study provides recent data at the national level. The NCS is revisited because it is an example of one of the few surveys that lends itself to biliteracy assessment. The chapter concludes with recommendations for national literacy assessments that are sensitive to language diversity and biliteracy and that are designed with input from the populations being assessed.

Motivations Behind Literacy and Intelligence Testing

Historically, literacy surveys have tended to use conventional and functional definitions of literacy in the United States. Widespread interest in measuring literacy and intelligence increased after the turn of the 20th century during a time of xenophobia toward non-English-speaking immigrants and racism toward African Americans and other racial minority groups. Literacy and intelligence test findings were repeatedly used to make cross-group comparisons, usually with race and ethnicity as the determining categories. With few exceptions, most attempts at national assessment have been conducted in English only. Literacy and prior schooling were largely ignored as factors in claims made for "innate" differences between groups. Literacy became a gatekeeping tool to bar immigrants from entering the United States when nativists began clamoring for restrictions (McKay & Weinstein-Shr, 1993). Literacy requirements were used to discriminate against African Americans at the polls (Leibowitz, 1969). Immigrant literacy-test bills were passed in Congress in 1896, 1904, and 1916. All received presidential vetoes and failed to become law until 1917, when wartime xenophobia bolstered support for restrictionism, and a bill was passed supporting a literacy test over President Wilson's veto. This literacy test required all immigrants 16 or more years of age to read a short passage from the Bible in their native language (Chermayeff, Wasserman, & Shapiro, 1991). During World War I, reports of high levels of failure by Army recruits on entrance tests became well publicized. This resulted in suspicion that U.S. Census data tended to overestimate the literacy rate for the nation (Venezky, Kaestle, & Sum, 1987). As a result, a massive testing campaign was initiated.

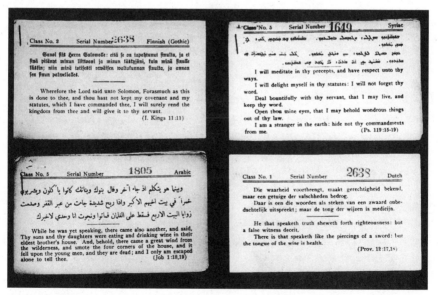

Cards with Bible passages in various languages that were used to test immigrants' literacy at Ellis Island, circa 1917.

Source: Chermayeff, Wasserman, & Shapiro, 1991, p. 121. Reprinted by permission.

During this period, intelligence testing became a national obsession. Corporate foundations underwrote studies on the inheritance of mental traits, eugenics, and race betterment. A committee on the heredity of feeble-mindedness included prominent researchers such as Edward Thorndike, who, with Lewis Terman of Stanford University, another pioneer in testing and measurement, supported sterilization of the feeble-minded. Thorndike and his student, Henry Garret, believed that those with lesser intelligence, as measured by standardized tests, were morally inferior. Although English literacy and some formal schooling were requisite for intelligence testing, researchers of the period paid little heed to language, class, and culture bias and presented their findings as "objective," "empirical" evidence that those of Anglo-Saxon origin were of "superior" intellectual and moral stock. In the United States, the so-called "scientific testing" movement was entangled in racism and linguicism (Karier, 1973; see also Gould, 1981).

In 1910, H. H. Goddard, who ran a school for "feeble-minded" children, translated Alfred Binet's intelligence test from French to English (Hakuta, 1986, p. 20). According to Mensh and Mensh (1991), although Binet originally intended to construct a test for classifying unsuccessful school performers of inferior intelligence, "it was impossible for him to create one that would do only that, i.e., function at only one extreme" (p. 23). Therefore, his test utilized "concepts of inferiority and superiority—each which requires the other" as "a device for universal ranking according to alleged mental worth" (p. 23). It was Binet's dream that his test would lead to "'a future where the social sphere would be better organized'" with each person working according to his or her know aptitude "'in such a way that no particle of psychic force should be lost for society. That would be an ideal city'" (cited in Mensh and Mensh, 1991, p. 23). In 1908, Elliot declared that "teachers of the elementary school ought to be able to sort the pupils by their *probable destinies*...[because] there was no more important function." (Kliebard, 1986, p. 123, emphasis added). Through "scientific" assessment, students could be tracked into manual training education or a college track. There was no sense in throwing good education money after those whose "probable destinies" could be divined in advance.

In 1916 Terman revised the Binet test and called it the Stanford-Binet. According to Weinberg (1983) it was normed on "1,000 white children of average social status born in California" (p. 60). Terman believed that

IQ tests would ultimately reveal "enormously significant racial differences in general intelligence, which cannot be wiped out by any scheme of mental culture" (Weinberg, 1983, p. 60). This view was diametrically opposed to that of Binet, who saw intelligence as a practical activity involving "the faculty of adapting oneself" (p. 59). Moreover, he "regarded with 'brutal pessimism' the view of intelligence as an unchangeable quantity" (p. 59).

It is necessary to remember that the rise of the testing movement and the push from expanded uses of restrictive literacy requirements coincided with the period of record immigration (as percentage of total population) and that a majority of the immigrants spoke languages other than English. Against this background, Goddard took the English-language version of the Stanford-Binet to Ellis Island in 1917 and administered it to newly arrived immigrants. In one test, he classified 25 of 30 adult Jews as "feeble-minded." "Following Goddard's lead, there was an almost immediate explosion of new tests and research" (Hakuta, 1986, p. 20). About nine percent of Ellis Island immigrants during this period were referred for mental testing to determine whether they were mentally impaired. Immigrants were put into inspection lines where they were inspected for behavior that might indicate mental instabilities that would burden the receiving society. Telling symptoms included "facetiousness, nail biting, smiling, or other eccentricities" such as an Englishman reacting to a question as if he were an Irishman (Chermayeff, Wasserman, & Shapiro, 1991, p. 137). If observed as acting in such a way,

> They were quickly chalked with an X, removed from the line, and taken to another room for an examination. There, doctors conducted a preliminary interview, asking immigrants about themselves and their families, where they came from, or similar questions. Perhaps they would ask an immigrant to solve a simple arithmetic problem or count backward from 20 to 1 or complete a puzzle. (Chermayeff, Wasserman, & Shapiro, 1991, p. 139)

One Polish immigrant woman noted the confusion experienced by immigrants during such interrogation. "They asked us questions. 'How much is two and one? How much is two and two?' But the next young girl... [was asked] 'How do you wash stairs, from the top or from the bottom?' She says, 'I don't go to America to wash stairs'" (Chermayeff, Wasserman, & Shapiro, 1991, p. 138).

Immigrants, clearly marked with Xs indicating suspected mental impairment, wait to be examined at Ellis Island.
Source: Chermayeff, Wasserman, & Shapiro, 1991, p. 138. Reprinted by permission.

Some of the immigration officers expressed skepticism about the mental testing because many confounding factors such as the "immigrants' diverse backgrounds, languages, cultures, and levels of education...affected their behavior" to such an extent that one "doctor recalled that the process of identifying mental incompetence...was 'always haphazard,' and that often fully competent people were held for examination" (Chermayeff, Wasserman & Shapiro, 1991, p. 139).

Meanwhile, on the military front, Lewis Terman sought to extend the use of the Stanford-Binet test even further and, with Goddard, convinced the army to test nearly two million draftees. Two English language tests were constructed: one for those who could read and write and another for "illiterates" and "foreigners" (who received instructions in pantomime). Comparisons among ethnic groups were made on the basis of literacy, national origin, and race. Europeans were racially classified into Nordics, Alpines, and Mediterranean races (Hakuta, 1986, p. 20), with Nordics at the top and Mediterraneans (Greeks and Italians) at the bottom. Italians, part of the Mediterranean group, were considered a "superior sort of Chinaman" (Wyman, 1993, p. 100).

In this peculiar scheme of classification, only English literacy counted as literacy. "Illiterates" and "foreigners" were lumped together. There was no serious consideration of native language literacy or prior schooling as factors influencing the results. Length of residency in the United States *was* a consideration, however. The test results were popularized in Carl Brigham's (1923) *A Study in American Intelligence*. The study concluded that immigrants of Alpine and Mediterranean races were inferior to the Nordic race. The study also found improved test scores based on length of residency in the United States, which, as Hakuta (1986) notes, "is obviously related to the knowledge of English and the level of acculturation" to U.S. society (p. 21). Nevertheless, Brigham discounted these biases. He also ignored the influence of non-English literacy and prior schooling. Imagine how bizarre the pantomimed test must have seemed to those newly arrived immigrants who were unfamiliar with such testing and who could not have suspected the racist assumptions behind the attempt to measure their intelligence. Because the data indicated that non-English-speaking Nordics had outperformed non-English-speaking Mediterraneans, Brigham concluded that the "underlying cause" of these differences was race rather than language (Hakuta, 1986, p. 21; see also Brigham, 1923, p. 174). Preoccupied with attempting to prove his racial differences hypotheses, Brigham ignored the possible influence of prior schooling, which would have involved practice in taking tests. Thus, in addition to a language bias, there was also a schooling bias. Had Mediterraneans out-performed Nordics, it is hard to image that Brigham would not have pursued the salience of other factors than race in his analysis of the data.

Brigham's racialization of the Stanford-Binet test data (see Chapter Five) proved beneficial for the political agenda of nativists and eugenicists:

In 1924, Congress passed a general immigration statute that established quotas for each country of origin. Immigration from favored countries—the "Nordiks"[sic]—were given higher quotas while those from "inferior" countries in eastern and southern Europe entered under lower quotas. Of the 27 states with sterilization laws by 1930, 20 had been passed since 1918, the end of World War I. Works by eugenicists such as Brigham were an important factor in the passage of this legislation. (Weinberg, 1983, p. 61)

In 1922, Army intelligence tests were critiqued by Alexander, who concluded that they were more tests of what one had learned in school than tests of aptitude for learning. According to Weinberg (1983), in 1924, a young African-American student at the University of Chicago, Horace Mann Bond, followed up on Alexander's studies and found a high correlation (.74) between schooling and intelligence, which helped confirm Alexander's conclusions. Bond further found that African Americans in Illinois averaged higher scores than Whites from four southern states. Speculating on the implications of these findings, Bond noted, "One wonders how Mr. Brigham squares the facts of southern white deficiency with his theory" (Weinberg, 1983, p. 63). Weinberg adds, "Would Brigham in other words claim that higher scoring northern whites had migrated selectively? Or, would he concede the overwhelming influence of differential opportunities," because leading testers of the day "such as Terman contended that racial status (as opposed to racial genetics) played only a minor role in the scores?" (p. 63). Despite these critiques, Brigham's work held sway during the 1920s, a period marked by "lynchings and comparatively low educational opportunities for blacks in the South...oppressions [that] were ignored by theorists of genetic inferiority" (p. 63).

In summary, the push to measure literacy and intelligence in the early decades of the twentieth century emerged during a period of xenophobia toward foreigners and racial prejudice toward African Americans and other language minorities. Some of the most famous founders of the modern testing and measurement movement used their purportedly "scientific" tools to affirm their own biases. The results of their studies influenced both public policies and popular stereotypes. Thus, when looking at the results of contemporary cross-group comparisons of literacy or intelligence, it is important to be aware of the abuses to which such information has been put.

Constructive Reasons for Measuring Literacy

Despite the negative legacy associated with efforts to measure literacy, there are also positive reasons to assess it. One of the more important reasons involves the use of literacy data in attempts to redress past discriminatory practices. There are many examples of such practices. During the nineteenth century, literacy requirements were used as preconditions for suffrage. In the mid-nineteenth century, they were used to disenfranchise English-speaking Irish voters. Following the end of their enslavement and initial enfranchisement, African-American males faced literacy requirements designed to bar them from voting (Leibowitz, 1969, 1974). Literacy requirements became one in a growing arsenal of Jim Crow measures that lead to the institutionalization of American apartheid. There was considerable irony in the use of literacy requirements against African Americans, because prior to the Civil War "compulsory ignorance laws" had made it a crime for blacks to receive literacy instruction in most southern states (Weinberg, 1995).

In an effort to redress these practices, Congress passed the Voting Rights Act in 1965 (Leibowitz, 1969). One of the Act's provisions called for "the use of ethnicity, voting, and literacy rates to identify possible violations of the act" (Macías, 1994, p. 40). In 1975, the scope of the Voting Rights Act was broadened by amendments focusing on non-English-language-background Latinos, Asian Americans, American Indians, and Alaskan natives. In 1982 Congress modified its definition of language minority by adding to it "no oral/comprehensive ability in English" and defined illiteracy as equivalent to "less than a fifth-grade education" (Macías, 1994, p. 40). Based on 1980 Census data, Congress required jurisdictions with a sufficient number of language minority groups to be identified. Whereas formerly, literacy tests and requirements had been used to restrict voting, the application of language and literacy assessment to the Voting Rights Act coincided with a general expansion of civil rights and a corresponding federal recognition of language minority rights in some legal domains (see Leibowitz, 1982). Just as language and literacy data are useful in attempting to redress past discrimination, so too they are essential in determining the extent of the need for specialized education programs such as bilingual and English as a second language (ESL) services for both children and adults. Without such data it is difficult to convince policymakers and politicians to allocate sufficient resources. (See Macías, 1993, and Macías & Spencer, 1984, for a discussion of technical issues in data collection.)

Definitions of Literacy and Biliteracy

There is little consensus among scholars and lay people concerning what it means to be literate. Literacy may be defined narrowly in terms of basic skills used in reading and writing or broadly, as social practices. Defining literacy is often problematic because the notion of what it involves is not static over time. Resnick and Resnick (1977), as well as a number of other scholars (e.g., Clifford, 1984; Scribner, 1988; Szwed, 1981), have noted that there has been a tendency for expectations regarding literacy to inflate over time, which makes intergenerational comparison difficult. The attempt to define literacy involves many questions, as Kaplan et al. (1984) has noted.

> Can one claim that literacy is the ability to write one's name? If so, is there any qualitative difference between being able to write one's name in an alphabetically graphized language versus one which is graphized in ideograms? Or does literacy imply some set of skills, e.g., the ability to complete a form, to address a letter, to compose a letter, to write a list, etc.? If literacy implies broader skills, what skills, in what combination, and to what degree? How does a definition of "basic" literacy correlate with the notion of "technical" literacy or with the notion of "literary" literacy?...What does it mean when a government claims that its citizens enjoy a certain percentage of literacy? Under such circumstances is literacy equally distributed among all segments of the population, or is it differentiated by sex, by economic status, by race, by religion, or by any number of other sociological variables? (p. X)

Given these inherent difficulties, researchers often do not proceed very far without attempting to constrain or operationalize the notion of literacy for purposes of measurement. Nevertheless, operational definitions rightly remain the subject of heated debate, and lack of consensus results in estimates of illiteracy that vary widely from 15 percent to 50 percent (Venezky, Kaestle, & Sum, 1987).

With these concerns in mind, anyone interested in measuring literacy confronts an array of competing contemporary definitions. The following list is representative but not exhaustive. Other definitions abound in the literature. In the United States, because definitions such as these are usually discussed in reference to English literacy only, implications for language diversity are addressed briefly.

1. Minimal literacy is the ability to read or write something, at some level, in some context(s). At one time the mere ability to write one's own name or read a simple passage aloud was taken as a sufficient indicator of literacy (Resnick & Resnick, 1977). During World War I, immigrants were required, as a precondition of entry, to demonstrate that they had minimal literacy abilities. They were required to read a short passage from the Bible in their native language.

2. Conventional literacy is the ability to use print in reading, writing, and comprehending "texts on familiar subjects and to understand" print within one's environment (Hunter & Harman, 1979, p. 7). Although the conventional definition seems straightforward enough, it is problematic for researchers because there is no consensus on what reading and writing are. In many language minority communities, texts on familiar subjects would include texts in languages other than English. It could also include religious texts, which are pretty high-level reading.

3. Basic literacy refers to the attainment of a level of literacy that allows for continued, self-sustained literacy development. This definition assumes some threshold level upon which one may build through one's own efforts (see Macías, 1990; Venezky, Wagner, & Cilberti, 1990). However, Mikulecky (1990) cautions that "there is little evidence that basic literacy in itself wields a magical transforming power for learning" (p. 26). For language minority individuals who have not yet acquired literacy, their native language provides the most accessible means for developing a level of literacy that allows for sustained development.

4. Functional literacy is the focus of much of the national debate over literacy. It refers to the ability to use print in order to achieve one's own goals and meet the demands of society by participating effectively within the family, community, and society—as a job holder, voter, consumer, information seeker, problem solver, and secular or religious group member. However, competencies for functional literacy education (more recently under the rubric of "life skills") are usually prescribed by middle-class educators according to their own norms and practices (see Hunter & Harman, 1979). Functional literacy subsumes *conventional* literacy; that is, it sees literacy as the ability to read, write, and comprehend texts on familiar subjects and instructions, directions, and labels necessary to get along within the immediate environment. It then extends the conventional definition to include the ability to use reading and writing to fulfill an economic or social purpose at a minimum level of competence (Hunter & Harman, 1979). Again, it is important to note that most of the abilities or skills assessed by measures of functional literacy are formulated by elite or professional groups who seek to predetermine what the groups being assessed need to know and the level of competency at which they need to know it.

Although they are held to address essential needs, functional literacy competencies are rarely grounded in ethnographic research based on what people themselves wish or need to do with literacy (see Weinstein-Shr, 1990, 1993b). Ethnographic studies (e.g., Klassen & Burnaby, 1993) indicate that those lacking English literacy and literacy in their native languages are often able to function successfully within their daily lives but are blocked from other opportunities for mobility due to a lack of schooling. Other studies (e.g., Taylor & Dorsey-Gaines, 1988) indicate that families in poverty often have more literacy skills than they are usually given credit for and are not necessarily liberated from their poverty by their literacy (see Chapter Five).

5. Restricted literacy refers to "participation in script activities" that remain "restricted to a minority of self-selected" people (Scribner & Cole, 1981, p. 238). It differs from state-supported mass literacy because it is acquired without formal schooling. There are language communities, such as the Vai in West Africa (see Chapter Three), where a script has been developed and informally taught outside of school. Vai literacy, as an example of restricted literacy, is functional because it is used in commerce and interpersonal communication, but it is not essential to all societal functional communication because "those who do not know it can get along quite well" without it (p. 238). Significantly, it "does not fulfill the expectations of those social scientists who consider literacy a prime mover in social change" as it does not necessarily "set off a dramatic modernizing sequence," nor has it been "accompanied by rapid developments in technology, art, and science" (p. 239). Restricted literacies do not compete with mass literacies (i.e., public school literacies); nevertheless, they offer rich possibilities for enhancing communication within groups and communities.

6. Vernacular literacy, according to Shuman (1993), is "unofficial" and "defined by its adherence to local rather than academic standards" involving a "presumed misalignment of a group...and institutional authority," or, more importantly, "choices of channel (i.e., speech or writing) and genres of communication (i.e., what can appropriately be said as opposed to what can appropriately be written)" (p. 267). Shuman contends that the "issue is not only varieties of writing, standard and local, but privileged channel and genre of communication" (p. 267). The notion of vernacular literacy blurs the distinction between oral and literate communication insofar as oral styles may be represented in writing. It may also involve the use of nonstandard as well as nonacademic varieties of language.

7. Elite literacy pertains to knowledge, skills, and academic credentials acquired in school to possess specialized knowledge or skills; knowledge (acquired through elite schools) becomes sociocultural capital for *strategic power* (Erickson, 1984; see Chapter Three). Elite literacy is typically legitimated by a university degree and especially through training in literature. Literacy is often represented as a kind of individual possession of knowledge and skills. Typically, however, education credentials such as diplomas and degrees, once attained, tend to be taken as evidence of literacy without the necessity to continue demonstrating mastery; they are markers of one's literate status. Thus, elite literacy is largely synonymous with formal education and with specific types of culturally and socially approved knowledge, especially in the prescribed standard language, as certified by recognized institutions of higher learning. Elite education often includes instruction in foreign languages. Ironically, while there has been considerable opposition to bilingual education and the development of literacy in two languages for language minority groups, there has been support for the development of high-status foreign languages as a basic component of elite education.

8. Analogical literacies refer to knowledge and skills specifically related to particular types of texts, such as cultural literacy,[1] computer literacy, mathematical literacy (numeracy), critical literacy, document literacy, and prose literacy. Macías (1990) has cautioned that the "uses of the term very often confuse the issues over literacy itself as well as the analogical uses, especially in debates about school curriculum...within this approach, numeracy and document processing, as well as uses of literacy (primarily writing), become secondary aspects of literacy study, not parts of the definition of literacy" (p. 19).

9. Literacies as social practices (as discussed in Chapter Three) refers to literacy practices embedded within social and ideological contexts. Practices involving reading and writing are to be analyzed within the contexts in which they are used. This definition has allowed for greater understanding of and sensitivity to language diversity (see Cook-Gumperz, 1986; Gee, 1990; Scribner & Cole, 1978, 1981; Street, 1984.)

Three Approaches to Measuring Literacy

Although there have been both uses and abuses in efforts to measure literacy, those efforts have been constrained in part by the methods available. Historically there have been three common ways of measuring literacy: (1) direct measures or tests, (2) self-reported measures, and (3) surrogate measures, which use a certain number of years of schooling as an indicator of literacy. One of the first direct measures of literacy was the ability to sign one's own name as opposed to merely making a mark on public documents (Clifford, 1984).

Self-Reported Measures of Literacy

The U.S. Census has been the primary source of national literacy data. Since 1850 the Census has collected *self-reported* literacy data (Venezky, Kaestle, & Sum, 1987). From 1850 to 1940, the Census determined literacy based on an individual's response to a question asking whether or not he or she had the ability to read or write a simple message in English or some other language. Those who answered "yes" were considered literate. Those who answered "no" were considered nonliterate (Kirsch & Guthrie, 1977-1978, p. 493). Meanwhile, because most people could read and write at some level, illiteracy was being extended to include people who could read and write, but who could not do so very well. Although researchers increasingly were concerned with the reliability of self-reported literacy data, the U.S. Census remained the primary national measure of literacy. Based on the Census in 1930, for example, the self-reported literacy rate was 97 percent for the Euro-American majority, 90 percent for foreign born, and 84 percent for Blacks (Venezky, Kaestle, & Sum, 1987).

There has been a tendency to distrust self-reported literacy information given the concern that individuals will inflate, or have an inflated view of, their abilities on self-reported survey questionnaires. This may, in part, be related to the structure of the questions asked, which require the respondent to make rather general claims about their abilities without specifying a context. For example, until 1940, the yes/no format of the Census question forced a simplistic dichotomization of literacy. Most of the adult population had at least rudimentary reading and writing abilities, and dichotomizing literacy into literacy/illiteracy was of little value.

There may be several explanations for the discrepancy between self-reported literacy data and direct measures. First, there may be a tendency for people to equate their formal education with their literacy abilities apart from how they actually cope and perform in real-world literacy events. Much of what is learned in school involves short-term memory. Thus, just because knowledge or skills were once mastered does not mean that they will be retained if there are no practical applications for them or no other incentives to maintain them. From this perspective, prior schooling may be confused with current literacy abilities. On the other hand, there may be a tendency for those with lesser schooling to deflate their actual literacy abilities; that is, they may down-play the skills they use on a daily basis if they associate survey questions about reading and writing with school-like reading and writing practices. For those who speak "nonstandard" (i.e., nondominant) varieties of English, or who have learned English as a second language, there may also be a tendency to indicate that they do not use the language very well—regardless of how they perform in English in their everyday lives. For example, a substantial portion of Chicanos surveyed in the National Chicano Survey indicated that they could not speak any language well. This may be more of a reflection of their lack of facility in school-taught language, or language variety, than of their linguistic abilities (Wiley, 1988).

There is, however, some evidence indicating that self-assessment can be a valuable tool when proper controls are used (LeBlanc & Painchaud, 1986). In one study sponsored by the Department of Education in 1982, the Census Bureau correlated self-reported data regarding English speaking proficiency on one survey with direct-measure data from the English Language Proficiency Survey (ELPS) and found a strong correlation between the two (McArthur, 1993, p. 4).

Surrogate Measures of Literacy

During the World War II era, the military again became interested in measuring literacy, as it had during World War I. During the war, trainers contended that draftees' abilities to follow written instructions on military matters were inadequate. The U.S. Army sought to determine the scope of its literacy problem in quantifiable terms. In 1940, the Army attempted to determine literacy based on a grade-level surrogate. First it equated completion of the fourth grade as the equivalent of literacy. In 1947, the standard was raised to completion of the fifth grade. In 1952, it settled on sixth grade (Hunter & Harman, 1979, p. 16; Venezky, Kaestle, & Sum, 1987, p. 12).

The grade-level surrogate was largely chosen for the convenience of having a readily accessible measure. Some scholars have argued that an eighth- or even twelfth-grade equivalency would be more appropriate (Venezky, Kaestle, & Sum, 1987). Still others contend that the number of school years completed is not an accurate measure of literacy skills.

Another concern is that there is no guarantee that skills acquired in school will be retained without ongoing practice (Hunter & Harman, 1979; Kirsch & Guthrie, 1977-1978).

The major limitation of the grade-level completion measure is that the number of years of schooling completed is no guarantee of skill mastery, because there is wide variation in individual abilities at any grade level and wide variation in the retention of skills taught. Its strength is that it does provide a measure of exposure to schooling that can be compared across groups; however, such comparisons provide no information about the quality of schooling received.

Direct Measures of Literacy

Given these concerns about grade-level achievement as a surrogate indicator, a number of attempts have been made at more direct measures of literacy. However, the problem of how to define literacy remained. Between 1950 and 1975, educational achievement was on the rise for all groups (see Chapter Five). Since most of the population was literate at some level, interest shifted to a focus on functional literacy. Functional literacy refers to an individual's ability to use print to meet both personal needs and the demands of society—those competencies needed to hold a job, vote, and be a consumer, information seeker, or problem solver. Functional literacy includes the conventional definition of being able to read, write, and comprehend texts on familiar subjects, instructions, directions, and labels necessary to get along within the immediate environment, as well as to perform an economic or social purpose at a minimum level of competence (Hunter & Harman, 1979).

In a review of approaches to measuring functional literacy, Kirsch and Guthrie (1977-1978) found a range of 1 to 20 percent for so-called "functional illiteracy." Among the various literacy tests, probably one of the best known is the Adult Performance Level (APL). The development of the APL was sponsored by the Office of Education, beginning in 1971. The APL attempted to assess adults between the ages of 18 and 65. It tested 65 competencies held to be necessary in successful adult living, concentrating on the areas of educational, economic, and employment success. The APL sought to determine three literacy levels—individuals who function with great difficulty, those who are functional but not proficient, and those who are highly proficient (Hunter & Harman, 1979). The underlying assumption was that the functional competencies represented and assessed by the test were necessary for a successful adult life. Based on the criteria established, approximately 20 percent of the APL sample was determined to be "functionally incompetent." An additional 30 percent was found to be "functioning with difficulty." Thus, the APL found only half of the adult population to be functionally competent (Kirsch & Guthrie, 1977-1978).

Direct measures are always preferable to self-reported and years of schooling. However, despite their alleged objectivity, they have serious drawbacks. One concern relates to their *ecological validity*, because direct measures are selected by experts who may not be familiar with the life circumstances of those being assessed. According to Hunter and Harman (1979), any objective criteria used for measurement are only as reliable and accurate as the judgments of the group that defines them. When criteria for assessment are determined, they may fail to anticipate the actual literacy needs, realities, or values of the people and communities being assessed. These concerns have been raised in connection with the APL, whose competencies were determined by academicians and adult basic education (ABE) administrators, based on a small sample of students enrolled in ABE programs. Those unable or unmotivated to enroll in programs were excluded from the sample. The APL failed to define success in terms other than economic and educational (Kirsch & Guthrie, 1977-1978).

Another limitation of direct measures relates to the assessment being a *simulation* of a real-world event. Test results represent an artificial or contrived approximation of an individual's actual ability to function (Erickson, 1984). The validity of simulation tests of literacy is a concern given their inauthenticity (Edelsky, 1986; Edelsky et al., 1983; see also Chapter Eight). Many of the tasks used in direct measures of literacy and reasoning ability (including the often-cited attempts by Greenfield, 1972; Luria, 1976; Scribner & Cole, 1978, 1981; and Vygotsky, 1978) are actually "tests of the ability to *use language in a certain way*. In particular they are tests of what we might call *explicitness*" (Gee, 1986, pp. 731-732, emphasis added). This means that general conclusions about literacy abilities drawn from the results of simulations or from in-school tests must be interpreted with great caution. Just because an individual cannot perform a task on a sit-down exam does not mean he or she is unable to perform the real-world task it is designed to simulate, nor does it mean that all tasks contrived by test makers represent things that people really have to do in order to function well in society.

Competency-based tests are particularly open to concerns about ecological validity. To return to, and extend, the admonition of Hunter and Harman (1979) at the beginning of this chapter, "If we take seriously the dynamic interaction between self-defined needs and the requirements of society, measurement of functional literacy becomes infinitely more elusive. Who but the person or group involved can really describe what 'effective functioning in one's own cultural group' really means?" (p. 19).

Beyond these issues there has been a long-standing question regarding language and cultural bias in standardized tests, as Wolfram and Christian (1980) contend. First, they note that the test situation is analogous to other circumstances, such as employment interviews, "where people are evaluated with standards of behavior from outside their community" (p. 179). They further observe that,

> Standardized tests have shown disproportionately lower scores for nonmainstream groups in our society. We should ask why this is so. High socioeconomic groups achieve the highest test scores, an achievement that could be due to some kind of inherent superiority. An alternative explanation is that proportionately higher scores for mainstream groups result from an environment that provides them with certain cultural advantages, and, in some cases, perhaps even physical ones such as proper nutrition or health care. A third possibility may reflect a bias built into the testing instruments themselves. It suggests that certain groups may be using language diversity to their advantage at the expense of others. (p. 179)

The test creates a social event in which the test administrator and the test taker have different expectations and agendas (Wolfram & Christian, p. 197). The test is, in fact an attempt to manipulate and evaluate the test taker's behavior. "While procedures for taking standardized tests are presumably the same everywhere, test takers may respond quite differently to those procedures" (p. 180).

Wolfram and Christian further note that the performance of a test taker may be emphasized by the language of the test as well as by other social factors, such as having outsiders asking them a lot of questions. In a testing situation, no aspect of culture is as likely to raise the issue of cultural boundaries in as conscious a way as language itself. This is especially the case for speakers of nondominant varieties of language, as Wolfram and Christian observe:

People who speak nonmainstream dialects are made aware at an early age that the *way* in which they express themselves, including the very form of the words and sentences they use, conflicts with the norms of the wider society. They are used to being corrected by teachers; they notice that when people in their community are speaking carefully at the most formal occasions, they tend to shift their language in the direction of the mainstream norms; they sometimes see or hear the typical speech of their community stereotyped and mocked. They can perceive a test on language abilities as an instrument designed to measure them according to someone else's standards, not their own. (p. 181)

This puts speakers of nondominant varieties of English at a disadvantage because rather than follow their "first intuitions about what is correct, [they must try to consider how] someone else would speak" (p. 182). Wolfram and Christian conclude that even "the most articulate person, the one best able to express complex thoughts clearly, may not be the one who receives the highest score" because the test lacks real-world validity for them (p. 182).

Summary: Strengths and Weaknesses of Various Approaches to Measuring Literacy

When measuring literacy skills, there is the potential that the testing itself may have negative results in the sense that it labels groups and certifies their incompetence. The positive role of measurement as an assessment tool should be to determine the kinds of literacy necessary for society as a whole and desired by individuals within their own communities. All three of the basic approaches to measurement (direct measures, surrogate measures, and self-reported measures) have strengths and limitations.

Given their attempts at objectivity, direct measures such as competency tests and simulations of real-life skills are generally preferable to self-reported measures, but they may be prescriptive and lack adequate controls for ecological validity. Because the amount of schooling represents a kind of status attainment, it is worth measuring in its own right. Self-reported measures are generally preferable to surrogate measures, since surrogate measures provide no guarantee of competency. Thresholds of functional literacy should not be taken as absolute cut-off points. Finally, no single approach can be taken as a foolproof means of assessing literacy.

What has been and still is missing in nearly all national surveys is a focus on literacy in languages other than English. This omission reinforces the common notion that English literacy—in the United States—is the only literacy worthy of measurement.

Conceptual Issues

Dichotomies, Thresholds, and Domains

In reporting literacy data, there has long been a tendency to dichotomize findings by imposing a boundary between literacy and illiteracy. Some authors have suggested that literacy should be conceptualized as a single set of skills measured along a continuum, while others argue that it is better portrayed as the ability to perform specific print-related practices in specific social contexts, thereby implying many literacies rather than one type of literacy (Heath, 1980; Scribner & Cole, 1981; Street, 1984). Unfortunately, national assessments using the latter definition are not very feasible. (See also Crandall & Imel, 1991, for a discussion of definition issues.)

One way to resolve the problem of dichotomizing literacy/illiteracy is to make more distinctions among various kinds of literacy and to see literacy as a continuum within various domains (Kirsch & Guthrie, 1977-1978). In an attempt to implement this approach, Kirsch and Jungeblut (1986, p. 64) devised three broad domains of literacy assessment:

(1) *prose literacy*: skills and strategies needed to understand and use information from texts that are frequently found in the home and community;

(2) *document literacy*: skills and strategies required to locate and use information contained in contextual materials that include travel maps, graphs, charts, indexes, forms, and schedules;

(3) *quantitative literacy:* knowledge and skills needed to apply arithmetic operations.

By conceptualizing literacy along continua within these domains, this approach attempts to break with the older practice of dichotomizing literacy/illiteracy. Nevertheless, a number of questions remain. Are all tasks involving documents distinct from those involving quantitative tasks? For example, tax forms would seem to involve both document-related skills and quantitative skills. Are skills that are identified as being specific to one domain (e.g., prose skills) all confined to that domain?

How do simulated tasks represent real-world tasks? How many of the skills assessed have been learned but forgotten due to lack of need or practice? There is evidence that literacy tasks assessed in one context do not necessarily transfer to another. For example, school-based literacy tasks do not necessarily carry over to work-related literacy tasks (Harste & Mikulecky, 1984; Mikulecky, 1990). Therefore, to what extent can we expect a test to realistically reflect individual capabilities? Moreover, in the interpretation of findings, threshold levels of competency (i.e., cut-off points based on scores) are established for each domain. Do these thresholds become functionally equivalent to the former dichotomization of literacy/illiteracy? In other words, have we merely exchanged the long-term concern about illiteracy for one over low levels of literacy?

Furthermore, does the notion of continuum hold up across languages or only within them? If literacy is embedded within social practices, is there a continuum that reflects these various social practices? It is likely that the very notion of a continuum of literacy skills is more a reflection of curriculum planners' attempts to provide a rational sequence of instruction than a reflection of what individuals know how to do in actual nonschool contexts.

What happens when these literacy domains are superimposed on a multilingual population? If the focus of the assessment is specifically English literacy, the relationship between literacy in English and in other languages in terms of how they function in various social domains is lost. Domain here refers to the situation in multilingual communities where languages are used for different purposes in different social contexts. Scribner and Cole (1978, 1981) elaborate on the Vai's use of Q'uranic literacy for religious practices, Vai literacy for interpersonal and business domains, and English literacy for academic instruction. Each language of literacy was tied to very specific social, economic, and religious domains. Additionally, literacy abilities were specific to literacy.

When Scribner and Cole (1981) compared Vai who were literate in school English with those who were Vai literate and Qur'anic literate, they found that Vai who had been educated in English medium schools could perform a larger number of specific tasks involving the ability to categorize, understand syllogisms, encode and decode texts, and give verbal explanations than those who were Vai literate or Qur'anic literate. Significantly, however, they could not perform all of the tasks as well. For example, in tests of memory ability, Qur'anic literates outperformed school English literates and Vai literates. This finding should come as no surprise since Qur'anic literates receive more practice in incremental recall. Similarly, Vai literates outperformed all others in tests involving semantic integration of syllables. Again, this should not be surprising since the Vai script is a syllabary (see Scribner & Cole, 1981, p. 253, for a detailed summary of their comparisons).

The majority of skills tested were associated with literacy skills practiced in school. If only English literacy (the language of the school) had been used to determine the distribution of literacy abilities, the literacy resources of the population would have been underestimated because many Vai had not been to English schools. For those schooled, biliterate Vai, it would be important to know which skills they had in languages other than English.

As they learned more and more about the Vai community through ethnographic work, Scribner and Cole were forced to refine their literacy assessment instruments. Given the linguistic diversity in the United States, a focus on English literacy only underestimates the literacy resources of the nation and stigmatizes those literate in other languages, but not in English. It also fails to inform us about how literacy in languages other than English operates in various social domains.

Limitations of National Measures of Literacy

National measures of literacy are influenced by the ideology of English monolingualism and the scholarly biases discussed in Chapter Two. Four types of limitations are particularly noteworthy. These are (1) ignoring literacy in languages other than English; (2) overemphasizing English oral language proficiency; (3) sampling biases; and (4) ambiguity in linguistic, ethnic, and racial identification.

1. Ignoring Literacy in Languages other than English. Measures of literacy in the United States are limited when they "implicitly or explicitly assume English literacy as the focus of the survey" (Macías, 1994, p. 20). Even when surveys collect background information on bilingualism and biliteracy, "this information is frequently ignored by researchers and policymakers" (p. 20). Regardless of the approach used to measure literacy, a major limitation of most national assessments has been the lack of attention to literacy in languages other than English. For the past two decades, the United States has undergone its second greatest period of foreign immigration; it now has one of the largest Spanish-speaking populations in the world (Simon, 1988). By failing to survey literacy in Spanish and other languages, literacy is equated with English literacy, and the literacy picture of the United States remains both incomplete and distorted. By concentrating only on English literacy, surveys inflate the perception of the extent of the "literacy crisis" in the United States and stigmatize many individuals who are literate in other languages. In educational policymaking and program planning, this exclusion fails to distinguish between insufficient initial literacy (in the native language) and insufficient English literacy.

2. Overemphasizing English Oral Language Proficiency. National demographic surveys often include questions regarding oral fluency in English or other languages at the same time that they neglect to seek information about literacy in languages other than English. Similarly, adult education programs for language minority populations seem to emphasize the acquisition of oral English and fail to survey native language literacy or even English literacy. Because primary language literacy provides a foundation for the acquisition of second language literacy (e.g., English literacy) there is a need for better data on native language literacy in both national surveys and in adult English as a second language programs.

3. Sampling Biases. Macías (1994) contends that there may also be a bias related to the sampling of language minorities. "There were significant problems with undercount of specific groups for the 1990 Census" (p. 30). Sampling characteristics tend to be based more on the characteristics of the general population than those of language, ethnicity, and social class. Unless oversampling is incorporated into surveys, generalizations based on those language minority persons sampled are unreliable. Moreover, because most "surveys were designed to assess English literacy, samples may have excluded individuals with little or no proficiency in English from being respondents" (p. 22). In the absence of bilingual surveyors and assessment instruments, "even if there is a substantial representation of language diversity in the sample, some subjects may be excluded from selection or from analysis because of their limited English proficiency" (p. 22). Such was the case of those limited-English-proficient (LEP) individuals excluded from the 1984 and 1986 National Assessment of Educational Progress (NAEP).

4. Ambiguity in Linguistic, Ethnic, and Racial Identification. Macías (1994) notes there is considerable ambiguity in how labels related to language background and ethnic identification are used in studies of literacy. "It has become an easy surrogate [for language background]...to use ethnic identifiers for language minorities. [This]...confuses the two categories" (p. 35). For example, if language minority groups are defined by "non-English household languages, then English monolinguals who are members of ethnic minority groups are excluded" (p. 35). Conversely, if "we define language minority groups as the same ethnic groups within which there are large numbers of non-English language background (NELB) speakers, this should be made clear" (p. 35).

Findings from National Literacy Surveys

The 1992 National Adult Literacy Survey

Background. The most current comprehensive data on English literacy in the United States comes from the National Adult Literacy Survey (NALS). The NALS grew out of a 1988 Congressional initiative in which the U.S. Department of Education was requested to gather information on the nation's literacy. In response, the Department's National Center for Education Statistics (NCES) and Division of Adult Education and Literacy chose to undertake a national household survey to assess the literacy skills of adults in the United States. Educational Testing Service (ETS) became the prime contractor and Westat Incorporated, its subcontractor (Macías, 1994; Wrigley, Chisman, & Ewen, 1993). The NALS survey builds on the model developed for the Young Adult Literacy Survey (YALS) that conceptualizes literacy along a continuum within three domains (prose, document, and quantitative literacy). Each of these domains is assessed through simulated real-world literacy tasks and seeks to determine five levels of literacy.

To the credit of its designers, the NALS survey is more sensitive to issues of ethnic diversity than most previous studies and included demographic questions related to language diversity. The NALS oversampled for Latinos and African Americans, and it provided both English and Spanish versions of the background questionnaire (Macías, 1994, p. 33). It also attempted to probe some of the diversity among the subgroups that it identifies as Hispanic/Mexican origin, Hispanic/Puerto Rican origin, Hispanic/Cuban origin, Hispanic/Central or South American origin, and Hispanic/Other. Given the diversity within other generically labeled groups (e.g., Asian/Pacific Islander), it is regrettable that further subgroup analysis was not attempted. Nevertheless, the attempt to identify some Latino subgroups represents an advance over most previous surveys. (See Macías, 1988, which also takes this approach in an analysis of Census data.)

The preface to the report (Kirsch, Jungeblut, Jenkins, & Kolstad, 1993) begins by noting recent demographic changes in the population: an increase of nearly 100 percent in the Asian or Pacific origin population between 1980 and 1990 (from 3.7 to 7.2 million) and an increase of 22 million in the Hispanic origin population, with some 32 million people who speak languages other than English. The authors state, "Given these patterns and changes, this is an opportune time to explore the literacy skills of adults in this nation" (p. ix). However, although the NALS only assessed English literacy, the fact that some 32 million people speak languages other than English has significance. Hence, although the NALS is more sensitive to language diversity than most prior surveys,[2] its focus is still on English literacy only.

Like most literacy surveys, the NALS was motivated by concerns about the preparedness of individuals and the nation as a whole to compete in a global economy. The preface quotes from the 1990 National Governor's Association's goals (endorsed by both Presidents Bush and Clinton):

> By the year 2000, every adult American will be literate and will possess the knowledge and skills necessary to compete in a global economy and exercise the rights and responsibilities of citizenship. (Kirsch et al., p. xi)

What the NALS does not ask about these goals is what kinds of literacy skills, in which languages, are necessary to compete in a "global economy" and whether one can exercise the rights and responsibilities of citizenship in languages other than English. Congress responded by passing the National Literacy Act of 1991 "to enhance the literacy and basic skills of adults" and "to strengthen and coordinate adult literacy programs" (p. xi). Endorsing the views of Carroll and Chall (1975, p. 11), the Act contends,

> "any national program for improving literacy skills would have to be based on the best possible information as to where the *deficits* are and how serious they are." Surprisingly, though, we do lack accurate and detailed information about literacy in our nation— including how many individuals have limited skills, who they are, and the severity of their problems. (p. xi)

Again, because the focus of the NALS is on English literacy, deficits implicitly become English literacy deficiencies, and recent ethnic and linguistic shifts become important only as they help to explain deficits in English literacy.

Initial Findings and Analyses. NALS findings made their way into the headlines of many of the nation's leading newspapers and magazines. The *Washington Post* article shown on the next page was typical. Among some of the more sensationalized findings were that some 40 to 44 million adults (21 to 23 percent of the nation's 191 million adults) could only perform at the lowest levels of tasks involving prose literacy. A whopping 90 million could not perform tasks above level two. A careful reading of the initial report, however, lends itself to a more prudent interpretation. For example, Kirsch et al. (1993) note that,

> The approximately 90 million adults who performed in Levels 1 and 2 did not necessarily perceive themselves as being "at risk." Across the literacy scales, 66 to 75 percent of adults in the lowest level and 93 to 97 percent in the second lowest level described themselves as being able to read or write English "well" or "very well." Moreover, only 14 to 25 percent of the adults in Level 1 and 4 to 12 percent in Level 2 said they get a lot of help from family members or friends with everyday prose, document, and quantitative literacy tasks. *It is therefore possible that their skills, while limited, allow them to meet some or most of their personal and occupational literacy needs.* (p. xv, emphasis added)

Thus, the NALS data should not be interpreted as indicating that 90 million people were nonfunctional. To do so is to fall into the trap of inventing a literacy crisis (see Welch & Freebody, 1993, pp. 14-16).

In attempting to account for the large number of individuals who functioned at the lowest level, Kirsch et al. (1993) explain, "Many factors help explain why so many adults demonstrated English literacy skills in the lowest proficiency level defined (Level 1). Twenty-one percent of the respondents who performed in this level were immigrants who may have been just learning to speak English" (p. xiv). Note that the emphasis here is on learning to speak English and that there is no discussion of prior literacy. Wrigley et al. (1993) maintain that "the NALS does not tell us how well nonnative speakers of English can deal with the language and literacy challenges in their daily lives. It only tells us they can read the kinds of items contained in the test" (p. 19). They also observe that because the NALS assumes familiarity with U.S.

The Washington Post

THURSDAY, SEPTEMBER 9, 1993

Literacy of 90 Million Is Deficient

U.S. Survey Sounds Alarm Over Skills in Reading, Arithmetic

The study "paints a picture of a society in which the vast majority of Americans do not know that they do not have the skills they need to earn a living."

—Education Secretary Richard W. Riley

society, it may be especially biased against newer arrivals. (See also Chisman, Wrigley, & Ewen, 1993.)

As with so many other standardized assessments of literacy, intelligence, or aptitude, the salient categories for comparison in the NALS are race, ethnicity, and language background.

> Black, American Indian/Alaskan Native, Hispanic, and Asian Pacific Islander adults were more likely than White adults to perform in the lowest two literacy levels. These performance differences are affected by many factors. For example, with the exception of Asian/Pacific Islander adults, individuals in these groups tended to have completed fewer years of schooling in this country than had White individuals. Further, many adults of Asian/Pacific Islander and Hispanic origin were born in other countries and were likely to have learned English as a second language. (Kirsch et al., p. xvi)

Given this emphasis, the report offers the following disclaimer:

> This report describes the literacy proficiencies of various subpopulations defined by characteristics such as age, sex, race, ethnicity, and educational background. While certain groups demonstrated lower literacy than others on the average, within each group there were some individuals who performed well and some who performed poorly....Such statements are only intended to highlight general patterns of differences among various groups and therefore do not capture the variability within each group. (p. 13)

This disclaimer addresses an important consideration not always acknowledged in cross-group comparisons, namely that variation within groups exceeds variation between groups. However, further analysis is still needed to identify those factors that would explain intergroup variations. The report deals with one of those factors, prior schooling. "Nearly two-thirds of those in Level 1 (62 percent) had terminated their education before completing high school" (p. xiv).

> It is impossible to identify the extent to which literacy shapes particular aspects of our lives or is, in turn, shaped by them. For example, there is a strong relationship between educational attainment and literacy proficiencies. On the one hand, it is likely that staying in school longer does strengthen an individual's skills. On the other hand, it is also true that those with more advanced skills tend to remain in school longer. (p. 13)

Similar to many prior surveys, NALS data indicated that Whites outperformed other groups. They averaged 26 to 80 points higher than any other ethnic and racial groups assessed (p. 33). In attempting to explain these differences, Kirsch et al. (1993) note that the amount of schooling respondents had received accounted for about 50 percent of the variance (p. 37). Given this, the question arises as to what accounts for the rest of the variance. Kirsch et al. speculate:

> In making comparisons here between white adults and those of either Hispanic or Asian/Pacific Islander origin, it is important to remember that the language spoken and country of birth may contribute substantially to proficiencies that are observed. (p. 38)

What is not clear from this statement is *how* language and country of origin contribute. Could it be that the test instrument and the situation are contributing factors, as Wolfram and Christian (1980) contend? Further exploration of this seems warranted. It is also noteworthy that African Americans were not included here as a language minority because many are native speakers of a different variety of English (see Chapter Seven). It is also particularly noteworthy that social class does not figure more overtly into the analysis because it might help account for some of the remaining variance between groups. It might also prove to be illuminating if class differences were explored both within and across groups.

Further analyses of the NALS are being conducted in which special attention will be given to language demographics, particularly at the state level. Pending these analyses, the value of the NALS as an indicator of the literacy abilities of language minorities remains mixed. On the one hand, there was a conscious attempt to oversample for groups more likely to be from language backgrounds other than English. There was also an attempt to collect more demographic data related to language diversity than in previous national assessments. Because there is the possibility to construct a biliteracy variable from the self-reported information collected in the exam, the "NALS bears close watching and deserves secondary analysis" (Macías, 1994, p. 39).

The National Chicano Survey

A high percentage of those who are held to be illiterate (in English) are literate in other languages; therefore, the failure to assess literacy abilities in other languages increases the appearance of wide-spread illiteracy and stigmatizes those who are literate in those languages. The

Figure 1.
Average Literacy Proficiencies of Young Adults, 1985 and 1992

PROSE

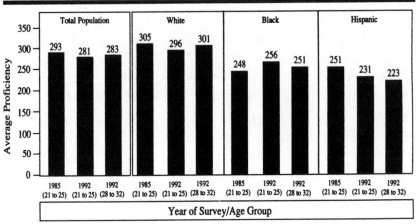

DOCUMENT

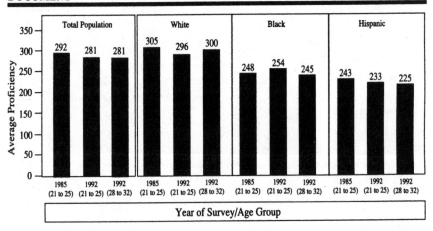

QUANTITATIVE

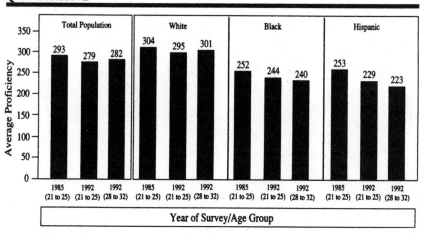

Source: Kirsch, Jungeblut, Jenkins, & Kolstad, 1993, p. 24. Reprinted by permission.

Figure 2.
Literacy Levels and Average Literacy Proficiencies, by Race/Ethnicity

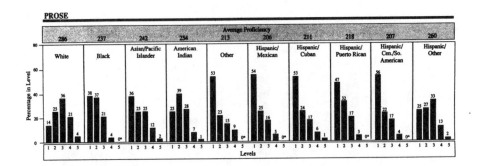

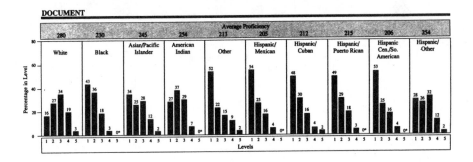

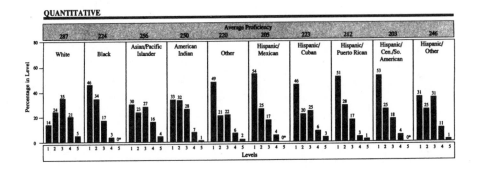

Source: Kirsch, Jungeblut, Jenkins, & Kolstad, 1993, p. 33. Reprinted by permission.

Figure 3.
Average Literacy Proficiencies, by Highest Level of Education Completed and Race/Ethnicity

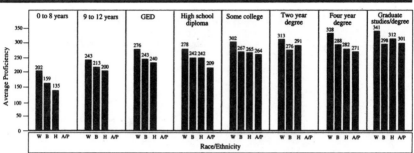

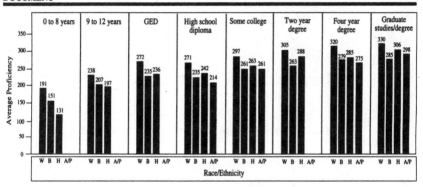

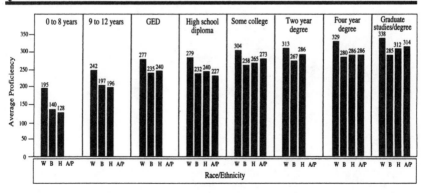

Source: Kirsch, Jungeblut, Jenkins, & Kolstad, 1993, p. 36. Reprinted by permission.

Figure 4.
Differences Between Adults in Various
Racial/Ethnic Groups in Average Literacy
Proficiencies and Average Years of Schooling

Differences Between White and Black Adults

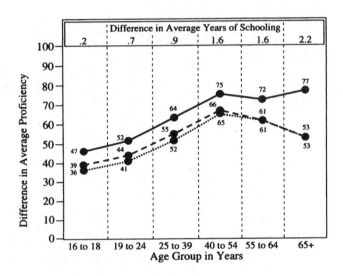

Differences Between White and Hispanic Adults

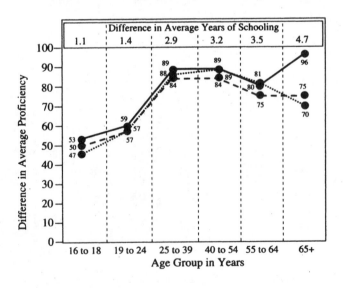

Differences Between White and Asian/Pacific Islander Adults

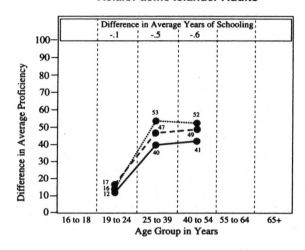

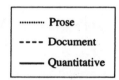

Source: Kirsch, Jungeblut, Jenkins, & Kolstad, 1993, p. 39. Reprinted by permission.

singular focus on English literacy, thus, tends to inflate the magnitude of the "literacy crisis." Consequently, there is a need to design national surveys that allow for an analysis of literacy across languages whenever possible. The National Chicano Survey is the only nationally representative survey to date that has allowed for such an analysis.

Background. The National Chicano Survey (NCS) was conducted in 1979 by the Institute for Social Research, with grants from the Ford Foundation and the National Institutes of Health. It was a bilingual survey of a nationally selected and representative sample of the Mexican-origin population in the United States. The NCS was not explicitly designed to measure language and literacy characteristics; rather, its purpose was to gather information about many different aspects of Chicano life, including social, demographic, political, and mental health characteristics "to compile a statistically representative and comprehensive body of empirical information about the social, economic and psychological status of Chicanos" (Arce, n.d., p. ii). Nevertheless, it is unique in that it allows for a focus on biliteracy through secondary analysis. The NCS was designed as a national sample (or, more accurately, as a sample representative of 90 percent of the national Chicano population) and provides opportunities for generalization regarding the U.S. Chicano population. The NCS collected self-reported language, literacy, and schooling data and involved no direct assessment. Though limited to self-reported information, its data tend to be far richer than those of the U.S. Census or other surveys such as the 1976 Survey of Income and Education (SIE). The NCS includes parallel literacy-related questions for English and Spanish, which allows for biliteracy assessment. The majority of the Chicano population in the United States is bilingual, and a biliteracy analysis allows for the determination of literacy characteristics of the population. The NCS also allows for the construction of a surrogate, years-of-schooling, measure of literacy.[3]

Limitations. Despite the strength of the NCS in allowing for biliteracy analysis, it has several limitations. For example, the literacy variables tend to dichotomize literacy and illiteracy and do not allow assessment based upon text types or within specific social settings.

Major Findings. Secondary data analyses of the NCS resulted in an overall Chicano literacy rate of 74 percent for the United States, with 52 percent English literate, 42 percent Spanish literate, and 22 percent biliterate in English and Spanish. If only English literacy had been measured, illiteracy would have been 48 percent as opposed to 26 percent by also measuring Spanish literacy (Macías, 1988; Wiley, 1988, 1990). (Tables 9, 10, and 11 provide further detail on biliteracy and grade-level achievement.)

Table 9.
Frequencies for Biliteracy in Four Values

Value Label	Frequency	Percent	Valid Percent	Cum. Percent
English Lit. Dominant	305	30.8	31.7	31.7
English/Spanish Bilit.	194	19.6	20.1	51.8
Spanish Lit. Dominant	214	21.6	22.2	74.0
Limited or Non-Literate	250	25.2	26.0	100.0
Missing Cases	28	2.8	missing	
Total	991	100.0	100.0	
Valid Cases = 979				

Source: Wiley, 1990, p. 116.

Table 10.
Frequencies for Grade Level Achievement

Value Label	Frequency	Percent	Valid Percent	Cum. Percent
Less than 6 yrs.	264	26.6	27.0	27.0
6 to 11 yrs.	392	39.6	40.0	67.0
More than 12 yrs.	323	32.6	33.0	100.0
Missing Cases	12	1.2	missing	
Total	991	100.0	100.0	
Valid Cases = 979				

Source: Wiley, 1990, p. 117.

Table 11.
Literacy by Selected Characteristics

	English Literate	Biliterate	Spanish Literate	Limited/Non-Literate
	#/%	#/%	#/%	#/%
Nativity				
U.S.	290/30.1	148/15.4	26/2.7	131/13.6
Mexico	15/1.6	46/4.8	188/19.5	119/12.4
Sex				
Male	109/11.3	74/7.7	103/10.7	98/10.2
Female	196/20.4	120/12.5	111/11.5	152/15.8
Age				
18-25	51/5.3	31/3.2	38/4.0	29/3.0
26-35	124/13.0	54/5.6	73/7.6	64/6.7
36-45	74/7.7	43/4.5	51/5.3	33/3.5
46-55	34/3.6	30/3.1	22/2.3	55/5.8
56-65	11/1.2	21/2.2	13/1.4	35/3.7
65 & Older	9/.9	12/1.3	17/1.8	32/3.3
Age of Immigration				
5 yrs. or less	5/1.4	5/1.4	4/1.1	9/2.5
6 to 8 yrs.	3/.8	3/.8	—	4/1.1
9 to 11 yrs.	3/.8	5/1.4	1/.3	3/.8
12 to 15 yrs.	1/.3	11/3.0	10/2.8	8/2.2
16 to 18 yrs.	—	7/1.9	30/8.3	23/6.4
19 yrs. or over	3/.8	15/4.1	140/38.7	69/19.1

Source: Wiley, 1990, p. 118.

Despite some of the design limitations of the NCS, Macías (1994) has concluded, "The design options for national surveys have to be widened to include the language and ethnic backgrounds for understanding English literacy as well as biliteracies;" thus, "it is not only possible, but very desirable to pursue another National Chicano Survey" (p. 38). Beyond a new NCS, similar studies of other groups are also desirable. Where cost prohibits direct assessments of native language literacy, surveys relying on self-reported data (using bilingual surveyors) could be undertaken.

Conclusion

In addition to the need to collect data that better reflect literacy and language diversity in the United States, there is a need to be aware of the history of efforts to measure literacy and intelligence and the uses to which some of those data are put. There is also a need to negotiate the kinds of information collected to better reflect the literacy needs and interests of the populations being surveyed. Quantitative data are needed to monitor the effectiveness of schools and adult education programs. However, there are limits to what can be assessed by direct measures or through self-reports. Thus, there is also a need for more ethnographic studies of literacy practices within various linguistic communities and between them and the dominant linguistic community. Beyond this, there is a limit to the utility of language and literacy data when it is linked solely to race, ethnicity, and culture. Greater attention needs to placed on social class as a factor both within and between groups.

Further Reading

Gould, S.J. (1981). *The mismeasure of man.* New York: Norton.

Details the misguided attempts of pseudo-scientists to establish a racial basis for intelligence. Implications of this study should not be lost for those interested in measuring literacy.

Macías, R.F. (1988). *Latino illiteracy in the United States.* Claremont, CA: Tomás Rivera Center. (ERIC Document Reproduction Service No. ED 321 608)

Presents comparative literacy data on major Latino subgroups based on analyses of the 1976 Survey of Income and Education (SIE), the 1979 National Chicano Survey (NCS), and the 1980 U.S. Census.

Macías, R.F. (1993). Language and ethnic classification of language minorities: Chicano and Latino students in the 1990s. *Hispanic Journal of Behavioral Sciences, 15*(2), 230-257.

Includes technical definitions that are used to operationalize data in national statistics on the Latino population as well as several data sources.

Macías, R.F. (1994). Inheriting sins while seeking absolution: Language diversity and national statistical data sets. In D. Spener (Ed.), *Adult biliteracy in the United States* (pp. 15-45). Washington, DC and McHenry, IL: Center for Applied Linguistics and Delta Systems.

Provides an important technical analysis of the issues related to defining and measuring literacy and provides examples of the strengths and limitations of several major national data sets.

Venezky, R.L, Wagner, D.A., & Ciliberti, B.S. (Eds.). (1990). *Toward defining literacy*. Newark, DE: International Reading Association.

Provides an overview of the issues associated with defining literacy focusing on scholarly and policy issues. Macías's critique of "mainstream" definitions is particularly relevant from the standpoint of literacy and language diversity in the United States.

Notes

[1] See Field (1992) and Walters (1992) for a critique of Hirsch's (1987) notion of cultural literacy.

[2] In addition to the test data, some demographic data were collected that allow for the constructions of a biliteracy variable. Further secondary data analysis may provide useful information based on self-reported data (Macías, 1994).

[3] The NCS used a household survey of individuals of Mexican descent living in Arizona, California, Colorado, Texas and Chicago, Illinois. Although the other states were excluded, the geographical scope of the study exceeded that of any previous study on Chicanos, and the survey covered a geographical area that included about 90 percent of the Mexican-origin population in the United States (Santos, 1985). In defining its sample population, the NCS treated "person of Mexican origin/descent" and "Chicano" as operationally synonymous. These terms were treated as encompassing both the native born, immigrants, and undocumented persons.

The survey was conducted from February through August of 1979. The sample design produced 12,000 eligible housing units of which 11,000 were actually screened using a five-minute screening instrument. Of these, 1,360 had at least one eligible member. Interviews were obtained from 991 respondents, thereby yielding a response rate of 73 percent. Forty-four percent of the respondents were residents of

California, about 35 percent were from Texas, 16 percent were from the Southwest, and just over 5 percent from the Northwest (i.e., the Chicago area). Face-to-face interviews were conducted in either English or Spanish (Santos, 1985, p. 20). Approximately 60 percent of the respondents were female, which reflects both a disproportionate representation in the population and a slightly higher refusal rate for men. Sixty-two percent of the respondents were born in the United States compared with 38 percent who were born in Mexico. The mean age of the respondents was 40.1 years for females and 39.6 years for males (Santos, 1985, p. 20-21). Fifty-two percent of the interviews were conducted in Spanish, and 48 percent were conducted in English (Arce, n.d., p. ii).

The survey questionnaire included a number of items useful in the analysis of educational achievement and literacy among Chicanos. These include both years-of-schooling data and self-assessment measures of literacy in both English and Spanish. By allowing for literacy assessment in both languages, the NCS facilitates a broader assessment of literacy than most national surveys and allows for a biliteracy comparison to educational achievement. In the survey, at the beginning of each interview, the respondents were given the option to use English or Spanish.

CHAPTER 5

Literacy, Schooling, and the Socioeconomic Divide

The idea of mobility hinges on the belief that there is equal opportunity in education and through education, opportunity for social mobility and a more equitable society....The germane point is that the idea of mobility through literacy and education remains persuasive, despite...the historical experience of most people. (Collins, 1991, p. 234-235)

In the 1980s, the release of the highly touted *A Nation at Risk* (National Commission on Excellence and Education) reinitiated debate over the nation's "literacy crisis," a predicament purportedly brought on by a lack of fundamental literacy skills in the United States. The report brought national polemics about literacy and education to a level not seen since the Sputnik Era. According to Welch and Freebody (1993), the literacy debate in the United States parallels that in other nations such as Canada where there has been "the ready ascription of the causes of the 'crisis' to areas of societal and political practice...notably about workers, immigrants, and the 'Back to Basics' school curriculum" (p. 15). The concern of these authors is that inappropriate education programs, mustered to solve the crisis, can be used "to further marginalize certain segments of society" (p. 15). Calls for higher national standards dominate much of the literacy debate in such a way that language minorities appear to be the cause of the crisis. Moreover, the "Back to Basics/teach 'em English" remedies that are offered are rooted in "a technicist definition of literacy" that has "underpinned the principal models of literacy in North America this century" (p. 15; see also de Castell & Luke, 1983; 1986). Although it would be pointless to argue that there is not a strong association between literacy and economic position, the concern here is how language minority populations are positioned in the debates about the crisis and whether the policy and program goals focused on them are appropriate.

This chapter reviews and critiques some of the common assumptions about the relationship between literacy and economic position and discusses their implications for language minority groups. It also presents data on the relationship among literacy, biliteracy, schooling, and employability. Data related to young adults and adolescent immigrants' schooling are presented with implications for policy and practice.

Naming the Disease While Blaming the Patient

Historically, social reformers have pointed to English illiteracy and underachievement in education as *causes* of crime, juvenile delinquency, and unemployment. In the nineteenth century, for example, the common school movement emerged, in part, as an educational remedy for problems associated with illiteracy. In the early decades of the twentieth century, adult Americanization programs were seen as a means for promoting linguistic assimilation, English literacy, and patriotism (see McClymer, 1982). Since then, illiteracy has continued to be depicted as a personal misery "whose public consequences—unemployment, crime, and so on—cannot be abated without" the assistance of educators (Brodkey, 1991, p. 44), despite advances in education. Therefore, educators must be made to understand the nature of the "disease" if they are to avoid offering educational placebos for problems that are really more fundamental.

Today, in the popular media and in policy debates, illiteracy and underachievement in education are also seen as indicators of a lack of national well-being and competitiveness. Illiteracy is associated with problems of the poor, immigrants, refugees, racial and ethnic minorities, and the non-English and limited English speaking. These labels are treated *as if they were similar*. The persistence of their use in popular media gives reason for pause and concern, since, as Brodkey (1991) contends, "all definitions of literacy project both a *literate self* and an *illiterate other*." They stipulate "the political as well as cultural terms on which the 'literate' wish to live with the 'illiterate' (p. 161).

Michael Lewis (1978) has observed that explanations for success and failure in this society take the form of a popular ideology or belief system that justifies (1) a "culture of inequality [and] mandates the existence of visible failure" and (2) "the persistence of major social problems" such as illiteracy (p. 192). In the culture of inequality, the illiterate and poor are caught in an ongoing cycle of failure and victimization that Lewis called the "calculus of estrangement" (p. 192). Lewis warned that the need for such victimization would intensify as the disparity between rich and poor widened. He observed that educational failure plays a unique role in the calculus of estrangement: "If the problem is educational failure, we do little except...to blame such failure on the backgrounds of those who fail; we certainly do not attempt extensive reform of those school systems which often appear inadequate" (p. 193). Being successful in society is thus attributed to an individual's ability to take advantage of educational opportunities and to become literate. As Collins (1991) concludes, "By defining the relevant measures of social position narrowly enough, social mobility seems to work: We succeed through our 'own' efforts, as represented by the match of education and job" (p. 235; see also Lankshear, 1987; Ryan, 1972).

Immigrant and native-born language minority groups have been particularly vulnerable to stigmatization because they fail to meet expectations of the majority. In order to blame them, it is necessary to assume that the educational system and the job market provide sufficient educational opportunities for all who use it. Rarely are the expectations of the majority, the equity of the educational system, or the opportunities within the job market questioned. Frequently, the existence of educational programs is taken as sufficient proof that equal opportunity and appropriate instruction have been provided. In a system of English-only instruction, the student is the target, and illiteracy in English is seen as the result of a personal, rather than systemic, failure. When specific education programs, such as bilingual education, are provided for language minority populations, critics attack the programs as inappropriate, because they are not English-only practices. Over the years, the impact of blaming the victim has influenced the way in which literacy issues are framed. Literacy problems persist generation after generation regardless of advances made in literacy and education. Thus, the persistence of a *perpetual literacy crisis* raises questions concerning how education reform efforts that offer only English literacy and basic skills education, but no access to good jobs, can address the more fundamental problems that result from economic inequity among individuals or solve structural problems within the economy.

Literacy and Socioeconomic Problems

At the macroeconomic level, the connections between literacy development and economic improvement are also not as causally linked as they appear in popular polemics, as Coulmas (1992) has observed:

> On the social level, affluence does not imply general literacy; witness the United States where mass functional illiteracy is, maybe, indicative of the unequal distribution of wealth, but not of social wealth as such. On the other hand, the reduction of illiteracy from 50 percent to 40 percent which was accomplished in Nicaragua by a literacy campaign during the 1980s will likely have no immediate or medium-term consequences for the development of social wealth in that country. Thus the socioeconomic value of literacy cannot be measured on a scale with linear progress. (p. 211)

It is also commonly argued that low literacy levels among a substantial portion of the total labor force must have a negative effect on the national economy because, "in a technological society, the need for the nation's workforce to be continuously replenished by adequately trained and functionally literate workers becomes increasingly important" (Vargas, 1986, p. 9), so important that "concerns about the human costs of limited literacy have, in a sense, been overshadowed by concerns about the economic and social costs" (Kirsch, Jungeblut, Jenkins, & Kolstad, 1993, p. x). Despite such concerns, the causality between literacy and national economic well being may be overestimated.

> What, maybe, the American example illustrates more clearly than any other is that a high level of economic and technological development is not incompatible with relatively high rates of illiteracy. As a matter of fact, in virtually all advanced countries that have taken the trouble to investigate the matter, it was found that functional illiteracy is much more pervasive a problem than had previously been thought. (Coulmas, 1992, p. 214)

What then of the impact of the mass literacy campaigns of the nineteenth century? Even when mass literacy campaigns intervened, social problems persisted. Graff (1979, 1987), who has studied the impact of such campaigns in Canadian history, locates the cause of economic and social problems not in illiteracy, but in social and economic inequality. He concludes,

> Criminal prosecution, and probably apprehension as well, derived from the facts of inequality. Punishment, stratification, and illiteracy too were rooted in the social structure; pervasive structures of inequality which emanated from the ethnic and sexual ascription ordered groups and individuals....Achievement of literacy or education had little impact upon these structures, and in many cases only reinforced them. (p. 210)

Graff (1987) contends that, whereas English literacy was touted as a remedy for the ills of Canadian immigrants in the nineteenth century, gains in literacy actually increased social stratification. Thus, historically, basic literacy education has been used as a normative agent. Both Street (1984) and Graff (1979) conclude that mass literacy campaigns hide a deeper motive, which is to pacify and manage those who do not match middle-class expectations.

The connection then between socioeconomic problems and illiteracy needs to be looked at in reverse. Illiteracy is more a result of socioeconomic problems than it is their cause. Literacy is obviously related to social and economic mobility, but the essential question is, Does literacy precede or follow gains in mobility? To answer this question, it is necessary to separate individual cases from general trends. There are examples of individuals coming from unprivileged backgrounds who became literate and ultimately successful. Nevertheless, the historical trend has been that upward mobility tends to follow, rather than precede, improvements in a family's economic position. Intergenerationally, children have tended to fare slightly better than their parents, at least until recently. Improved economic, political, and social position have more often been the result of long-term organized efforts to advance better working conditions and benefits than of merely increasing literacy. For example, the gains in economic position that occurred during the 1930s were more the result of the great expansion of unionism than gains in literacy. Many of those who joined the ranks of unions were from immigrant, language-minority backgrounds. Despite having been stigmatized for their lack of English literacy, they were able to improve their economic position through organized activity. With their improved economic position, their children benefited and increased their literacy levels. In other words, the next generation's rise in literacy reflected economic gains of the previous generation.

There are also constraints on how much impact being literate in and of itself can have on one's position. According to Coulmas (1992), "Those who can barely write their name do not have significantly better economic changes than those unable to write at all" (p. 211). Those who are literate, but who lack formal schooling and education credentials, usually cannot fully benefit in the job market from the literacy skills they do have. As taxpayers, they are short-changed because they contribute to services (such as higher education) in which they do not participate. Thus, they are unable to reap the full benefits of citizenship (Vargas, 1986). Often such people are recruited into adult literacy and English as a second language (ESL) programs with only a vague sense that improving their literacy and oral English skills will in some way do them some good. In the absence of formal education credentials, they are often blocked even though they acquire some degree of English literacy.

Profiles of the Association Between Literacy and Economic Position

When contemporary data on connections between English literacy, literacy in general, and educational achievement are analyzed, these data do indicate a correlation between lack of literacy and lower educational achievement in any language (and especially in English) and one's economic situation. However, these data are often mistakenly interpreted as indicating a causal relationship between literacy and economic position.

For example, Figure 5 indicates that only about one in four National Adult Literacy Survey (NALS) respondents living in poverty were able to perform at level three or higher on the prose, document, and quantitative literacy tasks (see Chapter Four regarding NALS literacy levels and task domains). Among those receiving food stamps, only one percent were able to perform level five tasks, compared with those who received interest from savings accounts or other bank accounts, of which 83 to 85 percent could perform level five tasks (see Figure 6).

Figure 5.
Percentages of Adults in Poverty, by Literacy Level

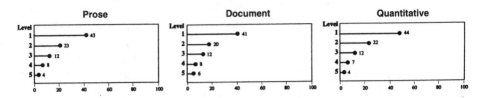

Source: Kirsch, Jungeblut, Jenkins, & Kolstad, 1993, p. 61. Reprinted by permission.

Figure 6.
Percentages of Adults Who Received Certain Types of Nonwage Income or Support in the Past 12 Months, by Literacy Level

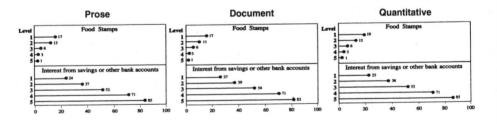

Source: Kirsch, Jungeblut, Jenkins, & Kolstad, 1993, p. 62. Reprinted by permission.

Figure 7.
Chicano Literacy by Family Income 1979

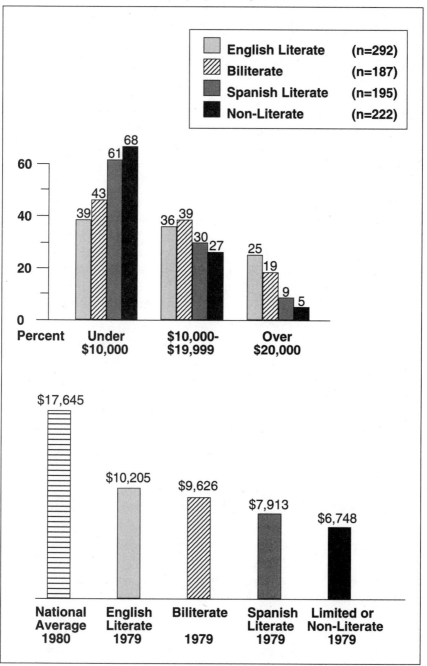

As indicated in Chapter Four, one of the limitations of the NALS is that it only directly assessed literacy in English. Thus, some comparison with the National Chicano Survey (NCS) is useful, since it allowed for an analysis of Spanish literacy and biliteracy in English and Spanish. Again, however, NCS data were based on self-reported information (see Chapter Four for a discussion of the strengths and limitations of self-reported data). Figure 7 compares language(s) of literacy among Chicanos by level of family income. The data indicate a strong association between English literacy and family income. However, Spanish literacy was also important. Those only literate in Spanish tended to have higher levels of literacy than nonliterates, which would seem to confirm the importance of assessing literacy in languages other than English. Family income among biliterates was only slightly lower than among those literate in only English. Interestingly, biliterates were slightly more likely to be employed than those only literate in English (68 percent to 62 percent) (Wiley, 1988, p. 168). As one would expect, the amount of schooling that one had attained also appeared to be very significant. Over 73 percent of those with twelve or more years of schooling were employed compared with only 50 percent of those with six to eleven years, and with only 42 percent of those with less than six years (Wiley, 1988, p. 259).

These data confirm that low levels of literacy and educational attainment do diminish employment prospects for language minorities. This points to the need to increase educational resources to promote English literacy for those who are already literate and to promote literacy in native languages for those who are not. However, literacy programs must be explicitly linked to improving both academic and economic opportunities. It is here that the agendas of policymakers, employers, and adult students are often at odds.

Playing Catch Up: The Dilemma of Rising Expectations and Rising Standards

As historical background to the perpetual literacy crisis, Resnick and Resnick (1977) note the impact of ever-rising standards for literacy. They provide a useful analysis of continually changing perceptions of being literate. They have analyzed several historical patterns of literacy education in Europe and the United States and conclude that current expectations regarding mass literacy have been held for, at most, three generations. In the past, literacy expectations were aimed at achieving a high level of literacy for elites but low levels for a large number of other individuals. Thus, recent calls for high levels of mass literacy can be seen as taking the standard that once applied only to elites and now applying it universally. This rapid rise of a standard for literacy raises the issue of the appropriateness of instructional goals because the clamor for higher standards does not always originate from the populations to which they will be applied. Whereas the emphasis for mass education was formerly on basic literacy skills, now criteria applied to literacy in the United States emphasize the ability to read new material and glean new information from it (p. 371).

The rise in expectations regarding literacy and education has not been without some negative consequences. Several authorities have argued that, as expectations have risen and as literacy competencies have increased throughout society, the widespread possession of any particular competency has come to be devalued. Levine (1982) observes that workers in the unskilled sector must increasingly demonstrate a level of competence higher than one that would have been respectable in an earlier generation. Collins (1979) has made a similar argument regarding the tendency to devalue educational credentials as these become widespread. Collins holds that there is often little relationship between educational credentials and job skills, and similar conclusions have been reached by others (e.g., Harste & Mikulecky, 1984; Mikulecky, 1990; O'Connor, 1993).

Extending this argument, Levine (1982) sees a parallel inflation and corresponding devaluation of literacy skills outside work. Individuals must attain minimal mastery to just pass as literate in public. As literacy programs and schools more effectively equip their students with literacy skills, the acceptability threshold continues to inflate. As a result of this inflation in literacy criteria, there appears to be no threshold where those with below-norm educational achievement can compete on an equal basis for jobs or command the same status as those above the norm. The implications of this for language minority groups in low socioeconomic strata means any marginal gains in educational achievement are minimized by gains made across all groups. For example, although it is generally acknowledged that open access to higher education in the late 1960s and the early 1970s led to dramatic gains in education among language minority groups, it is rarely pointed out that Whites who spoke only English also entered universities and colleges in record numbers (see Welch & Freebody, 1993).

Literacy and educational achievement gains within groups, from one generation to the next, are apparent. However, these gains must be seen as relative within the larger sociohistorical situation. Universal adult literacy and high school completion have become common expectations. Because groups are not usually compared only to themselves (e.g., African Americans in 1950 to African Americans in 1990), but to other groups as well, within-group gains have less significance when educational gains are being made in society generally. The job market worth of these gains may be negated by what Collins (1979) calls "credential inflation," which functions as follows: Even as ethnic, racial, and language minorities (of lower socioeconomic status) improve their literacy skills and educational performance, members of dominant groups are making gains, too. For example, between 1950 and 1975 major gains in educational achievement were made across all groups. Given an end to legal segregation and an expansion in educational opportunities generally, African Americans and Latinos showed dramatic gains in years of schooling completed. However, Whites also benefited from the expansion in educational opportunity, and they continue to maintain educational advantages.

In the quarter century between 1950 and 1975, relatively impressive educational gains were made by ethnic/racial minority groups in the United States. For example, average years of schooling for Black and Latino females increased from just over seven years in 1950 to about eleven years in 1975 (for a net gain of about fours years of schooling). The comparable gain for White females was only about two years, from just over ten years in 1950 to over twelve years in 1975. Thus, despite gains, Black and Latino women continue to lag behind White women in years of schooling. Black and Latino males also made similar progress when compared with White males, but continued to lag behind White males by about two years in the amount of schooling completed (ten plus years to twelve plus; see Hunter & Harman, 1979, p. 49, for a more detailed comparison).

These data indicate that despite gains in amount of education received by African Americans and Latinos, those gains tended to be somewhat negated by the educational gains among the White population. Thus, between 1950 and 1975, underrepresented groups were able to take advantage of additional educational opportunities, but they were not the sole beneficiaries of them.

Trends in Educational Progress Across
Ethnic and Linguistic Groups, 1979 to 1989

As Table 12 indicates, there was a substantial increase in the percentage of language minority children of school age between 1979 and 1989. What relationship is there between these increases and recent national trends in educational progress? There is no simple answer to this question since the data on educational progress (see Tables 12 and 13) can be interpreted based on which groups have (1) the highest and lowest percentages of below modal grade-level progress, or (2) the sharpest increases and declines in below modal grade-level performance between 1979 and 1989. When the former criterion is used, Whites from homes where only English was spoken had the lowest below modal grade percentage (22.3%; i.e., the highest educational progress) in 1979 and the second lowest (32.6%) in 1989.

However, data concerning educational progress across ethnic and linguistic groups indicate several surprising trends when increases/declines are compared (both within and between groups) from 1979 to 1989. Aggregated data for eight- to fifteen-year olds indicate that progress in school generally declined. Table 12 indicates that nearly 10% more students were below modal grade level in 1979 than in 1989. The sharpest increases in percentages of students below modal grade level were among White and Latino students (10.3% and 11.6% respectively) who come from homes where only English is spoken.[1] Comparatively, there was only a 1.1% increase among White students who come from homes where another language is spoken and only a 1.8% increase for Latino students from homes with similar language backgrounds. However, there was a net gain modal grade achievement among students in the "other" category. The majority of these students are probably of Asian ancestry.

Table 13 makes even finer distinctions between Latinos and non-Latinos by disaggregating data based on national origin. When this is done, the data indicate that the largest declines (i.e., increases in percentage of students below modal grade level) were at 9.9% for U.S.-born non-Latinos (from homes where only English is spoken) and 22.4% for those born outside the United States. However, even finer distinctions than language background and national origin need to be made to understand the educational and literacy needs of many students.

Table 12.

Race/Ethnicity, Language Spoken at Home, and Progress Through School of 8 to 15 Year Olds: 1979 and 1989

(Numbers in Thousands)

Year, Language, and Grade	Total	White	Black	Hispanic	Other
1979					
Enrolled in school*	26,741	20,611	3,857	1,783	490
% below modal grade	24.9	22.4	32.4	35.5	30.0
Speak only English at home	3,965	19,540	3,677	474	274
% below modal grade	24.0	22.3	32.8	27.0	22.8
Speak other language at home	2,098	619	53	1,238	188
% below modal grade	35.0	25.0	(B)	39.4	43.1
1989					
Enrolled in school*	25,572	18,028	3,884	2,668	992
% below modal grade	34.7	32.6	41.0	41.4	29.9
Speak only English at home	20,890	16,191	3,503	762	434
% below modal grade	34.2	32.6	41.2	38.6	27.7
Speak other language at home	2,961	615	88	1,768	489
% below modal grade	36.3	23.9	36.6	42.1	31.0

(B) The base of the derived figure is less than 75,000.

* Children for whom no language characteristics were reported are included in the totals but not shown separately.

Source: McArthur, 1993, p. 26. Based on U.S. Department of Commerce, Bureau of the Census, November Current Population Survey, 1979 and 1989. Reprinted by permission.

Table 13.
Progress Through School
(Numbers in Thousands)

Year, Ethnicity, Birth-place, and Percent Below Modal Grade	Total	Language Spoken at Home	
		Only English	Other
1979			
Hispanic*	1,783	474	1,238
% below modal grade	35.5	27.0	39.4
Born in 50 States and DC	1,365	455	910
% below modal grade	31.8	25.5	34.9
Born elsewhere	347	19	328
% below modal grade	52.4	(B)	51.8
Non-Hispanic*	24,958	23,491	860
% below modal grade	24.1	23.9	28.6
Born in 50 States and DC	23,753	23,184	569
% below modal grade	24.0	24.0	22.3
Born elsewhere	597	306	290
% below modal grade	31.1	21.5	41.3
1989			
Hispanic*	2,668	762	1,768
% below modal grade	41.4	38.6	42.1
Born in 50 States and DC	2,075	744	1,331
% below modal grade	40.1	39.1	40.7
Born elsewhere	396	14	381
% below modal grade	44.4	(B)**	45.3
Non-Hispanic*	22,904	20,128	1,192
% below modal grade	33.9	34.0	27.8
Born in 50 States and DC	20,598	19,784	813
% below modal grade	33.6	33.9	26.4
Born elsewhere	554	195	359
% below modal grade	36.1	43.9	31.8

* Totals for Hispanics and Non-Hispanics include some children whose country of birth and/or language was not reported.

**(B) Base is less than 75,000.

NOTE: Elsewhere includes Puerto Rico, the other U.S. outlying areas, and all other countries.

Source: McArthur, 1993, p. 27. Based on U.S. Department of Commerce, Bureau of the Census. October and November Current Population Survey, 1979 and 1989. Reprinted by permission.

Populations with Special Needs: Late Entrants

Frequently, policy discussions about students and adults who do not speak English concentrate only on that fact. By so doing, from the standpoint of educational equity, a major policy area of concern—students' educational histories—is overlooked (McDonnell & Hill, 1993; Stewart, 1993). In addition to knowing whether or not students know English and how much English they know, or what country they are from, it is also necessary to know about their native language literacy and prior schooling. Older school entrants present the greatest challenge and the largest proportion of the pool of likely candidates for adult ESL programs. As McDonnell and Hill (1993) observe,

> The instruction given older immigrant students depends profoundly on their academic preparation. *Immigrants who enter elementary school at grade three or above can have serious problems catching up with regular instruction.* Whether this happens in a particular case depends primarily on the student's social class and country of origin....However, students whose schooling was delayed or disrupted due to poverty and war are often far behind (p. 69-70, emphasis added).

It is difficult to estimate the size of this population, as McDonnell and Hill (1993) point out: "The limited visibility of immigrant students is evidenced in the lack of precise estimates of their numbers" (p. 2). Most of the available data on the immigrant population comes from the U.S. Census rather than from school data. Based on Census data, McDonnell and Hill report that five states (California, New York, Texas, Florida, and Illinois) account for 70 percent of the school-age immigrant population (p. 3). California has 41 percent of all the U.S. immigrant youth population, followed by New York with 12 percent. Among those cities with the largest percentages of immigrant youth are Los Angeles (21 percent), San Francisco (19 percent), and Miami/Dade County (18 percent) (p.3).

According to government sources in 1988, more than 76 percent of Mexican-born twenty-year olds in the United States had not completed high school compared with 21 percent for the U.S.-born population as a whole (Stewart, 1993, p. 23). Secondary data analysis of the 1979 National Chicano Survey (NCS) indicated that 80 percent of the Mexican-born population entered the United States at age of 15 or older. If these patterns have persisted, then the majority of Mexican immigrants enter the United States after the age of compulsory school attendance (age 16).

Students who immigrate at younger ages, especially those who enter the United States without grade-level equivalency, may still not be able to complete their education. Late-entrant adolescents are in a double bind because their lack of English interferes with their taking required classes for graduation if those courses are available only in English. Most of their high-school careers are spent learning English. Where available, bilingual programs can help these students develop literacy in their native language as they learn English. Unfortunately, the availability of bilingual programs at the high school and middle school levels is sorrowfully inadequate. Likewise, there is a need for content instruction in native languages at the adult level because students who must learn academic and vocational information are involved in a race against time.

For late-entrant students, adult ESL and adult basic education (ABE) programs usually are the only avenues that further the development of literacy. Yet, because ESL courses generally emphasize oral English, late entrants are not well served in the development of their literacy skills. Even when English literacy is offered, there is little articulation between ESL programs and programs that might lead to the kinds of academic and vocational credentials needed for job mobility (see Chisman, Wrigley, & Ewen, 1993; Wrigley, Chisman, & Ewen, 1993).

There has obviously been a lack of federal leadership in this area. McDonnell and Hill (1993) contend that the federal role has been restrained largely because of the overemphasis on the need to teach English to the exclusion of other educational issues:

> The localized impact of immigration means that the federal government has little incentive to address the unique needs of newcomers. On the other hand, the aspects of those students' schooling requirements most likely to gain widespread atten-tion—their need to learn English—is so intertwined with funda-mental cultural and political beliefs that it is rarely addressed as solely an educational issue. (p. 45)

Again, even as language minorities have made educational gains, the educational ante has been increased. For many, this has provided a disincentive to stay in school. A large number of English-speaking White students may likewise fail to see advantages to staying in school given the recent corporate trend toward "downsizing," which has led to a reduction of well-paying jobs in some industries even for native English speakers with higher levels of literacy and educational credentials. This has also led to increased job competition for groups that have historically been discriminated against or disadvantaged by lacking access to the traditional informal social networks that have been used by Whites to gain employment.[2]

In spite of these trends, Kirsch, Jungeblut, Jenkins, and Kolstad (1993) contend that, "although Americans today are, on the whole, better educated and more literate than any who preceded them, many employers say they are unable to find enough workers with the reading, writing, mathematical, and other competencies required in the workplace" (p. x). This commonly held view must be reconciled with the reality that many among the "educated" middle class are losing social position and mobility (see Phillips, 1993). As the highly English literate, college educated lose their jobs in aerospace and computer industries, an underclass, disproportionately populated by immigrants and other language minorities, appears to be growing. In a job market in which unemployment lines are increasingly populated by both the well educated and the undereducated, intergenerational mobility— once the hope of poor parents for their children—appears to be waning (Galbraith, 1992). No wonder that some are disenchanted by the lure of educational solutions to employment problems and fail to believe that education will give them a real advantage (see Gibson & Ogbu, 1991, for a related analysis).

Conflicting Agendas of Students, Programs, and Policymakers

National policy discourse and adult education program goals typically depict ESL instruction as instrumental in promoting cultural assimilation, economic mobility, and political participation. Programs usually describe their content in terms of (1) survival skills, (2) life skills, (3) academic English skills, or (4) employment skills. The connection between the curriculum and lofty policy goals often becomes fairly amorphous. The missing factor is a coherent delivery plan to offer a transition from ESL programs to academic programs in which students can receive credit. In vocational ESL programs, job skills are often geared to a specific job, which may or may not be tied to a career track. From the perspective of job mobility, all too often students, teachers, and policymakers know that English language skills are necessary but not sufficient to lead them to better jobs that usually require *both* English *and* educational credentials.

Students, employers, and policymakers often have conflicting goals. Students may be enticed to participate in educational programs by the lure that learning English will do them some good, but they may not find sufficient reason to continue participating. Employers are not necessarily interested in promoting ESL and literacy as goals in themselves, but see them as means for improved communication, safety, and efficiency in the work place. In fact,

> Improved mobility for the student is commonly touted as one of the major goals of literacy policy. Ironically, while the success of the learner in acquiring literacy skills may promote his or her mobility, it can pose a threat to individual employers in the following ways: The employer may grasp the benefits of workplace literacy in improving communication and efficiency, but how much internal mobility can the enterprise absorb? Some employers may feel they are supporting costly educational programs only to lose their investment when successful learners demand promotions, more pay, or move out of the enterprise to seek better opportunities elsewhere. Employees may feel frustrated when they successfully complete noncredit programs but still lack access to further training that "really counts," training that bestows diplomas, degrees, and credentials required for mobility. These issues are not easily resolved. They demonstrate that there are more fundamental structural issues that relate to whether programs will be successful in meeting the lofty goal of preparing students for full participation. (Wiley, 1993b, pp. 19-20)

Conclusion

If the national debate over the *perpetual literacy crisis* is to be elevated out of its discourse of blame and estrangement, more attention must be shifted to issues of educational equity and economic justice. From the standpoint of education for language minority populations, there must be a recognition that while the focus on English as it relates to mobility is necessary, it is not sufficient to remedy the great divide between those who have not had access to an equal education, either here in the United States or—if they are immigrants—in their countries of origin. Raising standards without looking at the special educational needs of specific groups does little except ensure that many will fail to meet them and thereby be certifiably underskilled and underqualified and will perpetuate the culture of blame.

Further Reading

Chisman, F.P., Wrigley, H.S., & Ewen, D.T. (1993). *ESL and the American dream.* Washington, DC: Southport Institute for Policy Analysis. (ERIC Document Reproduction Service ED 373 585)

Provides an overview of the condition of ESL instruction in the United States and notes contradictions and ambiguities in the goals of ESL programs that include both the development of oral English and literacy. The need for a coherent national ESL policy and for articulation among various types of providers is noted.

de Castell, S., & Luke, A. (1986). Models of literacy in North American schools: Social and historical conditions and consequences. In S. de Castell, A. Luke, & K. Egan (Eds.), *Literacy, society, and schooling* (pp. 87-109). Cambridge: Cambridge University Press.

Describes three major paradigms of literacy that have influenced debates over the alleged literacy crisis.

Freebody, P., & Welch, A.R. (Eds.). (1993). *Knowledge, culture, and power: International perspectives on literacy as policy and practice.* Pittsburgh: University of Pittsburgh Press.

This international collection has several important chapters on the relationship between literacy, social mobility, and economic development. See especially Chapters 1, 10, and 11.

Graff, H.J. (1979). *The literacy myth: Literacy and social structure in the 19th-century city.* New York: Academic Press.

Addresses the historical relationship between mass literacy campaigns and other socioeconomic agendas and explains why a singular focus on illiteracy fails to account for social and economic inequities.

Lankshear, C., with Lawler, M. (1987). *Literacy, schooling and revolution.* New York: Falmer.

Explores the uses of reading and writing in political contexts as they are shaped and influenced by the dominant interests of society. See especially Chapters 1, 4, and 6.

McDonnell, L.M., & Hill, P.T. (1993). *Newcomers in American schools: Meeting the educational needs of immigrant youth.* Santa Monica, CA: Rand.

Considers the special needs of immigrant youth and the limitations of the current educational delivery system. Implications for educational policy are explored.

Wrigley, H.S., Chisman, F.P., & Ewen, D.T. (1993). *Sparks of excellence: Program realities and promising practices in adult ESL.* Washington, DC: Southport Institute for Policy Analysis. (ERIC Document Reproduction Service No. ED 373 586)

Explores the limitations of current programmatic approaches and gives examples of innovative and promising practices.

Notes

[1] The decline for African Americans at 8.6% was also high and can be seen as reflecting the continued neglect and segregation found in many urban schools, documented in Kozol's (1991) *Savage Inequalities.*

[2] According to a recent study by Catteral of UCLA, a preponderance of jobs at the turn of the century "will be in areas that typically require only a high school education. And although only 25% of available jobs are likely to require a college degree, about 35% of students will have a diploma from a four-year institution" (as noted in Goldman, 1994). Moreover, federal policymakers now openly acknowledge that they are willing to accept a "natural" six percent jobless rate in an effort to thwart inflation (Risen, 1994).

CHAPTER 6
Language, Diversity, and the Ascription of Status

The ideology of blame discussed in Chapter Five is reflected in both popular and educational terminology about language use and abilities. Terminology can be both descriptive and ascriptive. When it is used ascriptively, it assigns a social status or social worth to those labeled by it. This is especially true in the case of "illiteracy," which necessarily refers to the absence of literacy in the rudimentary sense of the ability to read and write something at some level. A sense of social stigma is implied by the term *il*literate, since to be illiterate is to be "ignorant" and lacking in formal education. Moreover, illiteracy is a mark of "*inferiority* to an expected standard of familiarity with language and literature" (*American Heritage Dictionary of the English Language,* 1992, p. 899, emphasis added). Illiteracy at one time referred to lacking a "liberal education" (i.e., it meant not knowing Latin and Greek, even if one "could read in a vernacular language or handle accounts and correspondence") (Bailey & McArthur, 1992, p. 498).

To consciously avoid the stigma associated with the term "illiterate," the labels "preliterate" and "nonliterate" are preferred in academic discussions; yet illiterate persists in common usage. Terms such as "preliterate" carry a connotation of *expectation* that individuals and even whole societies will become literate. "Nonliteracy" carries no such expectation. The label "semiliterate" acknowledges literacy in the sense of being able to read and write at some level but implies the absence of formal education. From the perspective of language diversity, these labels take on special relevance. Speakers of nondominant varieties of English are sometimes looked down on as being less than literate (and unintelligent) because of characteristics of their oral language. Similarly, non-English-speaking people who are literate in languages other than English are treated as if they were illiterate simply because they do not speak English.

The racial, ethnic, and linguistic labeling that occurs in the popular media is also a problem.[1] Consider, for example, the census terminology used in reporting statistics. White (non-Hispanic), Hispanic, Black,

Asian/Pacific Islander, and American Indian represent a kind of grab bag of nonparallel human typecastings based upon rather fuzzy notions of race, culture, and geographical origin, and other dimensions of possible group identification, such as social class, are rarely represented. Individuals of Asian and Pacific geographical origin are melded into a Pan-Asian/Pacific group that seems to function as a quasi-racial category when, in fact, performance data among Asian/Pacific students vary widely. In California, for example, Cambodian American students have one of the lowest rates of admission to the University of California. Nevertheless, there has been considerable debate about whether they should be eligible for special educational assistance because Asians as an undifferentiated group tend to be over-represented and Cambodians are "Asian." "Hispanic" tends to be more of a cultural and linguistic designation. Despite the disclaimer on census forms that Hispanics can be members of any race, Hispanic now functions *like* a racial classification because Whites are considered a racial group. As a blanket term, Hispanic ignores distinctions among significant subgroups such as Chicanos, Cuban Americans, and Puerto Rican Americans, as well as distinctions between Hispanics born in the United States and Hispanic immigrants. Attempts to label and group people into these few categories may be called *racialization*. Miles (1989) defines racialization as "a process of delineation of group boundaries and an allocation of persons within those boundaries by primary reference to (supposedly) inherent and/or biological (usually phenotypical) characteristics. It is therefore an ideological process" (p. 74). A parallel process to racialization involves labeling people according to their language characteristics. Language labeling can be purely descriptive, such as "so and so is a Spanish speaker," but classifications such as "non-English speaker" ascribe status based upon what one does not speak rather than on what one speaks (see Wink, 1993).

This chapter begins with a discussion of status ascription based on language background, the types of labels routinely used in educational programs, and the attitudes often associated with them. This is followed by a discussion of the status of "nonstandard" (nondominant) varieties of language and the promotion of literacy in schools. Next, there is a discussion of African American Language and debates about its status and use in schools. The chapter concludes with implications for practice.

Status Ascription Based on Language

Depending on to whom one talks, bilingualism in the United States tends to be seen as either an asset or a curse. This ambivalence is reflected in educational policies that attempt to provide a *transition* for language minority students from their native languages to English as soon as possible and attempt to teach monolingual English speaking students *foreign* languages. In the first case, the United States fails to develop languages other than English, and in the second case, it spends millions to teach them. These policies are not as contradictory as they appear at first because they apply to two different populations. Transitional bilingual education was developed as a *remedial* program for students who had historically been discriminated against (see Lyons, 1990), whereas foreign language instruction is associated with an *elite* higher education tradition. Many of the opponents of bilingual education claim that they support foreign language instruction, in effect, denying dual language development for those who already speak a language other than English on the one hand, and supporting monolingual speakers of English learning a foreign language on the other.

Language is a marker of status. Like race and ethnicity, language provides one of the important means by which individuals and groups identify and distinguish themselves from others. Prejudice on the basis of language is not unlike other forms of prejudice and may work in conjunction with them or serve as a *surrogate* for them. Weinberg (1991) defines racism as a systematic, institutional procedure for excluding some and privileging others. It is premised not on the moral foundation of equal human worth, but on the belief that some are inherently superior to others. As a related, or surrogate, form of racism, discrimination on the basis of language may be called "linguicism." Linguicism has been defined as "the ideologies and structures which are used to legitimate, effectuate and reproduce an unequal division of power and resources (both material and nonmaterial) between groups which are in turn defined on the basis of language (i.e., the mother tongue)" (Phillipson, 1988, p. 339).

Linguistic ideology has affinities with the way racism is affirmed... [because] it essentially involves the dominant group/language presenting an idealized image of itself, stigmatizing the dominated group/language, and rationalizing the relationship between the two, always to the advantage of the dominant group/language.

It is of the essence of hegemony that injustices are internalized by both the dominant group and the dominated groups as being natural and legitimate. However, neither the structures nor the ideologies are static. Hegemony is lived experience which is in a constant process of negotiation, recreation and adjustment. It is therefore open to contestation. (Phillipson, 1988, pp. 341-343)

Historically, in the United States, language and literacy requirements, like racial policies, have served to bar individuals from immigrating, voting, and seeking employment in some occupations (see Leibowitz, 1969, 1974; McKay, 1993; McKay & Weinstein-Shr, 1993). Thus, through linguistic status ascription, language minority groups in various historical contexts have experienced exclusion on the basis of language and literacy that has been functionally parallel to racial exclusion. As with other forms of discrimination, language discrimination can be taken as the "denial of equal human worth."[2]

From LEPs to Lepers

The labels used by English language and literacy programs in the assessment and placement of students often ascribe a lower, language/literacy status to students who need English instruction (see Wink, 1993). At the high school, community college, and university levels, it is not uncommon to find some international and language minority students who wish to avoid taking ESL classes because they feel stigmatized by being known as "ESL students." They are embarrassed to be in courses that are often seen as remedial rather than as developmental. The fact that ESL classes often do not count for graduation credit does little to discourage their view.

Consider also the label "limited English proficient" (LEP). This term originated in the bilingual education legislation of 1968. Initially, it referred only to oral abilities in English. In 1978, it was extended to include reading and writing. It was "determined that English proficiency would be the exclusive criterion for the LEP population, irrespective of the person's proficiency in the non-English language" (Macías, 1994, p. 35). As an educational classification, the label is based solely on the language skills the student *lacks*—in terms of English only—rather than on those skills the student has in other languages. Abilities in other languages are thereby rendered invisible by the educational labeling. How such labels are tossed about in daily use, for example, in lunch room conversation, provides insight into the status ascribed to language minority students, as they have occasionally jokingly been referred to as "Lepers."

Labeling students solely on the basis of their English language proficiencies is also problematic in other ways. Macías (1993), for example, contends that educational assessments have tended to ignore relationships between languages, focusing instead on the notion of limited English proficiency alone. From an educational standpoint, this is significant since "programs and policies that were developed to address a student's limited English proficiency often ignore or de-emphasize race and ethnicity in general" (p. 231). It is important to note that "debates over bilingual education and cultural literacy are as much about race" and ethnicity as they are about language (Macías, 1993, p. 231; see also Crawford, 1992a, Chapter Six on "Hispanophobia").

Educational assessments also frequently ignore the social class of the students (or their prior social class in the case of refugees). Social class is usually a major determinant of educational opportunities. Students' prior educational histories need to be considered together with their English language proficiency. For children and adults, LEP and non-English language background (NELB) designations can inappropriately lead to an educational emphasis on English oral language development to the exclusion of an emphasis on English literacy or literacy in the students' native language (see Skutnabb-Kangas & Phillipson, 1989).

Literacy and Nondominant Varieties of Language

Illich (1979) has explored from an historical perspective the promotion of standardized languages of academic literacy as a means of social control and the role of schools in promoting those languages. In his provocative critique of the rise of modern schooling practices as they relate to vernacular language and literacy, Illich argues that instructional language policies impose a prescribed language in school. By so doing, vernacular values associated with local common languages are diminished. As an example, he maintains that the imposition of literacy (using standardized language) actually restricted vernacular functions of literacy in late 15th- and early 16th-century Spain. Rather than developing a tongue in common with others, people would have to receive it inauthentically through schools as socially sanctioned institutions. Thus, students would be formally taught the rules of grammar of their mother tongue as if it were Latin or a foreign language. Illich sees this change from the use of vernaculars to standardized mother tongues (by official sanction and imposition) as fostering the notion that the school is the only legitimate vehicle for promoting literacy:

> Now there would be no reading, no writing—if possible, no speaking, outside the educational sphere....We first allow standard language to degrade ethnic, black, or hillbilly language, and then spend money to teach their counterfeits as academic subjects. Administrators and entertainers, admen and newsmen, ethnic politicians and "radical" professionals form powerful interest groups, each fighting for a larger slice of the language pie. (1979, p. 55)

Illich's goal, in opposition to the monopoly of the educational establishment, calls for *de-schooling* society. Educational anarchism (see O'Neill, 1983) has never had a wide following in this country. However, whether one agrees with Illich's agenda or not, his observation underscores how the school's choice of language and its imposition of a standard are instruments of social control. For language minority populations, whose languages or regional and social varieties are not reflected in the schools, the relevance of these observations should not be lost because those who can impose their language and literacy practices as normative have a strategic advantage over those who cannot. The results of such an imposition advantage those whose language is chosen. In this regard, Bhatia (1984) concludes,

> Linguistic factors specific to ML [monolingual] societies govern the pattern of literacy. Some recent research indicates that the patterns within ML societies are neither randomly nor uniformly distributed. There is a systematic correlation between the rate of literacy and the distance between local dialects and the standard language....The relative difference in the distance between the high and low varieties of Tamil, Telugu, and Sihala plays an important role in the indices of literacy in...South Asia. A similar phenomenon has been observed in the United States, where the literacy rate among speakers of Black English is considerably lower than that for speakers of Standard English. (p. 28)

Again, the issue of whose language variety is taken as normative relates directly to who has advantages in the acquisition of literacy at school and who does not. Some students are advantaged because their language variety and their language practices become the norms for the rest of society. As the speakers of the standard language become advantaged, the speakers of other varieties become the disadvantaged. This is especially true when assessment and placement decisions about language levels and language proficiencies of students are based on standardized tests of academic English. Norms for standard language are based on written rather than oral varieties of language (Milroy & Milroy, 1985). Judgments made on the basis of these tests are determined and constrained by the instruments used. Moreover, when those tested speak, read, or write more than one language, judgments about language proficiency are constrained by the language of the test (see Cook-Gumperz, 1993; Hewitt & Inghilleri, 1993). Thus, our notions of language proficiency are influenced by "standard" and "literate" forms of the specific language of the assessment, which is the variety of language taught in schools.

The Case of African American Language

In a discussion of literacy and language diversity in the United States, it is important to include African American Language (AAL), because it is often seen as substandard and as a barrier to the acquisition of literacy. Although the majority of African Americans are native speakers of English, their linguistic history, related to their sociopolitical and economic history, is substantially different from that of many European-origin peoples in the United States. To understand the persistence of purportedly high rates of illiteracy and low rates of educational achievement among African Americans, it is important to take these factors into consideration by first confronting the legacy of stigmatization with which many African Americans are faced.

> The language of African Americans has often been portrayed as being "substandard," "illiterate," or "uneducated" unlike other language minority groups of color whose languages are at least seen as having linguistic legitimacy (Dandy, 1992).

Unlike most European-origin peoples who came to the United States either voluntarily or as political, religious, or economic refugees, the migration of most African-origin peoples was *forced* (see Ogbu, 1991; Ogbu & Matute-Bianchi, 1986). As a condition of enslavement, African Americans faced a policy of native language eradication. While enslaved, they were denied opportunities for schooling and acquiring English literacy, and they were barred from education by "compulsory ignorance laws" in many southern states (Weinberg, 1995). After the abolition of slavery, African Americans continued to be barred from equal participation in education, and English literacy requirements, in lieu of more blatantly racist measures, were often used to restrict their political participation (see Leibowitz, 1969).

Coming from a variety of largely West African-language backgrounds, and faced with English-speaking enslavers, African Americans developed an English creole.[3] African American speech was ascribed a lower status and developed a diglossic[4] relationship with higher status varieties of English. Roy (1987) explains,

> Over time, generations [of African Americans] had more and more contact with English through location, employment, and education and more of the stigmatized features were dropped and more of the forms hypothesized as English were added. Successive generations transmitted to their children a less marked,[5] creole system except in those areas where there was only minimal contact with English. This process of language change, a process of differential linguistic acculturation termed decreolizaton, is responsible for the movement of Plantation English Creole toward English and for the range of social, regional and individual dialects that have been described as Black English (BE) and Black English Vernacular that can be heard in the urban and rural Black communities today. (p. 232)

In contrast, European-origin immigrant groups and their offspring "with rare exceptions have not passed through the pidginization, creolization, and decreolization processes that are responsible for the wide range of language forms that are present in communities using Black English" (Roy, 1987, p. 237). Today, the high degree of correspondence between African-American speech and standard English obscures some of its systematic differences with the more dominant school-based variety of English (p. 233). These linguistic differences have sparked considerable debate over education policy for African Americans. Given these linguistic differences, some seek to accommodate what they see as "nonstandard" varieties of English in order to promote acquisition of standard English. A major legal challenge in 1979 (*Martin Luther King Jr. Elementary School Children v. Ann Arbor Board of Education*) asserted that the differences between the language of African Americans and the language of school were great enough to warrant accommodation by the schools. The suit was filed because, despite a district integration plan, African-American children performed at a significantly lower level than their White peers. The plaintiffs argued that the school's failure to take into account the language differences of their students was discriminatory. To prove the plaintiffs' position, it first had to be established that the children actually spoke a distinctly different variety of language. According to the presiding judge,

> This case is not an effort on the part of the plaintiffs to require that they be taught "black English," or that a dual language program be provided....It is a straightforward effort to require the court to intervene on the children's behalf to require the defendant School District Board to take appropriate action to teach them to read in the standard English of the school, the commercial world, the arts, the sciences, and the professions. This action is a cry for help in opening the doors to the establishment...*to keep another generation from becoming functionally illiterate.* (cited in Norgren & Nanda, 1988, p. 190, emphasis added)

Note that the judge's chief concern was "to keep another generation from becoming functionally illiterate" in standard English. Following extensive testimony by linguists, who demonstrated that African-American speech was systematically distinct from standard English, the Federal judge sided with the plaintiffs that the linguistic differences were significant enough to warrant special educational treatment (Labov, 1982). The decision sees the remedy for functional English illiteracy as one of *linguistic accommodation*. It is typical of solutions that see the language and educational problem to be that of African Americans'. The solution is seen as sensitizing teachers to systematic language differences, developing a more receptive attitude toward African-American speech, making differences between African-American speech and the dominant school-based variety more explicit, and avoiding biased assessment and testing practices.

Since the time of that decision, there is no indication that the attitudes of most teachers toward African American Language (AAL) have changed. Neither is there evidence that language differences have been accommodated in any systematic way in most public schools in the United States. Significantly, the decision ignored the more controversial issue of whether students should receive instruction in "Black English." Subsequently, for a number of years, there has been considerable controversy in the United States regarding the standing of AAL and the extent to which it should be used in the instruction of African-American children (see Dillard, 1972). For example, there have been occasional calls for the development of "dialect readers" to promote literacy among those whose speech is markedly different from speakers of the dominant variety. According to Wolfram (1994), in the 1970s, a series was developed for middle and high school students called *Bridge: A Cross-cultural Reading Program* (Simpkins, Simpkins, & Holt, 1977). The rationale for such materials is similar to the one for bilingual education, in other words, that language and literacy are better promoted when one learns in his or her own language before attempting to do so in a second language. This notion has been met with great opposition. Complicating the debate is the fact that many of the issues regarding the education of African-American children have been put forth by White social scientists such as Baratz (1973), Stewart (1964), and Wolfram and Fasold (1973). Occasionally, their intentions and prescriptions have been severely criticized by some commentators (e.g., Sledd, 1969, 1973; see also O'Neil's (1973) criticism of bidialectal instruction and Shuy's (1980) thoughts on the debate during the 1960s and 1970s). Wolfram (1994) observes,

> It is quite clear that vernacular dialects have been defined in our own society as inappropriate vehicles for literacy, and it is apparent that children are socialized regarding this functional differentiation from the onset of their socialization regarding literacy. In this respect, the U.S. situation is akin to some third-world situations, in which unwritten minority languages are considered inappropriate for literacy vis-à-vis official state languages even when knowledge of the official language is minimal or nonexistent. (p. 74)

In spite of such opposition, a small number of advocates continue to support literacy instruction in African American Language. Williams (1991), for example, advocates what is essentially a language maintenance policy. Maintenance bilingual policies attempt to cultivate the minority language of students while "strengthening their sense of cultural identity and affirming the rights of an ethnic minority group in a nation" (Baker, 1993, p. 152). Among the range of issues that such proposals encounter are the practical difficulties associated with the lack of materials, the cost of producing them, and the need for staff development—the same issues that have dogged bilingual education reform efforts. Williams agrees that there are significant phonological and grammatical differences in the language of African Americans based on the historical West African influences on AAL. However, he rejects the notion that the purported language problems reside in the speech of the student. Williams (1991) also rejects commonly used labels such as Black Dialect, Black English, or Black English Vernacular, because he contends that they ascribe a lower status to the language spoken by many African Americans and because they obscure its West African influences. He offers the label African American Language (AAL) as an alternative and, by so doing, equates AAL with English and other languages. Williams acknowledges a language problem only to the extent that it results from differential power between groups, English-speaking European American peoples and AAL-speaking African Americans, and the ability of the former to impose its language norms on the latter (see also Smith, 1993).

If we relate Williams's position to literacy policy, what are its implications? Readers in African American Language could be used to promote initial literacy in the native language variety spoken by those African Americans whose speech is markedly different from speakers of the dominant school variety of English. At least two arguments could be advanced for doing so. The first is analogous to the one underlying the use of native language instruction in bilingual education programs: Language and literacy are better promoted when one learns in his or her own language before attempting to do so in a second language. The second argument involves the use of language as a means of maintaining culture and cultural identity. Recently, in some alternative schools emphasizing an Afrocentric curriculum, AAL is being systematically taught much as standard English is in most public schools. This promotes its status and positively reinforces students' cultural identity. However, many researchers, teachers, and parents are vehemently opposed to teaching AAL and developing AAL readers, because they feel it would deprive students from learning the dominant, or power, language variety that is needed for full membership and participation in U.S. society. The issue of providing "bidialect" education has been hotly debated, as Wolfram (1994) observes:

> It is now two decades since the dialect reader controversy erupted and yet we still reap the effects of the phobia that it engendered in many education and popular circles. Applied social dialectologists are still often reminded by an unforgetting and unforgiving education establishment and general public that

a few of us once attempted to convince educators that it was at least worthwhile to experiment with dialect readers to see if they helped incipient readers gain access to the literate world. (p. 72)

From a linguistic standpoint Wolfram (1994) notes, "it is reasonable to hypothesize that the greater the mismatch between the spoken and written word, the greater the likelihood of processing difficulties in reading" (p. 75). Unfortunately, from a research standpoint, according to Wolfram, it is difficult to respond to this hypothesis, because "there still remain no carefully designed experimental studies that have examined this important research question in the United States in detail" (p. 75), although there are international examples where the divergence between language varieties used in and out of school is sufficient to cause developmental reading problems (see p. 76). In the United States, Wolfram believes the differences between AAL and the written standard are insufficient to interfere with reading development. In a related discussion, Ferreiro and Teberosky (1982) consider the implications of divergence from standard Spanish for some Indian children in South America and reach a similar conclusion. They believe that when the divergence is not too great and learners are allowed to read texts as they speak, reading in the dominant language is not a problem. The divergence between spoken and written language becomes a problem when teachers confuse reading (i.e., processing print for meaning) with pronunciation (i.e., speaking correctly). This is one reason why solely phonics-based approaches to reading are inappropriate for speakers of nondominant language varieties. Because phonics approaches assume that one must move from sound to meaning, students are presumed to be unable to read until they have mastered the sounds of the dominant variety. Given the prevalence of this approach, it is not difficult to see why speakers of nondominant varieties lose interest early in school and why adults are reluctant to go back.

Wolfram (1994) also notes that, given overall differences between oral and written language, even speakers of the dominant variety do not find an identical match between what they read and how they speak. Some prescriptivists would have us all talk like books. Writing, on the other hand, "may be more transparently influenced" by differences in language varieties; however, "it should be noted the influence of spoken language is not isomorphic" (p.75).

Conclusion and Recommendations

The issue of whether to teach AAL or standard English does not have to be framed as an either-or choice. Rather, students need to be aware of the characteristics of the varieties of language they speak, read, and write. For example, learning how to describe the systematic characteristic features of their own language can help native speakers of AAL to see where it is similar to standard academic English and where the two varieties differ. White students who speak Appalachian English could likewise benefit from systematically learning about their language. Similarly, speakers of standard English could benefit from learning about the differences between their spoken and written language and about the richness of other varieties such as AAL and Appalachian English. Such knowledge should help children and adults appreciate language differences and improve their attitudes toward language variation.

Language minorities are not the only people who could benefit from learning about language differences. Language prejudice is related to other forms of intolerance. In a society as racially, ethnically, and linguistically diverse as this one, children and adults need to learn more about the richness of their own language as well as other languages and varieties of language.

The question of whether AAL instruction should be part of a full-scale bilingual education program is more complex. The uses of AAL are not parallel to those of Spanish, for example, which has its own dominant varieties and nondominant varieties and its spoken and written forms. Given its diglossic relationship with English, AAL has been confined mostly to oral language and vernacular literacy practices. Allowing students to learn more about AAL and its use in "vernacular" writing will expose students to the richness of the language. As Wolfram (1994) notes, the work of a number of African-American writers such as Langston Hughes, Paul Dunbar, and Maya Angelou provide excellent examples. However, to develop a full AAL bilingual education program, a great deal more would be required of the language itself including extending its use to a wider range of social practices. Thus, a full-scale AAL-English bilingual program seems rather utopian.

With the range of language varieties represented in schools in the United States, it is essential that teachers have some minimal knowledge of and training in sociolinguistics, the study of language in its social contexts. Teachers need this knowledge to adequately assess their students' abilities and learning and to provide appropriate instruction. Both teachers and students need to better understand and appreciate language diversity. Without an understanding of language differences, language prejudice and status ascription based on language are perpetuated. Given the pervasiveness of bias toward nondominant varieties of language, language prejudices all too easily become surrogates for ethnic, racial, and class biases.

Further Reading

Dandy, E.B. (1992). Sensitizing teachers to cultural differences: An African American perspective. In D.E. Murray (Ed.), *Diversity as resource: Redefining cultural literacy* (pp. 87-112). Alexandria, VA: Teachers of English to Speakers of Other Languages.

Provides a practical introduction for teachers and suggestions for instructional projects (see also Dandy, 1991, *Black communications: Breaking down the barriers.* Chicago: African American Images).

Williams, S.W. (1991). Classroom use of African American language: Educational tool or social weapon? In C.E. Sleeter (Ed.), *Empowerment through multicultural education* (pp. 199-215). New York: State University of New York Press.

Identifies West African influences in AAL and provides several examples of how failure to note these influences results in inappropriate education for African Americans.

Wolfram, W. (1994). Bidialectal literacy in the United States. In D. Spener (Ed.), *Adult biliteracy in the United States* (pp. 71-88). Washington, DC and McHenry, IL: Center for Applied Linguistics and Delta Systems.

Provides background information on the status of AAL and the controversy regarding whether or not it should be used as a language of instruction. Also discusses instructional approaches.

Notes

[1] Sometimes language background is used as a substitute for race and ethnicity. In December 1993, the *Los Angeles Times* (Carvajal, 1993), for example, carried the headline: "When Languages Collide." Immediately below the headline there were two pie charts on demographic changes in the ethnic/racial composition of Orange County. The charts were introduced by the subheading: "Changing Ethnicity." Although language was used as the superordinate category, it was really only a surrogate for race and ethnicity.

[2] Meyer Weinberg has recently argued convincingly in several faculty seminars on racism at California State University, Long Beach, that related "isms" (racism, sexism, ageism) all share the common characteristic of denying equal human worth.

[3] In order to define "creole," it is first necessary to define "pidgin." A pidgin is a language with "limited vocabulary, and a reduced grammatical structure, and a narrow range of functions, compared to the languages which gave rise to them" (Crystal, 1987, p. 334). It is "the native language of no one" and develops "when members of two mutually unintelligible" languages attempt to communicate (Bright, 1992, p. 325). Typically, language contact occurs in connection with some form of colonization. Many pidgins are derived from politically and economically dominant European colonial languages; however, non-European derived pidgins can be found in areas where cross-linguistic contact has been common (Crystal, 1987, p. 334). When the next generation is born, the pidgin has its first native speakers and it becomes more complex; it becomes a creole. A creole then, unlike a pidgin, is a mother tongue. The process of a pidgin becoming a creole is called creolization. When a standard language begins to influence a creole, the process is called decreolization (Bright, 1992, p. 290).

[4] Diglossia refers to a "sociolinguistic situation where two very different varieties of a language co-occur throughout a speech community, each standardized to some degree, and each performing an individual range of social functions. The varieties are usually described as high (H) and low (L), corresponding broadly to a difference in formality" (Bright, 1992, p. 292).

[5] Markedness is an "analytic principle" used by linguistics "whereby pairs of linguistic features, seen as oppositions, are given values of positive or *marked* vs. neutral, negative, or unmarked" (Bright, 1992,

p. 314). When a language variety is marked, it may be seen as having either high (H) or low (L) status. In the context of Roy's statement, for successive generations to receive a less marked form of language means that it had fewer characteristics that contrasted with those of so-called "standard English."

CHAPTER 7
Literacy and Language Diversity in Sociocultural Contexts

Anthropologists who study literacy and social process have much to offer educational policy and practice. By helping to make explicit what social as well as educational resources adults bring with them, anthropologists can help educators to build on resources adults already have. By discovering the meanings and uses of literacy for members of diverse cultural communities, anthropologists can help educational planners take into account what adults want literacy to do for them. (Weinstein-Shr, 1993a, p. 291)

The more that literacy practices of schools are seen as the sole models for the ways people become literate, the more difficult it becomes to see other possibilities for acquiring literacy. As indicated in Chapter One, the popular media often perpetuate stereotypes about illiteracy. Concerning this point, Heath (1988a) observes,

> The public media today give much attention to the decline of literacy skills as measured in school settings and to the failure of students to acquire certain levels of literacy. However, the media pay little attention to occasions for literacy retention—to the actual uses of literacy in work settings, daily interactions in religious, economic, and legal institutions, and family habits of socializing the young into uses of literacy. (p. 349)

This chapter addresses literacy in the broader context of how it relates to social practices. It attempts to demonstrate the value of the social practices perspective (see Chapter Three) by looking at literacy in both school and community contexts and the relationship between them. The social practices perspective greatly adds to an understanding of literacy, yet there is still a need to view literacy practices not only *within* groups, but also *between* groups. It is likewise necessary to look at ways that school literacy practices and expectations privilege some and disadvantage others even as they enter school. It is one thing to talk about standards that all students should achieve by the end of the educational process; it is another to see how implicit expectations favoring one group affect others. Social practices viewed from an ideological perspective are likely to illuminate structural and institutional inequities that produce educational success and failure—often in spite of lofty goals and good intentions.

Ethnographic Studies of Literacy in Sociocultural Contexts

Ethnographic studies of literacy[1] describe what children and adults do with literacy in actual social and cultural contexts. They demonstrate the importance of studying literacy in a variety of linguistic, ethnocultural, and socioeconomic contexts by providing a more complete picture of functions of literacy in daily activities. Ethnographic studies have identified a wide range of community literacy practices, many of which are neither taught nor used as a basis for further learning in the schools. They are concerned with the literacy activities that people find both practical and meaningful such as those related to interpersonal communication, entertainment, and leisure. Rather than dichotomizing literacy and orality, ethnographic studies often focus on *literacy events* and analyze the interaction between those events. The literacy event is a useful conceptual tool for examining specific communities to determine "the actual forms and functions of oral and literate traditions and co-existing relationships between spoken and written language...in which a piece of writing is integral to the nature of participants' interactions and their interpretive processes" (Heath, 1988a, p. 350). For example, the following list summarizes the functions of literacy in just one community studied by Heath (1980):

(1) Literacy has an instrumental function. It provides practical information used in transportation or daily business transactions.

(2) It has social-interactional functions. It provides information useful in daily social communication, as illustrated by letter writing and the sending of greeting cards or the reading and writing of recipes.

(3) Literacy has a major news-related function.

(4) Literacy has a memory-supportive function, which is illustrated by the use of calendars, telephone books, and appointments books.

(5) Literacy substitutes for direct oral communication, as in the case of parents and teachers conveying messages by means of notes.

(6) Literacy provides a basis for the keeping of permanent records of an official nature.

(7) Literacy provides a basis to confirm beliefs that are already held, as in the case of appealing to authoritative texts such as dictionaries, code books, or religious texts. (summarized from pp. 128-129)

By expanding the range of social contexts in which reading and writing are studied, it is possible to de-school the notion of literacy and open it up to possibilities beyond the classroom. By so doing, we may find ways to move beyond stereotypic school-based notions of literacy and perhaps enrich those of the classroom. (See also Barton & Ivanic, 1991; Camitta, 1993; Cook-Gumperz & Keller-Cohen, 1993; Street 1993; Weinstein-Shr, 1993b.)

Ethnographic research allows concentration on literacy practices as they function within different communities. By focusing on literacy events, it is possible to see the interaction between oral and written modes of language use. Understanding literacy events within different communities helps us understand what children already know about language and literacy at the time they enter school. Such knowledge is useful to the schools because, as discussed in Chapter Three, one cannot equate literacy practices generally with school literacy practices specifically.

Literacy is often seen only in terms of what individuals can do with print. Can they read and write, and if so at what skill levels? Ethnographic studies, in contrast, see literacy as embedded in group-specific sociocultural practices. As Schieffelin and Cochran-Smith (1984) note,

To understand the observed behaviors of any social group, we have to know what literacy means to the group. We have to understand which genres are seen as appropriate to master at different points in time....Without serious consideration of what literacy means and does not mean for those people who are introduced to it, it will be impossible to make sense of the ways literacy organizes and is organized by different social groups. (pp. 20-22)

Schieffelin and Cochran-Smith (1984) arrived at this conclusion following several studies they undertook, two of which are briefly reviewed here. One study focused on the introduction of English literacy into a nonliterate community in New Guinea. Literacy was introduced by missionaries as a tool for changing the local religious beliefs and cultural practices. (Conditions in New Guinea have changed markedly since this study was undertaken.) According to Schieffelin and Cochran-Smith, literacy was introduced through its association with the practices of a foreign religion into a culture where an oral tradition predominated. Reading practices involved Bible reading and was taught by concentrating on syllabication with an emphasis on correct pronunciation. English-based (foreign) words were used for new concepts. The literacy practices introduced were passive, because they were limited to reading and reciting texts rather than writing or interpreting them. Under these circumstances, there appeared to be no incorporation of literacy into the traditional culture. Therefore, interaction between children and adults was not conducive to an intergenerational transmission of literacy. Children were discouraged from using or handling the books, because they were seen as valuable artifacts. Apart from its religious function, book reading had little relevance to the broader social practices of the community. In Scribner and Cole's (1981) terms, this is restricted literacy, because it is limited to specific religious practices and taught outside the domain of school. Further, it is literacy that is not tied to economic development, although there may have been individual economic incentives for associating with foreigners. From the social practices approach, literacy in this context can be seen in terms of its limited functions, associated with a rather narrow range of religious practices. From an ideological perspective, the literacy practices of one culture are being used to facilitate a change in the belief system of another. They are tools for conversion of one people to the beliefs of another. In this instance, the conversion appears not to be forced. (Historically, however, there are many examples where the literacy practices of one society have been forcibly imposed on another.)

Another study reported by Schieffelin and Cochran-Smith (1984) involved a Chinese-Vietnamese immigrant family in Philadelphia. This study helps break several stereotypes about literacy in immigrant families who speak languages other than English, but it also raises several questions. First, regarding the stereotypes, it is commonly assumed that children will have difficulty acquiring literacy (English literacy) if their parents do not speak English, because parents are assumed to be the principal literacy (English literacy) tutors of their children. It is also assumed (largely from an English-speaking, middle-class point of view) that a home must have plenty of (English) books and magazines to provide a literate environment (see Clark, 1976; Morrow, 1983). According to Schieffelin and Cochran-Smith (1984), in this family, as in many immigrant and refugee families, the parents are not literate in English, but they are literate in Chinese. There are not many books and magazines in the home, and the ones that are there are in Chinese. Nevertheless, Schieffelin and Cochran-Smith note that the children live in a very literate environment because "reading and writing are very important in their lives" (p. 19). For example, the children's father regularly reads letters from relatives aloud to the family, and family members frequently write letters. Similarly, in many language-minority households newspapers, magazines, and books in languages other than English allow adults to utilize their native language literacy and maintain currency within both their communities and the larger society.

Interaction with responsive adults is also stressed as being essential to the literacy development of children (e.g., Clark, 1976, 1984). However, in the case of the Chinese-Vietnamese family, the pattern for English literacy was reversed, with the child having to negotiate literacy events in English for his parents. Again, in immigrant and language-minority families, there is no reason to assume that the literacy practices of parents and children should parallel those of monolingual English-speaking, middle-class families. If the children are bilingual and have acquired some English literacy, they are likely to have to assist their parents with English literacy tasks. They become *access* persons or brokers for their parents by acting as translators and as scribes. This frequently involves them in literacy events that go well beyond those in which their monolingual peers are involved. What is not clear from Schieffelin and Cochran-Smith's account is to what extent the child was being coached by his parents during the interactions. Regarding parental support for the child's school work, they conclude,

Because he cannot receive assistance in school-related activities from his non-English-speaking parents, his requests for assistance are directed primarily to English-speaking adults who are outside his family network....Thus the non-English-speaking child must develop a range of social relationships that are very different from those of the English-speaking child, who may expect to receive assistance from family members. (Schieffelin & Cochran-Smith, 1984, p. 15)

Several issues emerge from this conclusion. First, if this child's literacy development is tied only to his access to English speakers, he must have been very fortunate to have these contacts, because many language minority children do not have these opportunities. Second, this is the type of conclusion that one might expect in situations where no bilingual education is available. If there were a bilingual program, this child's parents, who were literate in Chinese, could assist him with his academic school work while he was further developing English. However, other conclusions could be drawn if, for example, the school had a bilingual education or a family English literacy program. Then, the whole family could develop English literacy and utilize its literacy in Chinese. In the absence of a bilingual program, or a program to give him access to adults who could help him with the English-only curriculum, this child apparently had to fend for himself, and he had been lucky thus far.

Additional issues relate to what this child *did* know and whether the school recognized his knowledge and skills and built upon them. In a passive learning environment, his skills at negotiation—which were probably more developed than those of most of his monolingual peers—might not be recognized. If language and literacy skills are defined solely in terms of school practices, such children may never be allowed to shine in school. In this regard Wells (1986) offers several relevant observations and suggestions. He contends that too much emphasis is placed on age-grade comparisons of student performance and too little to mapping the individual progress of children. It is often assumed that children from lower socioeconomic backgrounds are deficient in their oral language abilities (a deficit view). In his own studies on the relationship between language use in the home and school, Wells found little support for a deficit view, especially when a variety of measures were used to evaluate language. He observed that teachers gave students far fewer opportunities for exploratory and collaborative talk than parents did, regardless of their social class. Thus, teachers can unwittingly reduce children to a passive role and under-assess their language abilities (see Barnes, 1976). Wells concluded that because schools value literacy at the expense of orality, schools may inadvertently be helping to accentuate the literacy disadvantage of some children by failing to incorporate oral language, which is the strength of many children especially in the lower grades.

Schieffelin and Cochran-Smith's (1984) work helps illustrate how literacy is tied to sociocultural practices and how a social practices perspective is valuable. It also demonstrates the value of micro-ethnographic approaches to investigating language use. However, in order to formulate literacy policies that are culturally sensitive, a macro-analysis of how they differentially impact groups is also needed. For such analyses, an ideological perspective is more powerful.

Much can also be learned from ethnographic studies of adults acquiring literacy. For example, in a study of Hmong adults living in Philadelphia, Weinstein-Shr (1993a) details the limitations of assessing students' abilities solely based on their performance in English as a second language classrooms. Weinstein-Shr compares two Hmong students—Pao Youa, an active leader in the Philadelphia Hmong community, and Chou Chang, a good student of English who does not wield any influence in his community. Her comparison of the capabilities of the two students *in* and *out* of class is particularly insightful:

> When I first met Pao Youa in the classroom, I could only see him as a dismally failing student with no hope for making it. Chou Chang, on the other hand, plodded through, allocated the time and resources necessary to complete enigmatic grammar exercises, learned the rules of classroom behavior, and came out with his high-school equivalency degree. A teacher who met these two men in the classroom would have missed much—she could not have imagined the kinds of resources at the command of the older student, nor could she have imagined the kinds of resources at the command of the star pupil, who would eventually leave Philadelphia in despair of his social isolation. (p.291)

Thus, if one were to rely solely on classroom assessments of functional English literacy, one could easily underestimate the abilities of a student who plodded through the classroom activities. In this regard, Taylor and Dorsey-Gaines (1988) have cogently admonished,

> If we are to teach, we must first examine our own assumptions about families and children, and we must be alert to the negative images in the literature ("dropouts come from stressful homes"). Instead of responding to "pathologies," we must recognize that

what we see may actually be healthy adaptations to an uncertain and stressful world. As teachers, researchers, and policymakers, we need to think about the children themselves and to try to imagine the contextual worlds of their day-to-day lives. (p. 203)

Ethnographic studies such as these underscore the fact that language-minority status in itself is not a liability and illustrate that students, whether children or adults, may have skills and abilities that are not noted, valued, or built upon in the schools. These studies also underscore the importance of having a *literacy network* that spans two languages, through which children can get the school-related help they need and through which adults can accomplish what they need in order to function. They also indicate that if literacy is viewed as a group resource (rather than as an individual's asset), there can be a better appreciation of both the resources and needs of the group.

Among some of the better known and most highly acclaimed ethnographic studies of literacy are those of Heath (1983, 1988a, 1988b), who sought to look at how home and school literacy events interact across several different communities. Based on the framework discussed in Chapter Three, Heath's Piedmont studies are located here largely within the social practices perspective for reasons to be explained (1983, 1988a, 1988b). Heath did extensive research in three separate communities in the Carolinas to which she gave the pseudonyms Maintown, Roadville, and Trackton. Maintown is described as a middle-class community; Roadville, as a working-class White community; and Trackton, a working-class Black community. Heath portrays all three communities as literate. Nevertheless, children from literate, working-class parents did not perform as well in the schools as their middle-class, mostly White, peers.

As Heath detailed the relationship between the literacy practices from each community, she documented the extent to which the literacy practices of each group matched the practices and expectations of the schools. Not surprisingly, she found that the literacy practices of the middle-class group corresponded closely to the literacy practices and expectations of the schools. "Children growing up in mainstream communities are expected to develop habits and values which attest to their membership in a 'literate society'" (1988b, p. 163).

Heath demonstrated that children from the other two communities often knew much more about language and literacy than they were credited for by the schools (see also Wells, 1986). Many such children are perceived as lacking school readiness skills and are thus labeled as *deficient at the point of entry*. Similarly, their parents and caretakers are often stereotyped as deficient in their ability to provide home support for their children. As the reasoning goes, if they are not deficient, why do such children continue to fail in the schools?

Heath's work helps dispel some of the common stereotypes surrounding literacy levels based on economic or racial divisions. Heath demonstrates how nonmainstream adults and children regularly participate in literacy events, although their communicative styles (i.e., their "ways with words") differ from those of the mostly White middle-class community. Thus, if illiteracy is not the problem, what is? On one level, it is the mismatch between literacy practices and expectations of the schools and those of the nonmainstream communities. But on a deeper level, it is a mismatch created by the imposition of mainstream norms on others at the point of entry. Terms such as "mainstream" and "Maintown" underscore the differential value attributed to the practices of the schools.

Given their closeness of fit with the schools, the mostly White middle-class children were then the most advantaged among the three groups. They were the most likely to make the initial adjustment to school and continue to do well. They had a head start that benefited them throughout their lives. Because schools historically have largely been the creations of middle-class Whites whose literacy practices are normative, success for this group comes as no surprise. All this suggests is that the schools reflect implicit class, linguistic, and cultural biases. Heath (1983) underscores the importance of these issues:

> Unless the boundaries between classrooms and communities can be broken, and the flow of cultural patterns between them encouraged, the schools will continue to legitimate and reproduce communities of townspeople who control and limit the potential progress of other communities and who themselves remain untouched by other values and ways of life. (p. 369)

Although these conclusions reflect an ideological perspective (see Chapter Three), Heath chose to concentrate on those "skills needed for teachers and students as individuals to make changes which were radical for them" (1983, p. 369). Her focus emphasizes a social practices perspective by concentrating on literacy events *within* each of the three communities. This approach goes a long way in attempting to depose literacy and cultural deficiency stereotypes that working-class Whites and African Americans often must endure. It also provides a basis for schools to recognize and incorporate some of the non-mainstream literacy practices Heath recommends.

A Critique of the Social Practices Studies from the Ideological Perspective

From an ideological perspective, however, additional analysis is needed. Specifically, there is a need to probe the way in which literacy practices function between the groups whose historical legacy has been one of racial discrimination, based on the differential power and authority between middle-class Whites and working-class African Americans. Thus, there is a need to go beyond description precisely because the norms of the White middle class dominate both the schools and the workplace. They provide an implicit mainstream norm against which the practices of working-class communities are assessed, as the following examples indicate:

> Roadville [White working-class] adults *do not* carry on or sustain in continually overlapping and interdependent fashion the linking of ways of taking meaning from books to ways of relating that knowledge to other aspects of the environment. They *do not* encourage decontextualization; in fact, they proscribe it in their own stories. They *do not* themselves make analytic statements or assert universal truths, except those related to their religious faith....Things *do not* have to follow logically so long as they fit the past experience of the individuals in the community. Thus, children learn to look for a specific moral in stories and to expect that story to fit their facts of reality explicitly. (Heath, 1988b, p. 180, emphasis added)

Similarly, characterizations of (African American working-class) Trackton residents imply a standard against which these practices are measured:

> There are *no* bedtime stories....Instead, during the time these activities would take place in Maintown and Roadville homes, Trackton children are enveloped in different kinds of social interactions. They are held, fed, talked about, and rewarded for nonverbal, and later verbal, renderings of events they witness....Children *do not* have labels or names of attributes of

items and events pointed out for them, and they are asked for reason-explanations *not* what-explanations....Children come to recognize similarities of pattern, though they *do not* name lines, points, or items which are similar between two items or situations. (Heath, 1988b, p. 180, emphasis added)

Although these characterizations are presented as descriptions, they could easily be construed as evaluations that imply deficits based on departures from, or the lack of, middle-class practices that are seen as normative. In this regard, Auerbach (1989) has observed: "Since authority is vested in those belonging to the mainstream culture, the literacy practices of the mainstream become the norm and have higher status in school contexts" (p. 173; see also Stuckey, 1991). Given that lower levels of literacy and educational achievement tend to persist for some groups across generations, more is needed to explain their lack of educational progress than differences in literacy practices. In a review that reflects an ideological perspective, Rosen (1985) finds much to praise about Heath's (1983) book, *Ways with Words*, but also observes,

Heath sets out...to satisfy a "need for a full description of the primary-face-to-face interactions of children from community cultures other than their own mainstream one"...and in the end "help working-class black and white children learn more effectively" (Heath, 1983, p. 3)....Here "working class" is being contrasted with "mainstream" (Heath, 1983, p. 4). What then does "mainstream" imply? Middle class?... It raises more questions than it answers: What are the fundamental determinants of class? How do the practices of everyday life relate to them? (p. 449)

Some clues are provided elsewhere in Heath's work (see 1988a) in answer to these questions. For example, everyday literacy practices such as applying for employment, working on the job, and seeking a loan are described. In these situations, Heath found that Trackton African Americans were usually not even required—or allowed—to use the literacy skills they had. In one instance, she reports that African Americans applying for millworker jobs had their applications filled out for them by White employment officers. When asked about this practice, the employment officers offered the explanation, "It is easier if we do it. This way, we get to talk to the client, ask questions not on the form, clarify immediately any questions they have, and, for our purposes, the whole thing is just cleaner" (Heath, 1988a, p. 362). What conclusions can be drawn here from an ideological perspective? Working-class African Americans were able to acquire and secure jobs (which even paid favorably against other types of employment that demanded greater literacy skills), but they were not empowered because they were not in control of the literacy events affecting their lives. Working-class people with little formal education were neither empowered nor disempowered by literacy. To understand the sociopolitical significance of their position, an analysis of their relationship with the dominant middle-class White community is needed. In this regard, Rosen (1985) further contends that racism and the unequal power between African Americans and Whites needs to be emphasized:

> Yes, indeed, communities have different social legacies. A major component of this legacy must be the experience of racism and its continued existence. Why has Heath chosen to warn us off? Black English is the expression and negotiation of Black experience. Racism does no more than lurk in the shadows of this text, raising questions which are not posed by Heath. (pp. 451-452)

Again, however, Heath's work (1988a) provides clues without explicitly focusing on racism. She describes situations outside the mills where African Americans lacked control over information and documents about themselves when interacting with bank, credit union, and loan-office personnel. Heath notes that typically they were asked questions about information in their folders without being able to look at the information. In this case, however, the lack of control of the literacy event was not as likely to go in the client's favor, because the client must respond to information about himself or herself that only the financial officer could see. As in the employment interviews mentioned above, these literacy events involved interactions between people with unequal social power, and only one person had control over its direction. Given the social roles that were ascribed in such literacy events, the oral performances of the interviewees took on greater significance than any use or display of their literacy skills.

This dynamic is significant in several respects. First, the so-called functional literacy skills of the interviewees were not important, because they are not allowed to be important. Second, by being placed in a passive oral response mode, the interviewees were judged only on the basis of oral language. One can suspect that these applicants were being socially evaluated based not on their literacy skills but on the extent to which their speech sounded "literate," that is, that it sounded like the speech of one who had been schooled. In communities dominated by members of one ethnic, racial, or speech community, members of that community control literacy events by virtue of their social position. As gatekeepers, their norms become the criteria for evaluating and ascribing social status to those with whom they interact—whether it be within schools as teachers, in offices as personnel officers or supervisors, or in banks and credit unions as loan officers.

Implications for Practice

There is considerable concern regarding the functions that schools play in helping to maintain stratification in society on the basis of their language policies and practices. A better understanding of the role that language, literacy, and cultural differences play in homes, the community, and the schools helps us to understand how social stratification is maintained and reproduced. However, the recognition that children and adult students come from communities with literacy practices that differ from those of the school in and of itself does little to ensure success for all if all we do is merely make aspects of the so-called "hidden curriculum" explicit. Knowledge of such biases can be acted upon. Several courses of action are possible: *adaptation, accommodation,* and *incorporation.*

Adaptation. Adaptation places most of the burden of change on those whose knowledge and practices are considered subordinate and, thereby, substandard. In schools and other social institutions, adaptation involves the expectation for children and adults, who are held to have substandard knowledge and skills, to acculturate or learn to match or measure up to the norms of those who control the schools, institutions, and workplace. Inside schools, this approach is often defended as maintaining standards (i.e., middle-class norms and practices). Applying this expectation to adults, Heath (1988a) contends,

> In work settings, *when others control* access to and restrict types of written information...especially those in financial and legal settings, Trackton residents recognize their *deficiency* of skills...not literacy skills, but knowledge of oral language uses which would enable them to obtain information about oral language uses....Learning how to do this *appropriately, so as not to seem to challenge a person in power,* is often critical to obtaining a

desired outcome and maintaining a job or reputation as a "satisfactory" applicant, or worker. (p. 365, emphasis added)

Accommodation. Accommodation applies more to the action of those who exercise social control by virtue of their role or position. Accommodation requires teachers, supervisors, personnel officers, and gatekeepers to have a better understanding of the communicative styles and literacy practices among their students. In schools historically, as Wright (1980) has indicated, working-class children had little opportunity to adapt to teacher-controlled question-and-answer dyads, because teachers typically did not model answers to their own questions. Teachers used a formal question register and expected students to answer in an equally formal recitation register. Student discourse was often limited to short-answer responses, which were scrutinized for being in the correct form more than for their content. Without making the expected form explicit, children (and previously unschooled adults; see Klassen & Burnaby, 1993; Miller, 1991) quickly learned that their oral performance was inadequate even if they did not know why. Today, as before, the expectation that working-class students will, and must, learn mainstream ways with words (based on middle-class norms) remains. This expectation implies deficits but seeks to accommodate them. Accommodation was the goal in the Ann Arbor case (see Chapter Six), and it continues to be endorsed (see Delpit, 1988). Accommodation can be seen as an appropriate response if there is no intention to alter standards. Teachers need to become aware of the cultural- and class-imposed biases of literacy practices expected and valued by the schools and become more sensitive to their students' lack of familiarity with these biases.

Incorporation. Because school practices tend to correspond more to middle-class literacy events and expectations regarding language use, one way to neutralize the advantages that the White middle-class students have is to incorporate some of the practices of other groups into school practices. This alternative requires study in those community practices that have not been valued previously by the schools and incorporating them into the curriculum. Heath (1988b) suggests as much:

> It must be admitted that a range of alternative ways of learning and displaying knowledge characterizes all highly school-successful adults in the advance stages of their careers. Knowing more about how these alternatives are learned at early ages in different

sociocultural conditions can help the school to provide opportunities for *all* students to avail themselves of these alternatives early in their school careers. For example, mainstream children can benefit from early exposure to Trackton's creative highly analogical styles of telling stories and giving explanations...to their repertoire of narrative types. (p. 181)

For working-class Black and White children and adults, this means that more attention should be directed to building on their strengths, rather than concentrating on their alleged deficiencies. For White middle-class children, it involves broadening their experience by exposing them to other ways of knowing and using language and literacy (see Edwards & Sienkewicz, 1990). It also means *surrendering a privileged position* by acknowledging that something can be learned from other groups. Surrendering the privilege, however, need not be taken as a retreat from high standards nor as imposing a hardship on the children of the middle-class since, as Heath contends, middle-class children can benefit by expanding their own possibilities for understanding and using language. Similarly, adults who have grown up with one set of language and literacy norms can be enriched by learning from the practices of others. Educational encounters with alternative ways of using language could do much to break down linguistic prejudice across groups.

In order for incorporation to occur, teachers need knowledge of the language, communication styles, and literacy practices of their students. A number of authors identify the kinds of knowledge needed, (e.g., Camitta, 1993; Dandy, 1992) but there are limits to how far such approaches can take us. As Shuman (1993) warns, the "issue is not only varieties of writing, standard and local, but privileged channels and genres of communication" (p. 267).

Incorporation obviously poses logistical problems for schools and classroom practice. First, schools face the problem that most teachers, in disproportion to their numbers even in racially and linguistically diverse areas of the country, tend to come from the White middle class. There is a need to break the racial and class monopoly on jobs in education that are disproportionately held by one group, because this imbalance is a contributing factor to what is called "reproduction." Reproduction involves the perpetual reinvention and continuation of social stratification through the social organization and practices of the schools.

As a second strategy for incorporation, Heath (1983) suggests turning teachers into learners and students into ethnographers. This is no simple task; her own efforts involved years of community and school ethnographic work. Short of being able to assign an ethnographer to every school—having a school anthropologist might be at least as useful as having a school psychologist—there are other possibilities. One possibility is to require ethnographic training within existing teacher education and staff development programs at all levels. Movement in this direction will confront the dominance of elitist attitudes and prescriptivism that grow out of misunderstandings and ignorance about language use in a diverse society.

Further Reading

Auerbach, E.R. (1989). Toward a social-contextual approach to family literacy. *Harvard Educational Review, 59*(2), 165-182.

Presents successful approaches to teaching parents to explore the uses of language and literacy within the home. Auerbach shows how community, workplace, and health care issues are incorporated into the curriculum and parents are taught how to advocate for their concerns with the schools.

Cook-Gumperz, J., & Keller-Cohen (Ed.). (1993). Alternative literacies: In school and beyond [Theme issue]. *Anthropology and Education Quarterly, 24* (4).

The editors of this volume contend that school literacy practices developed in the West have gradually privileged one kind of literacy. The articles explore possibilities for a more community-based and democratic form of literate discourse.

Dubin, F., & Kuhlman, N.A. (Eds.). (1992). *Cross-cultural literacy: Global perspectives in reading and writing.* Englewood Cliffs, NJ: Regents/Prentice Hall.

Contains case studies of literacy in different national and sociocultural contexts as well as several articles of relevance to the discussion in Chapters Three and Five.

Fishman, A. (1988). *Amish literacy: What and how it means.* Portsmouth, NH: Heinemann.

Focuses on the role of education and literacy in the Amish community from an ethnographic perspective and looks at the implications of their differences when they interact in classrooms of the dominant culture outside.

Heath, S.B. (1983). *Ways with words: Language, life and work in communities and classrooms.* Cambridge, England: Cambridge University Press.

This widely used and highly acclaimed work has become a neoclassic for many teachers and students. See Stucky (1991) below for a critique.

Street, B.V. (Ed.). (1993). *Cross-cultural approaches to literacy.* Cambridg, England: Cambridge University Press.

Builds on Street (1984) with a number of ethnographic studies that reflect either social practices or ideological perspectives.

Stuckey, J.E. (1991). *The violence of literacy.* Portsmouth, NH: Heinemann.

Provides an outspoken critique of the limitations of, and biases in, some ethnographic work. Its contentions regarding economic issues are also of relevance to issues raised in Chapter Five. Beginners may find this work tough going.

Taylor, D.M., & Dorsey-Gaines, C. (1988). *Growing up literate: Learning from inner-city families.* Portsmouth, NH: Heinemann.

This inner-city ethnographic study details the extent of literacy among those living under trying conditions in poverty and helps to debunk the notion that if people are poor they are probably illiterate.

Notes

[1] See, for example, Barton and Ivanic (1991); Camitta (1993); Cook-Gumperz and Keller-Cohen (1993); Delgado-Gaitán and Trueba (1991); Fishman (1988); Heath (1980, 1983, 1986, 1988a, 1988b); Schieffelin and Cochran-Smith (1984); Schieffelin and Gilmore (1986); Scollon and Scollon (1981); Street (1984, 1993); Taylor (1983); Taylor and Dorsey-Gaines (1988); and Trueba, Jacobs, and Kirton (1990).

CHAPTER 8

Contemporary Bilingual Education Theory and the Great Divide

Perhaps the rosiest future for bilingual education in the United States can be attained by dissolving the paradoxical attitude of admiration and pride for school-attained bilingualism on the one hand and scorn and shame for home-brewed immigrant bilinguals on the other. (Hakuta, 1986, p. 229)

Many of the issues raised in general discussions of literacy—particularly those related to the so-called "great divide" between literates and nonliterates (Street, 1984)—reappear in the debates over how best to promote English literacy among language minority groups. As discussed in Chapter Three, Olson (1977, 1984) argues that metalinguistic awareness underlies both literacy and academic success. Again, Olson sees differences in speech styles and varying degrees of metalinguistic awareness by children from different socioeconomic backgrounds as affecting the ease by which they become literate and adapt to formal schooling practices. These views presuppose a kind of *mismatch* between the language of the home, school, and textbook. From the perspective of a purported oral/literate great divide, this mismatch is assumed to result in cognitive limitations in the readiness of some language minority and lower-class children for basic literacy and formal education. When the discussion includes language minority children, the focus on language differences no longer relates only to registers, styles, or metalinguistic awareness within the same language but also to concerns over which language should be used to facilitate literacy and instruction—the students' home language (L1) or the language of the school (L2).

In this chapter, issues related to the great divide are revisited within the context of contemporary bilingual education theory in the United States. The central question addressed is, "To what extent are notions of an oral/literate and cognitive great divide reproduced, albeit unintentionally, in some of the commonly accepted constructs and hypotheses of bilingual education theory?" In attempting to address these issues, it is necessary to turn to a different research and literature base and to an influential contemporary framework that establishes guiding principles for language minority instruction and bilingual education.

Bilingual education in the United States has been instituted largely on the assumption that a linguistic mismatch puts language minority children at an inherent disadvantage when they begin instruction in school in a language other than their mother tongue. There is an ever-growing body of evidence that bilingual education is effective in promoting literacy and academic achievement among children when adequate resources are provided (e.g., Cummins, 1979, 1981, 1985; Cummins & Swain, 1986; Edelsky, 1986; Krashen & Biber, 1988; Merino & Lyons, 1990; Ramírez, 1992; Troike, 1978). While much of the literature on bilingual education has been directed at children, there is growing evidence that it also provides a promising alternative to typical adult English literacy and English as a second language (ESL) programs (e.g., Burtoff, 1985; Mélendez, 1990; Robson, 1982).

Despite the fact that these scholars are united in their support for bilingual education, their theoretical models often emerge from different assumptions about learning (see Chapter Three). Some are more reflective of an autonomous perspective, whereas others mirror assumptions of social practices and ideological perspectives. Others still are eclectic. Thus, as in most fields of education, within bilingual education there are contradictory forces at work. When researchers attempt to deal with issues that have sociopolitical significance, they often tend to approach these issues with the tools and constructs of their specific disciplines. Quite expectedly, their hypotheses and theories are influenced by their prior training. Progressive scholars often find themselves struggling against old assumptions within their own specializations. At first scholars may make small adjustments in the dominant models. They may devise slightly different labels to alter negative connotations associated with prior constructs. Nevertheless, they are still operating from the original, but weakened model. With each alteration, the dominant model reveals its loss of explanatory power. Contradictions within the dominant model become evident, and alternative hypotheses may emerge both within the discipline or from other fields, thereby making it is easy to drift into eclecticism.(See Kuhn, 1970.)

As noted in Chapter Three, criticism of the autonomous perspective in literacy studies (e.g., Scribner & Cole, 1981) has led to rebuttal, clarification, and revision of some of its components (see Goody, 1987; Olson, 1994). Street (1984, 1993) and Gee (1986, 1990) suggest that something analogous to a paradigm shift[1] has occurred, away from the autonomous perspective and toward a social practices and ideological perspective; however, this shift would appear to be far from complete because many researchers and practitioners continue to be influenced by tenets of earlier versions of the autonomous perspective. Because bilingual education also deals with literacy and biliteracy, it too has been influenced by competing perspectives and by a shift toward an ideological perspective. Some researchers and practitioners are consciously aware of the theoretical assumptions from which they operate. However, because others are somewhat more eclectic and less aware, there is a need to make these underlying assumptions more explicit in order to promote more consistency between theory and practice. There is likewise a need to determine the extent to which deficit theories associated with the autonomous perspective are reproduced in contemporary theory and practice.

As discussed in Chapter Five, *deficiency explanations* often locate problems in the individual rather than in a larger sociopolitical and socioeconomic frame of reference. During the 1960s and 1970s, many researchers began challenging theories that blamed the poor and minorities for being low achievers. Scholars from a variety of fields (e.g., anthropology, education, history, linguistics, psychology, and sociology) exhibited a heightened sense of professional social consciousness as they attacked deficit views in their respective specializations. Fresh from battles with colleagues in their own disciplines, scholars advocating either revised models or new paradigms often found themselves in cross-talk with their innovative peers from other disciplines. While struggling to improve the education of language minority groups, these mutual advocates of bilingual education have sometimes disputed aspects of each others' work.

A major assumption of this chapter is that much of the dispute among bilingual education theorists can be explained in terms of the persistence of great divide notions in contemporary frameworks. Some of their persistence may result from a misinterpretation of contemporary frameworks. However, it may also be the case that some of the more popular constructs in contemporary bilingual education theories lend themselves to a great divide interpretation. In any event, the extent to which assumptions underlying the autonomous perspective continue to exert an influence on language minority education merits examination. Such an examination is needed because school literacy has tended to reflect the practices, norms, expectations, and social class advantages of dominant groups (see Chapter Seven). Thus, there is a need to scrutinize the extent to which our notions about the cognitive effects associated with academic language proficiencies can reproduce aspects of the oral/literate divide and school literacy/non-school literacy divide.

Influential Constructs in Contemporary Bilingual Education Theory

Many of the major constructs in contemporary bilingual education theory grew out of research in Scandinavia and North America (Canada and the United States) during the 1970s and 1980s (see Baker, 1988, for an historical overview). Currently, the most influential school of thought in the United States draws largely, but not exclusively, from the work of Cummins (1976, 1979, 1981, 1984a, 1984b, 1985, 1986, 1989) and other scholars (see California State Department of Education, 1982; Cortés, 1986; Cummins & Swain, 1986; Krashen, 1981). Much of their work has struggled to overcome deficit theories and ill-conceived research formulated throughout much of the 20th century, and a number of these authors have tirelessly championed language minority rights (e.g., Skutnabb-Kangas & Cummins, 1988).

As Hakuta (1986) has chronicled, throughout much of this century, bilingualism has been either (1) ignored as a confounding factor in explaining lower levels of IQ across ethnic groups; or (2) has been construed as having negative, or "subtractive," consequences for intellectual development. However, by the 1960s and 1970s some studies (see Hakuta, 1986) began to indicate that bilinguals outper-formed their monolingual peers on various cognitive tasks, thus sug-gesting that there were additive effects associated with bilingualism. Lambert (1974) developed a psycho-social model of language acquisi-tion in an attempt to explain positive and negative effects of bilingual-ism. This model was to become a major influence in the field, as Baker (1993) observes:

> Additive and subtractive bilingualism have become important concepts in the explanation of research. Lambert's (1974) distinc-tion between additive and subtractive bilingualism has been used

in different ways. First, additive bilingualism is used to refer to positive cognitive outcomes from being bilingual....Subtractive bilingualism hence refers to the negative affective and cognitive effects of bilingualism (e.g., where both languages are "underdeveloped"). (p. 95)

According to some writers of the 1970s, subtractive bilingualism could result in the highly controversial notion of *double semilingualism*, which has been defined variously as "defective" or "imperfect" command of linguistic systems in two languages or the failure to learn them "properly" (see Skutnabb-Kangas, 1981, pp. 251-252). Later, a tripartite hierarchy was used to represent the cognitive effects of different types of bilingualism (see Cummins, 1981, p. 39, who follows Toukomaa & Skutnabb-Kangas, 1977, p. 29). Positive cognitive effects of bilingualism were associated with *proficient bilingualism* (i.e., having high levels of proficiency in two languages). Neither positive nor negative cognitive effects were associated with *partial bilingualism*, which was on a cognitive par with monolingualism because one had native-like proficiency in only one language. At the bottom of the scale was *limited bilingualism*, which recalls the notion of *semilingualism* because it was seen as having negative cognitive effects.

In comparison with early 20th-century views toward bilingualism, much progress had been made. Bilingualism was no longer associated solely with negative cognitive effects. Now it had become either a blessing, a curse, or of no consequence, depending on the threshold level of proficiency one had attained. However, much of the emphasis on the purported cognitive effects of bilingualism may be misguided. In this regard, Hakuta (1986) contends that a focus on cognitive effects tends "to abstract the bilinguals away from the social conditions in which they live and to focus only on their degree of bilingualism" (p. 42). He adds,

> The question of bilingualism and intelligence, whether they are linked positively or negatively will evaporate in the face of deeper issues surrounding both bilingualism and intelligence. The fundamental question is misguided, for it entails two key simplifying assumptions: The first assumption is that the effect of bilingualism—indeed, the human mind—can be reduced to a single dimension (ranging from good to bad). (p. 43)

Recognizing limitations associated with an autonomous perspective, a number of writers have attempted to recast terms such as "additive bilingualism" and "subtractive bilingualism" within a social practices or even ideological perspective. For example, Skutnabb-Kangas (1981) has suggested that "semilingualism cannot be regarded as a deficiency inherent in the *individual* but should rather be treated as one result of the (linguistically and otherwise) powerless circumstances, the (linguistic) oppression in which she has lived" (p. 249, emphasis and parentheses in the original). Cummins' (1989) empowerment approach (see Zanger, 1991, for a review) emphasizes additive as opposed to subtractive *contexts* for overcoming linguistic and cultural domination. Similarly, Baker (1993; following Landry, Allard, & Théberge, 1991) argues that a "wider use of additive and subtractive bilingualism relates to the enrichment or loss of minority language, culture and ethnolinguistic identity at a societal level" (p. 95).

These qualifications appear to represent an attempt to break with a rigid autonomous perspective that views those labeled as "limited bilinguals" as having cognitive deficiencies. From a social practices perspective, bilinguals can be seen as having had different experiences from those expected by the schools. From an ideological viewpoint, they have been oppressed and denied access to an equivalent education and held accountable to language norms and standards that have been imposed on them. They have not been given "a chance to learn" (Weinberg, 1995). Thus, the perspective that one takes (i.e., autonomous, social practices, ideological, or even eclectic) dictates whether one concentrates on cognitive or social and political effects of bilingualism.

Although repositioning terms such as additive and subtractive bilingualism and semilingualism within the social practices and ideological perspectives helps to reduce the sense of deficit associated with the autonomous perspective, by persisting in using these terms at all, there is a risk that cognitive deficit notions associated with the autonomous perspective will be reproduced.

As was noted in Chapter Six, categorization based on language proficiency is problematic because it ascribes status to students by reducing all of their abilities to a single dimension. Frequently, this is done only in reference to English. However, classification that acknowledges bilingualism can also result in status ascription and deficit labeling. When someone has been labeled a "partial" or "limited" bilingual, all of his or her language abilities have been treated as a totality. No distinction has been made in reference to oral abilities as opposed to literate abilities. Neither is there reference to the specific social contexts in which the assessments have been made—in other words, those in school as opposed to those in other contexts. Many tests designed to determine language ability frequently require literacy, and thereby equate language with literacy. This means that those classified as "proficient" bilinguals are apparently biliterate, and that they have probably been schooled in two languages. Unfortunately, this distinction is rarely made explicit. Similarly, so-called "partial" bilinguals are typically literate in one language, in other words, the language in which they received formal instruction, and they are probably not literate or fully schooled in a second. Those labeled as "limited" bilinguals are frequently orally fluent in a language that they have not been able to develop through schooling.

For these reasons, assumptions about literacy and schooling must be made explicit in assessments of language proficiency. Most normal human beings have command of their native languages, regardless of whether they are literate or not. Thus, to label people as "limited bilinguals" or "semilinguals," as was once the case, only stigmatizes them and confuses the discussion because it treats language as a global cognitive ability, much like the notion of IQ is treated.

Realizing problems associated with language classification, some researchers began to focus on cognitive differences related to different types of language proficiencies. They attempted to explain why some immigrant language minorities, for example, could attain conversational fluency (i.e., peer-appropriate L2 conversational skills) within two years of arrival in the new country, while their second language academic skills lagged behind native English speakers for five to seven years. Cummins (1981), for example, concluded that differences in the acquisition rates for oral and school-based literate language could be explained, in part, by differences in "cognitive demand." Initially, Cummins contended that there are two dimensions of language proficiency: one related to what he called Basic Interpersonal Communication Skills (BICS) and the other related to Cognitive Academic Language Proficiency (CALP). It is important to note that Cummins has subsequently replaced these terms. Nevertheless, as Edelsky (1991) notes, "they are catching on and being used by others" (p. 60).[2] Given their widespread usage, they are discussed here.

BICS and CALP were seen as relating to the cognitive demand that results from how language is contextualized. BICS refers to so-called *contextualized* language, which is usually characterized as less cognitively demanding. CALP is considered *less contextualized*, or *more abstract*, and *more cognitively demanding*. Because research indicated that peer-appropriate BICS could be achieved in only two years, concern over how to develop CALP became the major focus.

BICS and CALP, as two dimensions of language proficiency, were used to refute the notion that language proficiencies are developed separately according to the so-called separate underlying proficiency (SUP) model. Cummins and others rejected this model in favor of a *common underlying proficiency* (CUP) model, wherein the development of cognitively more demanding language (CALP) in L1 was seen as positively influencing its development in L2. It was assumed that L1 CALP had to be developed to a *threshold* level of proficiency that would allow for *transfer* to L2.

As was noted in Chapter Four, the attempt to define and measure literacy is problematic. So too is the attempt to define and operationalize notions of language proficiency and concepts like BICS and CALP. Fundamental assumptions must be explored concerning the relationship of language proficiency to school-based literacy, or even more basic, regarding the relationship of language proficiency to intelligence. Initially, Cummins followed Oller and Perkins (1980, p. 1):

> *"A single factor of global language proficiency* seems to account for the lion's share of variance in a wide variety of educational tests including nonverbal and verbal IQ measures, achievement batteries, and even personality inventories and affective measures...the results to date are preponderantly in favor of the assumption that language skill pervades every area of the school curriculum even more strongly than was ever thought by curriculum writers or testers." (cited by Cummins, 1985, p. 132, emphasis added)

These assumptions appear to fall squarely within the autonomous perspective since language proficiency is seen as global[3] and related to IQ even though a distinction is made between those aspects of language proficiency that are clearly related to school success and those that are not:

Academic and cognitive variables are strongly related to at least some measures of all four general language skills (listening, speaking, reading, and writing)...however, it seems apparent that not all aspects of language proficiency are cognitive/academic in nature. For example, in a first language context, *"conversational" aspects of proficiency* (e.g., phonology and fluency) *are clearly unrelated to academic and cognitive performance.* (Cummins, 1985, p.132; emphasis added)

Here, the framing of the issues tends to parallel the oral/literate divide of the autonomous perspective. Language proficiency is conceptualized as a kind of iceberg (this hierarchy parallels Bloom's 1956 taxonomy of cognitive abilities and recalls Chomsky's 1957 notion of deep structure). At the tip of the iceberg are those aspects of language that seem to be less related to academic success, whereas those at the bottom of the iceberg are considered cognitively demanding aspects that are more heavily related to academic success.

Figure 8.
Surface and Deep Levels of Language Proficiency

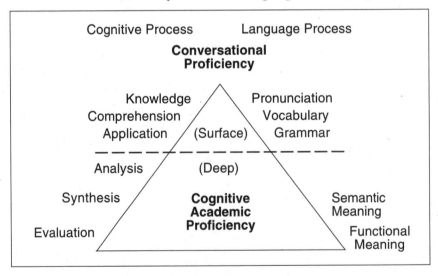

Source: Cummins, 1985, p. 138. Adapted with permission.

Later, Cummins dropped the formal labels of BICS and CALP and represented levels of proficiency as being tied to two continua: cognitive demand and contextual support.

Figure 9.
Communicative Quadrant: Range of Contextual Support and Degree of Cognitive Involvement

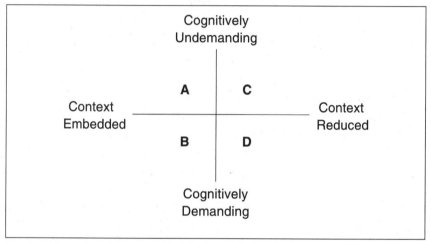

Source: Cummins, 1985, p. 139. Adapted with permission.

Quadrant A represents communication facilitated by the opportunity to negotiate meaning and the ability to get feedback and cues, whereas communication in Quadrant D is supported only by means of linguistic cues to meaning. It is apparent, based on this schema, that most reading and writing and other academic literacy tasks would fall in Quadrant D. Like the prior distinction between BICS and CALP, the differentiation here between cognitively undemanding/demanding language and context embedded/reduced was not intended as a strict dichotomy. However, the question remains as to whether it is generally interpreted as such.

The constructs of context and cognitive demand were used to help explain why second language students acquire interpersonal communication skills more quickly (within about two years) than peer-appropriate academic skills (which require about five to seven years). Appropriate[4] English as a second language (ESL) instruction helps students to acquire oral conversational language rapidly. However, because the major purpose of schooling is to develop students' abilities to comprehend and interpret texts, academic literacy must also be developed.

The assumption here is that academic tasks are more cognitively demanding because they require a *cognitively deeper* language proficiency. This deeper *common underlying proficiency* is seen as being developed through a language, but its purported cognitive effects are seen as not being specific to it. According to Cummins,

> In concrete terms what this principle means is that [for example] in a Spanish-English bilingual programme, Spanish instruction that develops first language reading skills for Spanish-speaking students is not just developing Spanish skills, it is also developing a deeper conceptual and linguistic proficiency that is strongly related to the development of English literacy and general academic skills. (1985, p. 143)

To illustrate the notion of common underlying proficiency, Cummins drew on the metaphor of a dual-tipped single iceberg. The peaks represent surface features of proficiency in two languages and the singular base represents the common underlying academic proficiency as illustrated in Figure 10.

Figure 10.
Iceberg Representing a Common
Underlying Language Proficiency

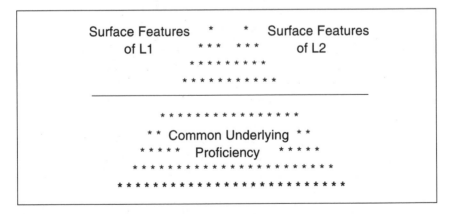

Source: Cummins, 1985, p. 143. Adapted with permission.

The Contextual Interaction Model

The question of whether instruction should be initiated in L1 or L2 depends on several factors in addition to language. In a pioneering Canadian immersion[5] program study, the St. Lambert experiment (Lambert & Tucker, 1972; also see Baker, 1988, for a review), monolingual English-speaking children were given academic instruction through French rather than English. In both English language development and academic achievement, they performed as well as or better than their peers who had received instruction in English. At first glance, these findings would seem to support the opponents of bilingual education who argue that schools should not waste students' time in L1 instruction; rather they should provide instruction immediately in L2 unless factors other than language are taken into consideration.

However, the Contextual Interaction Model showed the relationship between language of instruction and other factors that have an impact on learning. The early model was formulated by California's Office of Bilingual Education (OBE) drawing most heavily on the work of Cummins and, to a lesser extent, on the work of Krashen (1981), Terrell (1981), and several other scholars. The model attempted to show the relationship between student background factors and educational treatments. Its basic components are shown in Figure 11.

Figure 11.
The Contextual Interaction Model
for Language Minority Students (Initial Version)

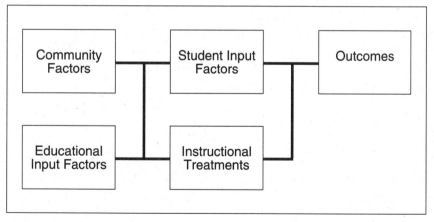

Source: California State Department of Education, Office of Bilingual Education, 1982, p. 4. Adapted with permission.

The model assumes an interaction between the school and the student:

> In this model, community background factors, such as language use patterns in the home and community and attitudes toward the student's home language (L1) and second language (L2) contribute to student input factors which the child brings to the educational setting. These factors, such as L1 and L2 proficiency, self-esteem, levels of academic achievement, and motivation to acquire L2 and maintain L1, are in constant interaction with instructional treatments, resulting in various cognitive and affective student outcomes. (California State Department of Education, 1982, p. 4)

According to OBE, the Contextual Interaction Model rested on five empirically supported hypotheses or principles that describe how student background factors interact with (or should determine the choice of) educational treatments to promote three goals. These goals were (1) ultimate proficiency in English, (2) academic achievement, and (3) positive psychosocial adjustment.

The five principles that support these goals were summarized as:

1. The extent to which the proficiencies of bilingual students are jointly developed in L1 and L2 is positively associated with academic achievement.

This principle assumed that a linguistic threshold underlies success in school. Success was seen as occurring when the home language was maintained and the school language was developed. In the absence of this, negative effects were expected in the form of subtractive bilingualism, which resulted from neither maintaining the home language nor developing the school language. Subtractive bilingualism was seen as producing limited bilinguals, who would have difficulties in attaining initial (school) literacy (CA State Dept. of Ed., 1982, pp. 5-7).

2. Language proficiency involves two dimensions: the ability to communicate in basic interactive tasks (BICS) and the ability to use language in literacy/academic tasks (CALP).

This principle reflected Donaldson's (1978) constructs of *context* and *cognitive demand*. It was argued that academic programs must develop both dimensions of language to ensure academic success (CA State Dept. of Ed., 1982, pp. 7-9).

3. Developing the L1 skills of language minority students in academic tasks supports for the development of similar proficiencies in L2.

Based on the notion of a *common underlying proficiency*, the assumption was that (school) literacy training in L1 provided a basis for, and later transferred to, L2 (CA State Dept. of Ed., 1982, pp. 9-12).

4. The acquisition of basic communication skills in L2 is facilitated by the provision of "comprehensible input" and a supportive affective environment.

Here the model drew largely on one of Krashen's (1981) hypotheses related to his Monitor Model. The assumption was that "basic" (that is, cognitively undemanding) second language skills must be developed in the L2 before "academic" proficiencies could be developed. Consequently, linguistic input could not be too cognitively demanding, and the learning environment would have to be supportive of the student (CA State Dept. of Ed., 1982, pp. 12-15).

5. Interactions between students and teachers and among students themselves are affected by how the students' status is perceived.

Based on studies of the role of self-perception and teacher perception and their effect on academic achievement, it was also concluded that students themselves and their teachers must have a positive perception of the students in order to promote academic success. Using the students' L1 in initial instruction was seen as having positive psychosocial and cognitive benefits (CA State Dept. of Ed., 1982, pp. 15-18).

It is important to note that this model, as presented, was not solely Cummins's or Krashen's but represented a synthesis by others who tried to create a coherent paradigm that would link together a number of factors known to influence the acquisition of English (as a second language) and promote academic achievement.

In time, Cortés (1986) reconceptualized the model. Most importantly, the interaction between its various components was seen to be dynamic both *synchronically* (i.e., at a single point in time) and *diachronically* (i.e., over time). In Cortés's synthesis,

> The examination of a wide variety of societal and school factors, including their interaction both at one point in time and dynamically over time, provides the essence of the Contextual Interaction Model. This model rejects single-cause explanations [of school success and failure] and instead seeks to incorporate a

multiplicity of factors that may influence educational achievement. It rejects static correlations and instead substitutes the consideration of observable dynamic interactions over time in an attempt to assess causation. It rejects the examination of societal and school factors outside of a specific context and instead examines the dynamic operation of these multiple factors within a specific context in order to identify different ways in which sociocultural factors interact with and influence educational achievement and experience. (p. 23)

The Significance of the Contextual Interaction Model

The earlier version of the Contextual Interaction Model provided a useful framework for bilingual education. Before it was developed, embattled advocates of bilingual education were hard pressed to defend it when the research appeared to show that cognitive academic language proficiencies could be developed by bypassing instruction in L1. The model helped to explain under what conditions the maintenance of L1 is desirable and why initial literacy instruction in L1 poses no long-term threat to success in L2. Its main strengths were that it took into account the status of L1 in relation to L2 in the community and that it saw language as being related to a sense of self-concept. From a political standpoint, the model's simplicity (five principles and explanatory charts) added a sense of legitimacy to the arguments of proponents of bilingual education. Cortés's (1986) synthesis represented an improvement over the initial version.

The contextual interaction theory provided a model for *transitional* bilingual education programs.[6] In a transitional program, students receive primary language (L1) instruction to (1) keep pace academically with English-speaking students and (2) eventually acquire enough English to keep pace in English-only classrooms. The research of Cummins and others indicates that given enough time to develop academic literacy in L1 (while simultaneously developing oral language and literacy in L2), students can successfully make the transition to instruction mediated through L2. If they are transitioned too quickly, most students will not be able to keep pace with native speakers of English because they will not have developed academic English. They will not have enough school-based literacy skills in English to compete with native speakers of English in academic subjects taught in English.

It is important to remember, however, that the contextual interaction model is eclectic and draws from a variety of disciplines. Some of its elements reflect the influence of an autonomous perspective, especially those related to language proficiency, cognitive demand, and contexualization. Others can be seen to reflect aspects of both the social practices and ideological perspectives—such as those that embrace promoting the status and incorporation of language minority languages and cultures (e.g., Cummins, 1989).

Critiques of Troublesome Constructs in Contemporary Bilingual Education Theory

Given the interdisciplinary work being done in the field of bilingual education, it is understandable that researchers trained in one discipline might borrow attractive aspects from another without fully discerning contradictions and theoretical inconsistencies that emerge by so doing. It is suggested here that such eclecticism currently dominates language minority education in the United States. In any event, linguistic and literacy-related constructs associated with popular frameworks have had significant influence and are the source of much concern from the standpoint of reproducing notions of the great divide.

The Use of Inauthentic Test Data in Determining Language Proficiency

A major concern relates to the authenticity of using school-test data as a means of determining language proficiencies. To establish the notion of a linguistic threshold, for example, it is necessary to determine levels of language proficiency. Although the notion of a linguistic threshold was not intended to imply a cognitive dividing line, it is difficult to make any other interpretation because purportedly cognitively higher order language abilities are located above the line. In fact levels of proficiency, both above and below the threshold, must be operationalized. They are derived from test scores based on specific language and literacy tests of the school. These tests, in turn, reflect particular literacy practices and social expectations favoring groups that control institutions. Also, because school tests are based on "standard" academic language, there is an implicit bias against language variation within L1 (i.e., there is a bias against speakers of nonstandard and creolized varieties of L1). In interpreting results based on standardized tests, practitioners sometimes claim that students have "no language," meaning that they have no standard academic language. Such claims recall the notion of semilingualism. Language tests classify, sort, and track students based on an autonomous view of language use and ability in which it is assumed that the results represent a window on the cognitive abilities of those assessed.

Edelsky, whose work is located consistently in the ideological perspective in this book, has been particularly critical of many of the popular assumptions underlying current bilingual education theory (Edelsky, 1991; Edelsky et al., 1983). Edelsky et al. (1983) contended, "It [current bilingual education theory] is wrong in a basic premise concerning literacy and wrong in relying primarily on data from tests and test settings" (p. 1). A careful reading of her critique indicates a deeply rooted philosophical dispute between those of the social practices and ideological perspectives and those influenced by autonomous perspectives (i.e., those who rely on psychometric/positivist approaches to assessment and skills-based approaches to instruction). Edelsky et al. (1983) rejected the ecological validity of test data and its relationship to normal instructional practice:

> Once one accepts the equivalencies reading test = reading and exercises-with-artificial-texts = proper literacy instruction, then it becomes necessary to explain failure on the tests and exercises by blaming the learner, the teacher, the language of instruction, anything but examining the validity of how literacy (or language proficiency or learning) was conceptualized in the first place. (p. 4)

Again, it is important to note that this criticism echoes concerns raised within the great divide debate in the general field of literacy.

Semilingualism and Related Notions

Martin-Jones and Romaine (1986), with Edelsky et al. (1983), have contended that the persistence of terms such as "semilingualism" and "subtractive bilingualism" or "less than native-like competence" carry with them underlying assumptions of cognitive deficit. They have noted that the "literature on 'semilingualism' abounds with terms such as 'full competence,' 'threshold level,' 'additive' and 'subtractive bilingualism'" (Martin-Jones & Romaine, 1986, p. 32). Implicit within the notions of semilingualism and linguistic competence is a "container" metaphor. The container is depicted as either being "full or partially full. Terms such as 'semilingualism' are...misleading because they implicitly foster the belief that there is such a thing as an ideal, fully competent monolingual or bilingual speaker who has a full or complete version of a language" (Martin-Jones & Romaine, 1986, p. 32).

Edelsky et al. (1983) were particularly concerned about the confusion caused by the construct of semilingualism:

[It is not] a strictly linguistic concept at all, but a concept pertaining to cognitive aspects of the language, understanding of the meanings of abstract concepts, synonyms, etc., as well as vocabulary. This is also a description of cognitive academic language. In other words, low proficiency in academic language is not due to semilingualism; it is semilingualism—another tautology. (p. 10)

Edelsky et al. (1983) preferred to interpret linguistic performance associated with semilingualism as language differences rather than as cognitive/language deficiencies. Many language minority children and adults possess neither the standard (dominant) language nor the prestige dialect in their presumed L1, and some students may not even be native speakers of their presumed L1. Thus, L1 assessment may also involve L1 social dialect biases. For example, in Southern California, some immigrant children and adults from Central and South America and from Mexico are assumed to be native speakers of Spanish, when in fact, they speak Indian languages. Based on standardized assessments in English or Spanish, they would be labeled subtractive bilinguals, having no mastery of either language. If there are subtractive bilinguals, there must be a monolingual equivalent, such as subtractive monolinguals. What language or schooling characteristics would they have? Most likely they would be people who had little opportunity for formal education. Possibly they would speak a nonstandard variety of a language. Based upon these characteristics would it be fair to label them as cognitively deficient, or merely unschooled in the standard language?

Given these questions, it is essential that we be absolutely clear on the implications of the labels we apply. Cummins (1989) appears to have recognized this issue, because he cites the work of Labov (1970, 1973) to refute the notion that speakers of nonstandard language varieties are cognitively deficient. This is an important caveat. However, it is one that Cummins's readers might easily miss given its lack of elaboration and reconciliation with the overall framework.

In summary, the continued use of terms like "additive" and "subtractive bilingualism" can foster and reproduce stereotypes about the cognitive limitations of students. Even though Cummins and others have dropped semilingualism, additive and subtractive bilingualism—even when applied to social and political contexts of education—tend to perpetuate a deficit metaphor in which it is difficult to separate cognitive deficiencies from social and political inequities.

The Notions of BICS, CALP, and Cognitive Demand

Edelsky et al. (1983; see also Edelsky, 1991) have rejected so-called "Cognitive Academic Language Proficiency" (CALP) as being merely an artifact of "test-wiseness" (pp. 5-6); in other words, "the ability to produce or match printed synonyms or vocabulary items." Thus, "native-like competence in a language was not defined as fluency but as scores on tests of vocabulary and synonyms" (pp. 5-6). CALP, then, reflects the ability to perform specific, school-based, sociocultural literacy practices. Edelsky et al. also noted that tests utilize linguistic texts that may not be representative of other kinds of texts (which might be more familiar to the test taker).They concluded that CALP's relationship to schooling is "tautological" because the definition of school success is Cognitive Academic Language Proficiency, and the definition of CALP is operationalized as one's ability to perform on school tests (pp. 8-9). Again, the concerns regarding BICS and CALP and, more recently, over the constructs of *contextually embedded/ reduced language* and *cognitively demanding/undemanding language* parallel those concerning the great divide in Chapter Three.

Specifically, they recall debates over purported cognitive differences between nonliterates and literates and between literacy without schooling and literacy with schooling. Significantly, Cummins has noted the similarities between his framework and those of Donaldson (1978) and Olson (1977), which he identifies as "related frameworks" (Cummins, 1981, p. 17). Cummins cites Donaldson as supporting "the distinction between embedded and disembedded thought and language" (p. 18) and Olson's claims regarding the differences between oral language development and literacy (Cummins, 1981, p. 19). All of these frameworks share the view that oral language is less cognitively demanding than literate academic language because it utilizes both linguistic, extra-linguistic, and nonlinguistic cues. Noting these similarities, Cummins (1981) offers an important qualification:

Although the distinctions between "embedded-disembedded" (Donaldson, 1978) "utterance-text" (Olson, 1977) and "conversation-composition" (Bereiter & Scardamalia, 1981) were developed independently and in relation to a different set of data, they share the essential characteristics of the distinctions outlined in the present theoretical framework. The major difference is that the failure of other frameworks to distinguish explicitly between the cognitive and contextual aspects of communicative activities might incorrectly suggest that context-reduced communication (literate tradition) is *intrinsically* more cognitively demanding than context-embedded communication (oral tradition). (Cummins, 1981, p. 20, emphasis in the original)

This is a significant caveat because his framework, and those cited in support of it, seem to emphasize this very point—that literate academic language *is intrinsically* more cognitively demanding than oral language. If this is a misreading (see Cummins, 1983), it would seem to result from a lack of elaboration in the framework.

Edelsky et al. (1983) also claimed that the distinction between BICS and CALP was "absurd" because logic and metaphor and other abstract aspects of communication occur in face-to-face communication as well as in written communication. Again, in fairness, it must be emphasized that Cummins moved away from the labels BICS and CALP and replaced them with the notions of *cognitive demand* (i.e., cognitively demanding language versus cognitively undemanding language as two poles of one continuum) and *context* (i.e., context-embedded language and context-reduced language as poles of another continuum). However, Spolsky (1984) warns that in using such terms, one runs the risk of falling into the same trap as Bernstein (1971)[7] by applying "value laden labels." Unfortunately, merely abandoning the labels of BICS and CALP did not resolve the basic problem that results from the notion of context reduced/embedded communication. In this regard, Wald (1984) contends that unless the distinctions between "concrete" and "abstract" communication (or here between "context-embedded" and "context-reduced" communication) are clearly specified and elaborated, they can generate more confusion than clarity.

Several other prominent scholars have expressed similar concerns about implicit class biases in establishing levels of language proficiency. Troike (1984), for example, echoes the concerns of Edelsky et al. as he observes,

The general (language-mediated) cognitive-intellectual ability which he [Cummins] posits may be largely an artifact of test results that actually reflect acculturation approximations to middle-class Western cultural norms and behaviors. If we are to avoid reifying tautologies, we must be cautious about prematurely moving to draw conclusions or formulate models on the basis of inadequate and incompletely understood data. (p. 51)

In addition, CALP and so-called "context-reduced language," as these terms have been used in practice, are solely associated with the language of school. This creates a problem because,

> even in monolingual communities there is often a big gap between the language used in intimate settings such as the home, and the public language which characterizes interactions in instructional settings such as the school. It is this publicly sanctioned language that children are expected to learn, display, and be tested in at school. (Martin-Jones & Romaine, 1986, p. 26)

Martin-Jones and Romaine (1986; see also Romaine, 1989) have argued that different cognitive demands are associated with different kinds of social practices in a particular language and in a particular social context. Recalling the work of Scribner and Cole (1981; see Chapter Three), they observe,

> The fact that literate Vai did not do better on CALP-type tests than non-literates makes the distinction between CALP and BICS suspect, if both are seen as independent of rather than shaped by the language context in which they are acquired and used....The type of literacy-related skills described by Cummins are, in fact, quite culture-specific: that is, *they are specific to the cultural setting of the school.* (Martin-Jones & Romaine, 1986, p. 30; emphasis added)

The central point here is that cognitive effects cannot be separated from their sociocultural contexts. Since school represents such a sociocultural/social class-based context, we must ask whose culture and whose literacy practices it represents and why so many are found to be deficient when measured against its standards.

Thus, language proficiency is important in understanding academic success not because it is associated with universal cognitive thresholds, or common underlying language proficiencies, but because it is associated with the norms, practices, and expectations of those whose language, cultural, and class practices are embodied in the schools. Failing to appreciate this, we are left with the illusion that school practices involve universal, higher order cognitive functions and that all other uses of language are merely basic.

To draw these conclusions is not to retreat from the importance of language in education or the choice of language for instruction. Rather, it is to locate language within broader cultural and class contexts and to recognize that notions of language proficiency can continue to be used as gatekeeping mechanisms in schools. Thus, notions of language proficiency must address the dominance of L1 and L2 high-status varieties of language over L1 and L2 low-status varieties. As discussed earlier, historically, high-status varieties of language have been associated with the literate tradition, with standard language, with schooling, and frequently with the language norms and practices of the middle class whose culture is reaffirmed and transmitted by the schools. A similar split between spoken vernacular and a rhetorical, standard school language has been noted among linguistic minorities (Martin-Jones & Romaine, 1986). Those whose speech deviates from that standard are disadvantaged.

The Decontextualization Hypothesis
In some of his later work, for example, Cummins (1989) replaced BICS and CALP with other terminology. For example, "conversational" language proficiency has become a substitute for BICS, and "academic" language proficiency replaces CALP. Again, these are to be seen as poles on a language continuum rather than as opposites. He also emphasized that these poles are not identical with the distinction between oral and written language (see 1989, pp. 29-30). However, despite the shift in terminology, this approach appears compatible with the so-called "decontextualization hypothesis," which treats texts as autonomous. Tannen (1982) contends that the decontextualization hypothesis emerges from the great divide literature on orality versus literacy in the work of Goody and Watt (1963), Havelock (1963), Olson (1977, 1984), and Ong (1982) (see Chapter Three). Cummins did add the important qualification that oral interactions, both in and out of school, can also be decontextualized:

> Written uses do tend to require explicit and decontextualized use
> of language, since the communicative partner is not present and
> a shared context often cannot be assumed, but many oral lan-
> guage interactions, both in school and outside school, are also

decontextualized to a greater or lesser extent and thus would be characterized as academic....A central aspect of what I have termed "academic" language proficiency is the ability to make complex meanings explicit in either oral or written modalities by means of *language itself* rather than by means of paralinguistic cues (e.g., gestures, intonation, etc.). Experience of these uses of language in oral interactions prior to school clearly helps to prepare children to use and understand the increasingly decontextualized language demands of school. (1989, p. 30, emphasis in the original)

Here there appears to be an effort to bridge the oral/literate divide. This qualification represents an important clarification of prior discussions. Nevertheless, the continued reliance on the notion of decontextualized language remains problematic. Tannen's (1982) work, in particular, points to the limitations of the decontextualization hypothesis. For example, in a cross-group study of young adult Greek- and U.S.-born women performing a story retelling task, she observed that the U.S.-born women approached the task as one of providing elaborate detail, sticking to the facts, and presenting them in proper order, whereas the Greek women took more interpretive license, and as a result, told more interesting stories by ascribing roles and motives to their characters. Tannen observed that whereas the U.S.-born women might be seen as having taken a decontextualized approach, both groups had, in fact, approached the task with a different sense of context. The Greek women seemed more concerned with affect than detail and accuracy because they saw the context as one of storytelling (what Edwards and Sienkewicz, 1990, would call emphasizing "performance"). The U.S.-born women seemed to interpret the task as being within a school or academic context that demanded detail and factual accuracy. Noting that a social context is always operative, it is easy to seen why Tannen concludes that there is

a growing dissatisfaction with the notion that any discourse can be decontextualized and that what has been thought "literate" is in fact associated with formal schooling....The emphasis on correct memory for detail, chronological sequence, and getting facts straight without personal evaluation, which the Americans in this study exhibited, is associated with this kind of literate or school-based strategy....The point here is not that the Greeks are oral and the Americans literate....Quite the contrary, the findings of the study demonstrate that these oral and literate strategies all appear in oral language. (1982, pp. 40-41)

Tannen offers another example of how oral and written language have similarities achieved by different strategies in her discussion of the "cohesion hypothesis," wherein "spoken discourse establishes cohesion through paralinguistic features whereas written discourse does so through lexicalization" (1982, p. 41). From this hypothesis, it is possible to see that both oral and written discourse require cohesion but achieve it through different means. This hypothesis suggests another way in which oral and written language have parallel, but not identical, functions. Again, the issue is not one of contextualized versus decontextualized language; rather it is a question of what strategies are used to achieve communicative goals (see Tannen, 1987, p. 85; see also Edwards & Sienkewicz, 1990).

The Notions of Threshold Level and Transfer

Other areas of contention relate to the notions of threshold and transfer. The work of several researchers provides some support for some threshold level of language ability necessary for L2 literacy development. Clarke (1980), for example, has considered this question in the context of learning to read a second language. Clarke maintained that inadequate oral abilities in a second language can cause those who read proficiently in their first language to short-circuit when attempting to read in a second language.

However, Hudson (1981) argues that more than just second language oral proficiency is necessary to prevent a "short-circuit" when reading in a second language. Although some threshold level of oral proficiency is important in determining the ability to read in a second language, there may be other factors, such as schema or background knowledge, that may cause the reader to "short-circuit" (Andersson & Barnitz, 1984). Other researchers have noted the importance of discourse narrative structures in reading development (see Durán, 1985, who argues that the role of story structures is one of the earliest modes of discourse acquired by children).

Closely tied to the notion of threshold is the idea of transfer, since it is hypothesized that a certain level of language proficiency must be achieved in L1 before positive cognitive benefits can be transferred to L2. When we attempt to apply the notion of transfer of language proficiency to CALP or academic language, additional issues emerge. If

CALP is in fact "test-wiseness" as Edelsky et al. (1983) contend, transfer must involve much more than just language. It must include knowledge of specific school-defined literacy practices. As Odlin (1989) observes,

> The comparative success of literate bilinguals does not as clearly indicate the importance of language transfer in the sense of native language influence as it indicates the importance of *transfer of training*. That is, literate bilinguals may have an advantage not just because of their linguistic skills but also because of problem-solving skills that they may have acquired in the course of their education. (pp. 134-135, emphasis added)

To the extent that students have learned how to do certain school-based literacy practices in L1, they are able to transfer that knowledge to parallel literacy practices in L2. Or, in Scribner and Cole's terms, transfer includes not just language but also knowledge of literacy practices. In this regard, Odlin reviews Linnarud's (1978) studies on cross-language composition abilities (of Swedish-English bilinguals) as evidence that bilinguals who are good writers in one language are likely to be good writers in their other language, and conversely, poor writers in one tend to also be poor writers in their other language. Although these findings support the notion of a common underlying language proficiency, qualification is necessary because writing task, genre, and text discourse styles between Swedish and English would have to be similar in order for there to be transfer.[8] More is involved in transfer than merely knowledge of language as (autonomous) code because social expectations and rules of appropriateness are embedded in literacy practices.

Odlin reviews other studies (e.g., Genesee, 1979) involving transfer of literacy abilities among three languages, where there is evidence that the similarity in the writing systems positively affects transfer. Tests of Canadian children who were literate in French, English, and Hebrew indicated higher correlations on reading scores between French and English than between either of them and Hebrew, which has a different script. There is also evidence that transfer involves knowledge that is more specifically related to the linguistic system, when those systems share commonalties. "Studies of trilingualism indicate that the more similar the linguistic structures in two languages are, the greater the likelihood of transfer" (Odlin, 1989, p. 141). This also extends to languages that share a large number of cognates. Odlin cautions, however, "If an English speaker does not understand *ambitious*, for example, the similarity of it to French *ambitieux* will be of little help in understanding the French word" (p. 135). However, Odlin cautions that "studies of language awareness indicate that the importance of language distance depends very much on the *perceptions* of that distance by learners" (p. 141, emphasis in the original). Studies such as these suggest that the notion of transfer as it relates to literacy processes and practices needs much more elaboration.

Attempts to Operationalize Constructs for Practitioners

Although Cummins has attempted to clarify and refine his position, some of his interpreters have attempted to apply his framework in rather simplistic ways, which suggests either that his readers have missed his qualifications or that the framework is not sufficiently elaborated. Staff development handouts such as those adapted in Figure 12 have circulated since the 1980s.

Figure 12.
The Communicative Quadrant Operationalized

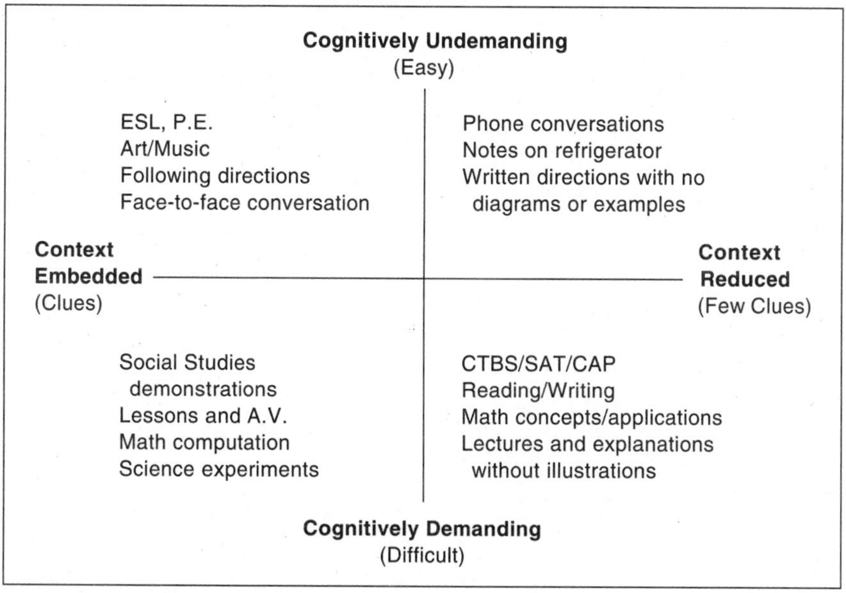

```
                     Cognitively Undemanding
                            (Easy)

      ESL, P.E.                      Phone conversations
      Art/Music                      Notes on refrigerator
      Following directions           Written directions with no
      Face-to-face conversation          diagrams or examples

Context                                                    Context
Embedded  ——————————————————————————————————————————————  Reduced
(Clues)                                                    (Few Clues)

      Social Studies                 CTBS/SAT/CAP
        demonstrations               Reading/Writing
      Lessons and A.V.               Math concepts/applications
      Math computation               Lectures and explanations
      Science experiments                without illustrations

                      Cognitively Demanding
                           (Difficult)
```

(Authorship of the handout from which this grid is adapted is unclear, although the California State Department of Education was referenced. Many such handouts have been developed and circulated by staff development personnel who, with all good intentions, have liberally, and in an ad hoc manner, attempted to "clarify" and "operationalize" various constructs of contemporary theory.)

This attempt to operationalize Cummins's quadrant into examples familiar to teachers illustrates some of the concerns that Edelsky (1991), Spolsky (1984), and Wald (1984) have expressed. The terms and examples chosen to operationalize constructs like contextualization and cognitive demand are inescapably value laden and arbitrary. The categorization is confused and inaccurate. Even more problematic is the lack of parallelism in the chart. ESL, science experiments, and reading/writing are hardly comparable activities.

Professional development materials such as these illustrate the limitations of applying constructs in practice that have not been fully elaborated at the theoretical level. Insofar as theory is a guide to practice, it must be sufficiently clear and elaborated to be applicable. Some commentators have provided much better discussions of the curricular relevance of some of these constructs (e.g., see Baker, 1993, especially pp. 142-144). However, care must be taken to avoid simplistic reductionism. In this regard, the observations of Wald (1984) have relevance.

> Unless some of the basic concepts...are refined for further clarity and informed by specific sociocultural settings,...the framework will remain an academic abstraction incapable of making contact between the language resources developing among the students independently of academic contexts and the development of literacy skills necessary for academic achievement. (p. 68)

As part of that elaboration, it would seem necessary to rid the framework of those constructs that are compatible with an autonomous view of language use. This would avoid the pitfalls of false dichotomies such as the alleged cognitive differences between concrete and abstract speech. It would require dropping the decontextualization hypothesis, which continues to be a central tenet of the framework. It would require more elaboration on the interrelationships between oral and literate language strategies (Tannen, 1987) in order to debunk the myth of orality versus literacy (Tannen, 1982; see also Edwards & Sienkewicz, 1990). It would also require focusing more on social than on cognitive factors affecting language development (Troike, 1984) and on the cultural factors that affect language and literacy practices in the schools (Delgado-Gaitán & Trueba, 1991; Philips, 1972, 1983; Trueba, 1989; Trueba, Jacobs, & Kirton, 1990).

Additional Issues in Research on Literacy Instruction for Language Minority Learners

Besides these issues, there are a number of other theoretical and technical concerns related to literacy in bilingual education that are worthy of a more in-depth discussion than is feasible in this volume. A few of these issues are discussed briefly here as they relate to grade-school and adult education.

K-12 Issues

It is commonly assumed that language minority learners enter bilingual and ESL programs with considerable linguistic deficiencies that make their acquisition of English literacy difficult. However, in a major review of the literature related to reading in bilingual programs, Fillmore and Valadez (1986) note that research findings are mixed on the extent to which various language proficiencies affect L2 reading. They note that some studies indicate that L2 reading difficulties may be due to an inadequate development of L2 oral language; others indicate that L2 learners may have difficulty learning to speak and read in L2 simultaneously. However, L1 readers can study L2 oral language and learn to read in L1 as separate tasks. They also note that bilingual children score higher in L2 achievement tests if they have learned to read in their L1 first. These findings tend to support Cummins's transfer hypotheses (1981, 1984a, 1985). However, several authorities would qualify or take issue with these claims. Goodman, Goodman, and Flores (1979) contend that, while it is easier to become literate in a second language once one has developed literacy in any language, one need not have a highly developed oral productive and receptive ability in the second language to become literate in a second language. Rather, the receptive skills are more essential. Edelsky (1986) makes a similar claim for children's writing. She maintains that transferability of writing skills is not constant across contexts; it varies with the context. This suggests, at least in the case of writing, that skills are not transferable based upon a common underlying language proficiency, but are situation-specific, as Scribner and Cole (1978, 1981) have contended. Furthermore, she argues that students learning to write in English and Spanish have been able to keep the two languages separate without one interfering with the other. She also maintains that a rigid learning sequence (e.g., first learning L2 orally before learning L2 reading and writing) does not have to be adhered to.

Other works have addressed the implications of language varieties and functions of literacy for literacy development and literacy instruction (e.g., Penfield, 1982; Trueba, 1984, 1989). Valadez (1981) has addressed both issues as they apply to writing. She maintains that before effective literacy instruction can be planned for language minority students, it is necessary to understand the significance of literacy for members of these groups outside the classroom. In order to motivate students to write in an alien environment (i.e., the classroom), it may be necessary (at least initially) to allow them to write in the language or dialect in which they are the most comfortable (see also Williams, 1991). Valadez (1981) also contends that students' motivation to write must be nurtured before emphasis is placed on rules of form. Once students have the motivation to write, the language arts teacher or some other critic might suggest rules of rhetoric that can enhance the message they wish to convey. She concludes that there "are benefits which accrue to those who discover that they can write, who feel the power that the written word gives, (as Paulo Freire teaches, and as our graffiti writers express), and will improve academic achievement in the language arts and in other areas of the school curriculum" (p. 177).

Adult Issues

Much of the available research on language minority status and literacy acquisition has focused on school-age children and to some extent on adolescents. This is due in part to greater access to children and adolescents as research subjects. Adult language minority issues also provide a less lucrative market for research and publication. While it is likely that many of the issues related to child L2 language and literacy acquisition are of relevance to adults, much more research and theoretical work is necessary to determine the extent to which this is true. For example, studies are needed that focus on the effects of prior schooling, life experience, and aging on literacy development. In most controlled studies of older learners to date, "older" typically means that the subjects in these studies were in their teens (Hatch, 1983). Thus, the role of age and the aging process relative to second language learning is unclear. It is known that aging seems to have some relationship to language loss. However, its relationship to ability and motivation (within the contexts of normal adult life) to learn a second language and to develop literacy in a first or second language are unclear (Wiley, 1986).

When reading studies of adult second language and literacy development, it is necessary to pay close attention to who was being studied. Much of the adult second language acquisition literature is based on studies of those who are highly literate in L1, in other words, university ESL students who have already received extensive schooling. There is a much smaller body of literature on the acquisition of language and literacy by adult language minorities in noncollege environments. Ethnographic studies of a variety of populations are necessary, since groups vary according to language and cultural background, social class, and age (see Weinstein-Shr, 1995). The ethnographic studies that have been done are useful, since they deal with actual literacy practices of adults and the treatment of adult language minorities by the majority. Important examples include Auerbach's (1989) and Weinstein-Shr and Quintero's (1995) work on family literacy; Miller's (1991) study of access issues faced by Hmong adults in California; Klassen and Burnaby's (1993) work on adult immigrants in Canada; Weinstein-Shr's (Weinstein, 1984; Weinstein-Shr, 1993a) studies on the Hmong in Philadelphia; and the work being done on biliteracy by Hornberger (1989; Hornberger & Hardman, 1994) and Farr (1994).

It is also important to consider the reasons why adult learners enter programs, because unlike children, they are not required to attend. Curricula need to be matched with student aims and needs, particularly with adults. Learner profiles and needs assessments are essential in program, curriculum, and instructional planning. According to Wrigley and Guth (1992), adult students have many reasons for enrolling in programs. In one survey, students were asked, "Why would an adult want to go (back) to school and learn to read and write in English?" Responses from students indicated what they wanted:

- to become more independent; to not have to rely on friends and family to translate; to not be at the mercy of kids who "interpret" school notices and report cards creatively; to be able to go to appointments alone;
- to gain access to "better jobs"; to help children succeed; to teach children how to make it through the school system;
- to give something back to the community; to help others; to support the school by becoming a teacher or an aide;
- to feel like "somebody" and get some respect; to have others realize that they are dealing with someone who is smart and has

ideas; to avoid feeling that all communication breakdown is the fault of the speaker;

- to be involved in education for its own sake; to do something worthwhile for oneself. (Wrigley & Guth, 1992, p. 10)

There is also a need for programs to negotiate with students in the development of curricula so that curricula are not imposed. Adult learners need to be involved in deciding what types of study they will undertake based on their needs, goals, and interests. By so doing, they can exercise language choices. Rather than having English be the sole language used in literacy instruction, adult learners should be allowed to choose the language of instruction where possible. Programs for adults need to be concerned with which language provides the most immediate access to the knowledge they need and the best foundation for continued learning. The choice of one language of instruction does not preclude the development of another—it may, in fact, enhance it.

There are, however, limitations in trying to involve students in decisions about literacy curricula. As Crandall (1979) has maintained, students cannot truly negotiate their learning unless they can make informed choices. Choices are constrained by (1) the availability of trained teachers and materials; (2) the language and literacy practices that need to be learned and the situations in which they will be used; (3) the difficulty or ease of transferring prior literacy skills from L1 to L2; and (4) the amount of time allowed for literacy training (see also Chisman, et al., 1993; Wrigley, et al., 1993).

Implications for Policy and Practice

As Dumont (1972) observed many years ago, in the absence of bilingual programs and culturally appropriate instruction, "education for most students is an either-or proposition: Participate by teacher-school established norms or withdraw. It is being able to speak English or silence" (p. 368). If students are to benefit from educational programs, they must also have opportunities to develop their literacy skills by building on their linguistic, literacy, and cultural resources.

To promote literacy through bilingual education, there is a need to carefully distinguish those aspects of instruction that are related specifically to language from those that involve cultural differences and socioeconomic inequities. There is a need to scrutinize contemporary bilingual education theory for those constructs that reproduce the great divide. Notions of academic language proficiency and decontextualization, as they are often used, are particularly problematic because they confound language with schooling and equate a higher cognitive status to the language and literacy practices of school. Academic language proficiency seems to equate broadly with schooling. Schooling is not a neutral process. It involves class and culturally specific forms of socialization. Language and literacy development in schools is always carried out in specific social contexts involving specific literacy practices. Thus, from the social practices and ideological perspectives, there should be no cognitive mystique about academic language proficiency.

Similarly, it is necessary to reconsider what we mean by language transfer and to disentangle language transfer from transfer of school-based training. Since much of what falls under the rubric of academic language proficiency involves academic socialization to specific literacy practices, it would be better to concentrate more explicitly on those specific practices rather than on some amorphous level of proficiency that is not specific to any particular context.

A rationale for transitional bilingual education can be provided in relatively straightforward terms without reference to these troublesome constructs. Students need to develop school-based literacy in a language that they understand if they are to keep pace academically with their peers who already understand the language of instruction. If they must spend all of their instructional time learning the dominant language of instruction before they are allowed to study academic content, they will fall behind those who already understand the language of instruction. For language minority children and adults, the native language usually provides the most immediate means for participating in school literacy practices. While school literacy knowledge and skills are being developed in the native language, they can also learn the dominant language of instruction. When their L2 oral language is sufficiently developed, they can participate in L2 academic classrooms effectively if they have practiced parallel activities in their L1. Reframing the issues in this way shifts the focus from academic language as an autonomous entity to language and literacy practices as context-specific activities.

However, even when stated in these terms, this rationale refers only to a transitional bilingual education model. Transitional programs are designed for linguistic assimilation into classrooms dominated by the majority language. They are not necessarily routes for linguistic equality in the long term. At best, transitional bilingual education *accommodates* minority languages. In order to *promote* bilingualism and biliteracy, language diversity must be seen as a resource in its own right (Ruíz, 1984).

Beyond this, *literacy*—not just participation in school English instruction—must be seen as a goal. In this regard, Edelsky et al. (1983) contend that literacy can best be promoted if there is a shift away from the acquisition of nonsensical skills. They further argue that,

- Language instruction needs to be purposeful and contain "messageful content."
- The goal of instruction should not be improved test performance by children who are "literate impostors," i.e., those who can perform meaningless manipulations of surface structure.
- Oral communicative competence provides the basis for literacy. Consequently, the school and community should accept the child's entry abilities as a legitimate foundation for future learning.
- Interpersonal uses of language (oral and written) should become more of a focus in the school to foster authentic literacy development.
- It is possible to first become truly literate before learning school literacy. (summarized from pp. 13-14)

The assumption underlying these conclusions is that much of what is called literacy in schools is artificial and inauthentic and that much of what passes for academic language proficiency and decontextualized language practice is, in fact, not reflective of higher order cognitive abilities at all. Rather, these types of activities are class-based, culturally biased activities that many students experience as meaningless. Thus, they should be looked at with great care.

In order to promote languages and literacies, educational policies must be guided by both theoretical principles and a desire to include the voices of those who have often been excluded. Rather than imposing uniform national standards on all groups, as many contemporary educational reformers advocate, there is a need for greater exploration of alternative literacies (see Cook-Gumperz & Keller-Cohen, 1993; Wrigley, 1993) and alternative approaches to schooling. New educational models must emerge from a negotiation with the populations to be served (see Edelsky & Hudelson, 1991). Such a negotiation is more likely to occur when schools employ bilingual and bicultural personnel who represent the communities being served at all levels.

Further Reading

Baker, C. (1993). *Foundations of bilingual education and bilingualism.* Philadelphia: Multilingual Matters.

This comprehensive and accessible introduction to issues in language minority instruction details and critiques a range of educational options by considering the societal and academic goals of these approaches as well as many important theroetical and practical issues. It is highly recommended both for students new to the field and their teachers.

Cummins, J. (1983). Analysis-by-rhetoric: Reading the text or the reader's own projections? A reply to Edelsky et al. *Applied Linguistics, 4*(1), 23-41.

This article provides a reply to Edelsky et al. (1983) below. These two works should be read together.

Cummins, J. (1989). *Empowering minority students.* Sacramento, CA: California Association for Bilingual Education.

This work provides a later version of Cummins's theories. In addition to the theoretical issues addressed in this chapter, its practical suggestions and discussion of anti-racist education are valuable.

Edelsky, C. (1991). *With literacy and justice for all: Rethinking the social in language and education.* London: Falmer Press.

In this volume, Edelsky extends her views beyond her earlier (1986) work and updates her critique of Cummins's work.

Edelsky, C., Hudelson, S., Flores, B., Barkin, F., Altweger, B., & Kristina, J. (1983). Semilingualism and language deficit. *Applied Linguistics, 4*(1), 3-22.

This article provides a critical examination of Cummins's early work. Read it with Cummins's reply (1983) above.

Hakuta, K. (1986). *Mirror of language: The debate on bilingualism.* New York: Basic Books.

Although this work does not explicitly address literacy issues, it provides a comprehensive overview of issues related to bilingualism and to concerns raised in this chapter.

Martin-Jones, M., & Romaine, S. (1986). Semilingualism: A half-baked theory of communicative competence. *Applied Linguistics, 7*(1), 26-38.

This article raises concerns related to those of Edelsky et al. (1983).

Rivera, C. (Ed.). (1984). *Language proficiency and academic achievement.* Avon, England: Multilingual Matters.

This collection entertains the responses of a number of well-known researchers to Cummins's earlier work. The contributions by Cummins, Troike, and Wald have particular relevance for this chapter.

Romaine, S. (1989). *Bilingualism.* Oxford, England: Blackwell.

This volume provides a comprehensive general introduction to issues related to bilingualism and updates issues raised in Martin-Jones and Romaine (1986).

Notes

[1] Although it is not suggested here that models in literacy studies have the same gravity as paradigms do for the natural sciences, Kuhn's (1970) classic work on paradigm shift in science has general relevance to this discussion.

[2] In California, since the mid 1980s, these and related constructs have been an essential part of the content required in state examinations for bilingual education credentials and the related Language Development Specialist, and for new Cross-Cultural Language and Academic Development Credentials. Therefore, these constructs have become a major part of both university-level teacher education and district-level inservice training. The popular *CALLA* approach in ESL instruction (see Chamot & O'Malley, 1986, 1987; O'Malley & Chamot, 1990) also incorporates these constructs.

[3] The notion of a "global" language proficiency has come under increasing scrutiny and has been rejected by some writers (see Nunan, 1988, especially Chapter Eight).

[4] Communicative ESL approaches such as the Natural Approach (Krashen & Terrell, 1983), as opposed to grammar-based approaches (which assume that one must learn grammar before one can learn to communicate), have proven particularly effective for both children and adults.

[5] Baker (1993, p. 153) defines immersion programs as bilingual programs for language majority children, which has an initial bilingual emphasis on L2 and which has as its aims pluralism, societal enrichment, and bilingualism and biliteracy.

[6] Transitional bilingual programs are based on the goal of linguistic assimilation into the dominant language (see Baker, 1993, Chapter Eleven, for an analysis of the various types of programs). Although many advocates of bilingual education in the United States support two-way or dual immersion programs for all students, transitional bilingual programs have been more common largely due to constraints on federal funding and pressure from opponents of bilingual education.

[7] Bernstein (1971) hypothesized that the (White) English-speaking working class was socialized toward a concrete, shared, "restricted code" in language use, whereas the (White) English-speaking middle class was socialized toward a more abstract "elaborated code." According to this view, because schools use elaborated codes, middle-class children are advantaged in schools. This advantage influences the reproduction of social classes, because those who can use the school code outperform those who cannot use it as effectively. Bernstein's characterizations of restricted versus elaborated codes appear to be roughly parallel to Cummins's earlier BICS/CALP and subsequent notions of "cognitively demanding/undemanding" language and context embedded/reduced distinctions. See Labov (1970) and Leacock (1972) for substantive discussions regarding the adequacy of nonstandard, "oral" varieties of language.

[8] See Kaplan (1966, 1986) for a related discussion that reaches the controversial conclusion that there is an intervening factor of different cultural thought patterns in which L1 thought patterns interfere with the quality of L2 compositions.

CHAPTER 9

The Impact of Literacy
Policies and Practices
on Language Minority Learners

What emerges as the key question in examining literacy theories, practices, and research is not whether they recognize variable and contextual aspects of literacy, but whether they consider how this diversity positions learners, teachers, and researchers with respect to existing inequities and relations of domination and subordination. (Auerbach, 1991, p. 80)

This chapter reviews societal attitudes, social and educational policies, and pedagogical practices and their impact on language minority groups in the United States. It attempts to locate these attitudes, policies, and practices within the three perspectives on literacy education and research (autonomous, social practices, and ideological) and suggests areas where further research and reflection on policies and practices related to literacy are needed. As was discussed in Chapter Three, the three perspectives on the study of literacy differ because they (1) employ different units of analysis (e.g., individual factors versus group factors); (2) place different emphases on intergroup power relations; and (3) interpret differently the roles of the social scientist and the teacher in the processes of conducting research and teaching (Tollefson, 1991). In Chapters Three and Seven, the influence of these perspectives on general literacy theory and ethnographic research, respectively, was noted. Here, their implications are addressed further.

Policy discussions regarding the education of immigrants and other language minority groups are often focused on issues of impact, which usually means cost to the country. Less frequently is public debate centered on the impact of policy, or its absence, on language minorities themselves. Consider, for example, the way that public and educational policy issues affecting refugees have been framed. In the early 1980s, members of a congressional fact-finding committee on refugee

188

affairs called a meeting of a group of education and health care providers. The committee was attempting to assess the impact of refugee resettlement. The federal refugee agenda under the new Reagan administration was aimed at reducing the impact, in other words, reducing the costs, of refugee resettlement on the federal government. Subsequently, there was a shift toward employment training and job-related English skills. The impact of this change in federal policy was reciprocal, since refugees were affected by these policy changes as well. The impact of the new policy on them was reduced social, health, and educational support. For those who successfully acquired entry-level jobs, it meant that they would earn only minimum wage. For those with families to support, it meant the loss of medical treatment for their family members. Thus, the impact of the policy changes on people was increased marginalization and a greater struggle to survive.

The Impact of Societal Attitudes toward Language Minorities

As discussed in Chapter Five, most analyses regarding second language acquisition and literacy emphasize individual motivation to learn a language. Such analyses can be located within the autonomous perspective, since they fail to take societal and structural economic factors affecting learning into account. Perdue's (1984) investigation of adult immigrant workers in Europe moves beyond the autonomous perspective and provides some clues regarding the impact of social obstacles on adults when they are trying to learn and use a second language. For example, Perdue found that adults, particularly those of lower socioeconomic status, often felt discouraged from attempting to use a language they were trying to learn because of intolerant language attitudes and expectations of the majority. He observed that many speakers of a dominant language expect immigrants and language minorities to use their language, and more importantly, to use it as well as a native speaker would. Perdue concluded that the inability of language minority adults to do so reinforces the language prejudice of many among the majority who often stigmatize the L2 non-native-speaker. Feeling the impact of this stigmatization, the non-native speaker avoids situations where he or she might feel less than competent and, thereby, loses the opportunity to use, practice, or experiment with the second language.

In situations of contact with members of a dominant language group, language minorities are frequently in a subordinated social position. Klassen and Burnaby's (1993) analysis of Canadian immigrants and Miller's (1991) study of Hmong refugees in the United States support the importance of focusing on social and ideological issues related to second language and literacy acquisition. Miller explores institutional barriers that discourage adult immigrant students from participating in classroom practices that they perceive as alien and threatening. These studies indicate a need for additional research on how language attitudes of dominant groups affect the motivation of language minority groups to acquire second language and literacy. Similarly, there is a need to study teacher attitudes toward language minorities to see how those attitudes affect the motivation of language minorities to learn.

Finally, there is a need to consider how, for various groups, social class tensions persist after members of these groups immigrate. Klassen and Burnaby (1993), for example, note tensions among Central American immigrant students based on social class conflicts that existed prior to immigration and reappeared in Canadian ESL classrooms. Their work indicates that we need to know more about students than just their national origin or the dominant language in their home country. There are often differences in social class, language background, and ethnicity within the source countries.

The Impact of Immigration and Educational Policies

Immigration and education policies have a profound impact on language minority adults. For example, in the United States, under the 1986 Immigration Reform and Control Act (IRCA), undocumented immigrants and refugees who met several conditions were entitled to become legal citizens of the United States. If these adults participated in amnesty-related classes, which required a minimum of 40 hours of instruction in ESL and U.S. history (out of a 60-hour program in most cases), most were entitled to permanent resident status (Spener, 1994, p. 5). Hundreds of thousands of people responded, swamping adult education programs with new students "they were not adequately prepared to serve" (p. 5). Spener points out, "Regardless of its quality, 60 hours of instruction...is an impossibly short amount of time to achieve significant gains in spoken English proficiency, much less English literacy" (p. 6). As many students completed the amnesty program, they sought further education. Many of these students had lacked opportunities for schooling in their native languages and thereby lacked a foundation in literacy. Both the educational requirements of the program and the availability of services are issues that needed to be considered because educational standards and requirements cannot have a positive impact unless adequate resources and training are provided.

Choice of language of instruction also has an impact on students who seek opportunities to acquire literacy. Which languages are used for instruction depends on a number of factors, including the availability of native language teachers and materials and the goals of the students. There are sound pedagogical reasons for developing literacy in the native language first. To do so does not exclude or ignore instruction in English; rather, it adds another educational option.

> If an individual who is literate in his or her mother tongue is more likely to become a proficient speaker, reader, and writer of English than one who is illiterate in the mother tongue, and if in turn such proficiency and literacy in the English language increases that individual's potential to be a skilled and productive worker in the U.S. economy, then a rationale for biliteracy as both an educational goal and an instructional approach for language minority adults can be conscientiously made. (Spener, 1994, p. 7)

Spener (1994) further observes that in spite of their strong motivation to learn English, many immigrants must attempt to learn it under conditions that are far from ideal since they work in low- and semi-skilled jobs while doing so. He concludes,

> In addition to the difficulty of finding time to study English each day after family and work responsibilities are taken care of, both immigrants and U.S.-born limited English speakers too often find themselves working low-skill, low-wage jobs where they either work primarily alongside other immigrants (with whom they interact in their shared native language or in their limited English) or at jobs where they are required to engage in only limited verbal communication with anyone. The potential for them to acquire English informally through interaction with native English speakers is thus limited as well. Denying access to job-related training by making it available only to literate, proficient English speakers (native or not) only compounds the problem of lack of contact

with English by making it more difficult for language minority adults to break into higher skill jobs where they are more likely to interact with native English speakers. (p. 8)

A fact that is often ignored is that the United States is dependent on the importation of foreign labor, interestingly, at both the lower and the upper ends of the economic scale and educational ladder. Those with little formal education need both native language literacy *and* English language and literacy development to improve their job mobility. However, for many, there are insufficient opportunities for such training. In a number of states, most agricultural labor is performed by immigrant and migrant laborers, many of whom come from Mexico. There are few educational opportunities for these workers, and there is little in the way of an educational or occupational ladder for them.

Historically, in the United States, labor has been imported. Southern agriculture prior to the Civil War, particularly in the cotton and tobacco industries, was dependent upon imported, involuntary laborers (slaves) and their descendants. There was no mobility ladder for these workers, and illiteracy—in other words, *compulsory ignorance*—was mandatory (Weinberg, 1995). In California, Chinese immigrants were instrumental in developing the state's agriculture. They became targets of exclusionary immigration policies in the 1880s and were subsequently replaced by Japanese and Fillipino workers who experienced a similar fate. Ultimately, in California, these groups were replaced by a labor force that was predominately of Mexican origin. As each group toiled in the fields, their children were all too often discriminated against or— at best—relegated to inferior schools. These examples also point to limitations of autonomous explanations about the relationship between "illiteracy" (and "educational under-achievement") and poverty and national competitiveness.

At the other end of the educational ladder, the United States has frequently benefitted from importing educated foreign labor. Currently, a high percentage of the nation's technical brain power is imported. A large number of foreign students complete their education in U.S. colleges and universities. Many of these biliterate students remain in the United States working in technical fields. The impact of their educational costs on this country is negligible because most of their educational expenses were paid by their home countries or by their families if they were wealthy. Many pay for their education at premium foreign student tuition rates. Thus, while the strain that these students place on U.S. educational resources is minimal, the U.S. corporations that employ them benefit by not having been taxed to support their education. Similarly, when there are shortages of nurses in the health care fields, many nurses, from the Philippines and Korea, for example, are imported. Since many of these nurses have received most of their education elsewhere, the total educational costs for such skilled labor are not borne by the United States.

The Impact of Educational Policies and Resources on Language Majority Youth

The next generation of adult language minority students are now enrolled in many U.S. schools. These students, along with a large number of monolingual English-speaking students, are frequently receiving an inadequate education in under-funded schools with scarce resources and inappropriate educational programs. In this regard, McDonnell and Hill (1993) note that, "Problems of these districts are geographically localized" (p. 107). They observe that Latino and African-American youth are heavily concentrated in a small number of urban areas. For example, nearly 75% of all Latino immigrant youth are concentrated in just eleven cities. Forty percent of all African Americans live in these five cities: Los Angeles, Miami/Dade County, Houston, New York, and Chicago. "Together these five cities educate nearly 1 in 20" U.S. students of school age (McDonnell & Hill, 1993, p. 108).

National agendas fail to address the special needs of students in these areas. As McDonnell and Hill (1993) note, recent national agendas for school reform, which began in the Bush administration and were continued under Clinton's, fail because they assume that schools have enough money "to improve their own performance, if only efforts are properly focused by means of goals, standards, and accountability measures" (p. 107). Under current operational conditions, the push for national standards and accountability measures will probably only increase the perception of widespread educational failure and of a national literacy crisis, because the resources are not available to make meaningful reforms possible. As McDonnell and Hill observe,

> Current reform proposals do not contemplate the creation of new curricula for students who cannot profit from full-time instruction in English, nor do they remedy the shortages of teachers and texts that can provide a bridge between immigrant students' native languages and English. (p. 108)

Recently, however, there has been some positive movement in this direction. In California, for example, requirements for some new teaching credentials include an emphasis on specially designed academic instruction in English for language minority students. The purpose of such instruction is to provide students access to the core academic curriculum as quickly as possible. These instructional approaches represent an advance over the "sink or swim" English-only approaches of the past, which made no distinction between the needs of monolingual English-speaking students and language minority students. Nevertheless, if access to academic content is to be provided equally to all students, there is also a need for native language instruction for those who cannot benefit from even specially designed academic instruction in English and the need for increased funding if these new initiatives are to have a positive impact.

However, important as the issue of appropriate language of instruction is, by itself it is not sufficient to address all problems associated with educational inequities. Students whose native language is English also cannot get an equal chance to learn in schools that are inadequately funded and where teachers lack appropriate training. Thus, reform efforts that merely emphasize raising standards and demanding accountability will not lead to meaningful change when "students have only limited access to relevant curricula" (McDonnell & Hill, 1993, p. 110).

A larger issue of accountability also needs to be addressed. Typically, accountability refers to making schools responsible for maintaining standards. However, as McDonnell and Hill (1993) contend,

> Accountability implies a reciprocal relationship between schools and the broader community. Schools are to produce educational outcomes desired by the community, but in return, the community needs to provide the legitimacy and support to make those outcomes possible. In its highest form, accountability is a social contract—an acceptance of shared responsibility between schools and the larger society. (p. 110)

School reform efforts related to literacy development have both a broad and a narrow focus. Their goals are often broad and lofty; they attempt to impose a uniform, monocultural standard on everyone. At the local level, however, such reform is to be carried out by individual schools that have different levels of funding and resources. Reform carried out under these conditions of inequality merely sets up the conditions for persistent failure and blame.

Ideally, reform efforts should involve equal access to meaningful curricula and equitable funding. However, even if such were the case, additional questions would have to be raised: First, if dropout rates were substantially reduced, would schools in many areas of the nation be able to accommodate all of the students they would need to serve? Second, if the literacy and educational achievement of high school students and adult learners increased dramatically, would all those qualified to work find jobs and be paid at a level at which they could live their lives with dignity? Frank answers to these questions should indicate that merely raising literacy standards and improving the quality of education is not enough. Social and economic conditions must also be improved.

The Impact of Pedagogy

Instructional practices also affect the ability of students to become literate. Instructional practices are guided, whether consciously or not, by the various perspectives identified in Chapter Three (autonomous, social practices, and ideological). These perspectives are reflected in various instructional trends. For example, Auerbach (1991) has identified four recent tends in adult literacy pedagogy that reflect these approaches.

The first involves educators using ethnographic methods to determine specifically which literacy practices should be taught. For example, in workplace literacy programs it is common to teach adults the specific practices and skills that will enable them to do their jobs more efficiently. Auerbach notes that this approach, which reflects an autonomous perspective, "arose in response to the conceptions of literacy as a monolithic set of skills, it has, in some cases, given rise to a new prescriptivism" (p. 77). Thus, merely using ethnographic techniques to first describe and then prescribe literacy practices for instruction without critically analyzing those practices has little advantage over prescribing an autonomous set of skills for the learner to acquire.

A second pedagogical trend that Auerbach observes is the attempt to involve adults more in curricular decisions. She notes that some educators mistakenly equate learner involvement in curricular choices with empowerment. However, a focus on personal learning goals alone as a means to empower learners who are generally marginalized in this country "may undermine the possibilities for collective action and obscure the limitations on their power as isolated individuals to shape their environment, thus leading to self-blame" (1991, p. 78).

A third trend has been to overemphasize the transformative and empowering aspects of literacy while politicizing the content of literacy instruction. Auerbach (1991) cites early interpretations of Freire's work in developing countries, where rapid social change was occurring, as an example. Such interpretations, with superficial applications to U.S. contexts, tended to become simplistic and dogmatic and contained "the seed of a new danger, namely that of reproducing relations of authority and dominance between teacher and student by substituting one body of knowledge received for another" (p. 78). Such approaches have tended to leave learners with an "idealized and mystified view of literacy that can only lead to disillusionment when learners discovered that literacy alone doesn't open up new political possibilities" (pp. 78-79).

The fourth pedagogical trend identified by Auerbach involves integrating learner voices and experiences into the curriculum while at the same time developing their abilities to undertake critical social analysis. This approach (described in Auerbach, 1992) emerges from an ideological orientation. Auerbach (1991) summarizes it as follows:

> It focuses on transforming both the content and the process of literacy education in order to challenge inequities in the broader society. In terms of content, this means centering instruction on lived reality of learners as it relates to the broader social context.... In terms of process, it means problematizing reality as the basis for dialogue, critical analysis, the collaborative construction of knowledge, and action outside the classroom. (p. 79)

For socially and economically marginalized students, this latter trend has made a positive impact on students in programs that have been able to implement it (see Nash, Cason, Rhum, McGrail, & Gomez-Sanford, 1992, for descriptions of its implementation).

Conclusion

If policymakers, program designers, and teachers are to make a more positive impact on the education of language minority students, there is a need to expand on practices that integrate the languages and perspectives of learners into educational programs and curricula. By engaging in discussions and debate with others outside the domains of our daily work, we may find that, in addition to voicing our common frustrations, we can improve the educational experience and opportunities of our students. For teachers working within the constraints of declining resources and limited opportunities for professional development and collaboration, the task is wearisome. Change is slow and meandering, and those committed to it must be in for the long haul (see Fullan, 1994).

In concluding this discussion on literacy and language diversity in the United States, there is one guiding principle against which theory, policy, and practice can be evaluated: *All normal people can learn to do what they have had the opportunity, need, and desire to do in a language they understand.* Since most language minorities are normal people, if a disproportionate number appear to have literacy problems, we must re-examine our literacy theories, research, policies, and practices to try to determine why this is so.

As was stressed in Chapter Two, literacy problems do not result from language diversity; rather, the perception of a literacy crisis is magnified by ignoring literacy in languages other than English and by blaming those who have not had an opportunity for a meaningful education. (See Chapter Five.) On the national level, the literacy "crisis" in the United States is largely invented and re-invented as cover for an economic system that is unable to employ all who can work and for the failings of an educational system that is neither adequately funded nor designed to meet the educational needs of all its students.

However, given the importance of educational credentials, which are acquired through formal instruction, lack of schooling is a problem for many people. Schooling documents one's literacy; therefore, schooling is important not merely for its purported cognitive effects, but for its social effects. Given the importance of schooling, there is both a need to improve access to it and to incorporate diverse languages, language styles and varieties, and literacy practices into it. The most direct way to achieve this is to promote two-way bilingual immersion programs for all students. Beyond this there is also a need to recognize the value of literacies developed and nurtured outside of schools so that we can appreciate and build on the richness of our language diversity.

Further Reading

Auerbach, E.R. (1992). *Making meaning, making change: Participatory curriculum development for adult ESL literacy*. Washington, DC and McHenry, IL: Center for Applied Linguistics and Delta Systems.

This work provides a "how to do it" introduction to adult ESL literacy instruction with an ideological perspective.

Crandall, J., & Peyton, J.K. (Eds.). (1993). *Approaches to adult ESL literacy instruction*. Washington, DC and McHenry, IL: Center for Applied Linguistics and Delta Systems.

This collection provides contributions from well-known specialists in adult ESL literacy education. The work reflects a broad range of orientations that reflect different perspectives identified in this chapter and in Chapter Three.

Rodby, J. (1992). *Appropriating literacy: Writing and reading in English as a second language*. Portsmouth, NH: Boynton/Cook, Heinemann.

This work is theoretical, practical, and interdisciplinary in scope. Its practical examples are drawn from university and adult ESL contexts.

Wrigley, H.S., & Guth, J.A. (1992). *Bringing literacy to life: Issues and options in adult ESL*. San Mateo, CA: Aguirre International. (Now available from San Diego, CA: Dominie Press.)

This work provides a comprehensive and eclectic introduction to issues in adult ESL literacy education. It is one of the few works that includes a discussion of adult native language and biliteracy issues for practitioners.

REFERENCES

American Heritage Dictionary of the English Language (3rd ed.). (1992). Boston: Houghton Mifflin.

Andersson, B.V., & Barnitz, J.G. (1984). Cross-cultural schemata and reading comprehension instruction. *Journal of Reading, 28*(2), 102-108.

Arce, C.H. (n.d.). *Mexican origin people in the United States: The 1979 National Chicano Survey: Variable dictionary, codebook and related materials.* Ann Arbor, MI: Institute for Social Research.

Aronowitz, S., & Giroux, H. (1985). *Education under siege: The conservative, liberal, and radical debate over schooling.* South Hadley, MA: Bergin & Garvey.

Auerbach, E.R. (1989). Toward a social-contextual approach to family literacy. *Harvard Educational Review, 59*, 165-182.

Auerbach, E.R. (1991). Literacy and ideology. In W. Grabe & R.B. Kaplan (Eds.), *Annual Review of Applied Linguistics* (pp. 71-86). New York: Cambridge University Press.

Auerbach, E.R. (1992). *Making meaning, making change: Participatory curriculum development for adult ESL literacy.* Washington, DC and McHenry, IL: Center for Applied Linguistics and Delta Systems.

Bailey, R.W., & McArthur, T. (1992). Illiteracy. In T. McArthur (Ed.), *The Oxford companion to the English language* (pp. 498-499). Oxford, England: Oxford University Press.

Baker, C. (1988). *Key issues in bilingualism and bilingual education.* Philadelphia: Multilingual Matters.

Baker, C. (1993). *Foundations of bilingual education and bilingualism.* Philadelphia: Multilingual Matters.

Baratz, J.C. (1973). Teaching reading in an urban Negro school system. In R.H. Bentley & S.D. Crawford (Eds.), *Black language reader* (pp. 154-171). Glenview, IL: Scott Foresman.

Barnes, D. (1976). *From communication to curriculum.* London: Penguin Books.

199

Barton, D., & Ivanic, R. (Eds.). (1991). *Writing in the community*. London: Sage.

Bernstein, B. (1971). *Class, codes and control*. London: Routledge and Kegan Paul.

Bhatia, T.K. (1984). Literacy in monolingual societies. In R.B. Kaplan (Ed.), *Annual review of applied linguistics* (pp. 23-38). Rowley, MA: Newbury House.

Bloom, B.S. (Ed.). (1956). *Taxonomy of educational objectives: The classification of educational goals, Handbook I: Cognitive domain*. New York: Longman.

Bowles, S., & Gintis, H. (1976). *Schooling in capitalist America*. New York: Basic Books.

Brigham, C.C. (1923). *A study in American intelligence*. Princeton, NJ: Princeton University Press.

Bright, W. (Ed.). (1992). *International encyclopedia of linguistics, Vol. IV*. New York: Oxford University Press.

Brodkey, L. (1991). Tropics of literacy. In C. Mitchell & K. Weiler (Eds.), *Rewriting literacy: Culture and the discourse of the other* (pp. 161-168). New York: Bergin & Garvey.

Burtoff, M. (1985). *Haitian Creole literacy evaluation study*. Washington, DC: Center for Applied Linguistics.

California State Department of Education, Office of Bilingual Education. (1982). *Basic principles for the education of language-minority students: An overview, 1982*. Sacramento, CA: Author.

Camitta, M. (1993). Vernacular writing: Varieties of literacy among Philadelphia high school students. In B. Street (Ed.), *Cross-cultural approaches to literacy* (pp. 228-246). Cambridge, England: Cambridge University Press.

Carroll, J.B., & Chall, J.S. (Eds.). (1975). *Toward a literate society: A report from the National Academy of Education*. New York: McGraw-Hill.

Carter, T.P., & Segura, R.D. (1979). *Mexican Americans in school: A decade of change*. New York: College Entrance Examination Board.

Carvajal, D. (1993, December 19). When languages collide. *Los Angeles Times* (Orange County Edition), p. A1.

Chamot, A.U., & O'Malley, J.M. (1986). *A cognitive academic language learning approach: An ESL content-based curriculum.* Wheaton, MD: National Clearinghouse for Bilingual Education.

Chamot, A.U., & O'Malley, J.M. (1987). The cognitive academic language learning approach: A bridge to the mainstream. *TESOL Quarterly, 21,* 227-249.

Chermayeff, I., Wasserman, F., & Shapiro, M.J. (1991*). Ellis Island: An illustrated history of the immigrant experience.* New York: MacMillan.

Chisman, F.P., Wrigley, H.S., & Ewen, D.T. (1993). *ESL and the American dream.* Washington, DC: Southport Institute for Policy Analysis.

Chomsky, N. (1957). *Syntactic structures.* The Hague, Netherlands: Mouton.

Clark, M.M. (1976). *Young fluent readers.* London: Heinemann Educational Books.

Clark, M.M. (1984). Literacy at home and at school: Insights from young fluent readers. In H. Goelman, A.A. Oberg, & F. Smith (Eds.), *Awakening to literacy* (pp. 122-130). Portsmouth, NH: Heinemann.

Clarke, M. (1980). The short circuit hypothesis of ESL reading—Or when language competence interferes with reading performance. *Modern Language Journal, 64*(2), 203-209.

Clifford, G.J. (1984). Buch und lesen: Historical perspectives on literacy and schooling. *Review of Educational Research, 54,* 472-500.

Collins, J. (1991). Hegemonic practice: Literacy and standard language in public education. In C. Mitchell & K. Weiler (Eds.), *Rewriting literacy: Culture and the discourse of the other* (pp. 229-253). New York: Bergin & Garvey.

Collins, R. (1979). *The credential society: An historical sociology of education and stratification.* New York: Academic Press.

Cook-Gumperz, J. (Ed.). (1986). *The social construction of literacy.* Cambridge, England: Cambridge University Press.

Cook-Gumperz, J. (1993). Dilemmas of identity: Oral and written literacies in the making of a basic writing student. *Anthropology & Education Quarterly, 24,* 336-356.

Cook-Gumperz, J., & Keller-Cohen, D. (Eds.). (1993). Alternative literacies: In school and beyond [Theme issue]. *Anthropology & Education Quarterly, 24*(4).

Cortés, C.E. (1986). The education of language minority students: A contextual interaction model. In California State Department of Education (Ed.), *Beyond language: Social and cultural factors in schooling* (pp. 3-33). Los Angeles: California State University, Evaluation, Dissemination, and Assessment Center.

Coulmas, F. (1992). *Language and economy.* Oxford, England: Blackwell.

Crandall, J.A. (1979). *Language in education: Theory and practice, 22.* Arlington, VA: Center for Applied Linguistics.

Crandall, J., & Imel, S. (1991). Issues in adult literacy education. *The ERIC Review, 1*(2), 2-7.

Crandall, J., & Peyton, J.K. (Eds.) (1993). *Approaches to adult ESL literacy instruction.* Washington, DC and McHenry, IL: Center for Applied Linguistics and Delta Systems.

Crawford, J. (1991). *Bilingual education: History, politics, theory, and practice* (2nd ed.). Los Angeles: Bilingual Education Services.

Crawford, J. (1992a). *Hold your tongue: Bilingualism and the politics of "English Only."* Reading, MA: Addison-Wesley.

Crawford, J. (Ed.). (1992b). *Language loyalties: A source book on the Official English controversy.* Chicago: University of Chicago Press.

Crystal, D. (1987). *The Cambridge encyclopedia of language.* Cambridge, England: Cambridge University Press.

Cummins, J. (1976). The influence of bilingualism on cognitive growth: A synthesis of research findings and explanatory hypotheses. *Working Papers on Bilingualism, 9*, 1-43.

Cummins, J. (1979). Linguistic interdependence and the educational development of bilingual children. *Review of Educational Research, 49*, 222-251.

Cummins, J. (1981). The role of primary language development in promoting educational success for language minority students. In California State Department of Education, Office of Bilingual Education (Ed.), *Schooling and language minority students: A theoretical framework* (pp. 3-49). Los Angeles: California State University, Evaluation, Dissemination and Assessment Center.

Cummins, J. (1983). Analysis-by-rhetoric: Reading the text or the reader's own projections? A reply to Edelsky et al. *Applied Linguistics, 4*(1), 23-41.

Cummins, J. (1984a). Wanted: A theoretical framework for relating language proficiency to academic achievement among bilingual students. In C. Rivera (Ed.), *Language proficiency and academic achievement* (pp. 2-19). Avon, England: Multilingual Matters.

Cummins, J. (1984b). Language proficiency and academic achievement revisited: A response. In C. Rivera (Ed.), *Language proficiency and academic achievement* (pp. 71-76). Avon, England: Multilingual Matters.

Cummins, J. (1985). *Bilingualism and special education: Issues in assessment and pedagogy.* San Diego, CA: College-Hill Press.

Cummins, J. (1986). Empowering minority students: A framework for intervention. *Harvard Educational Review, 56,* 18-36.

Cummins, J. (1989). *Empowering minority students.* Sacramento, CA: California Association for Bilingual Education.

Cummins, J., & Swain, M. (1986). *Bilingualism in education.* New York: Longman.

Dandy, E.B. (1991). *Black communications: Breaking down the barriers.* Chicago: African American Images.

Dandy, E.B. (1992). Sensitizing teachers to cultural differences: An African American perspective. In D.E. Murray (Ed.), *Diversity as resource: Redefining cultural literacy* (pp. 87-112). Alexandria, VA: Teachers of English to Speakers of Other Languages.

Darder, A. (1991). *Culture and power in the classroom: A critical foundation for bicultural education.* New York: Bergin & Garvey.

de Castell, S., & Luke, A. (1983). Defining "literacy" in North American schools: Social and historical consequences. *Journal of Curriculum Studies, 15,* 373-389.

de Castell, S., & Luke, A. (1986). Models of literacy in North American schools: Social and historical conditions and consequences. In S. de Castell, A. Luke, & K. Egan (Eds.), *Literacy, society, and schooling* (pp. 87-109). Cambridge, MA: Cambridge University Press.

Delgado-Gaitán, C. (1990). *Literacy for empowerment: The role of parents in children's education.* New York: Falmer Press.

Delgado-Gaitán, C., & Trueba, H.T. (1991). *Crossing cultural borders: Education for immigrant families in America.* New York: Falmer Press.

Delpit, L.D. (1988). The silenced dialogue: Power and pedagogy in educating other people's children. *Harvard Educational Review, 58*, 280-298.

Dillard, J.L. (1972). *Black English: Its history and usage in the United States.* New York: Vintage/Random House.

Donaldson, M. (1978). *Children's minds.* Glasgow, Scotland: Collins.

Dubin, F., & Kuhlman, N.A. (Eds.). *Cross-cultural literacy: Global perspectives on reading and writing.* Englewood Cliffs, NJ: Regents/Prentice-Hall.

Dumont, R.V., Jr. (1972). Learning English and how to be silent in Sioux and Cherokee classrooms. In C. Cazden, V. John, & D. Hymes (Eds.), *Functions of language in the classroom* (pp. 344-369). Prospect Heights, IL: Waveland Press.

Durán, R.P. (1985). Discourse skills of bilingual children: Precursors of literacy. *International Journal of the Sociology of Language, 53,* 99-114.

Edelsky, C. (1986). *Writing in a bilingual program: Había una vez.* Norwood, NJ: Ablex.

Edelsky, C. (1991). *With literacy and justice for all: Rethinking the social in language and education.* London: Falmer Press.

Edelsky, C., and Hudelson, S. (1991). Contextual complexities: Written language policies for bilingual programs. In S. Benesch (Ed.), *ESL in America: Myths and possibilities* (pp. 75-90). Portsmouth, NH: Boynton/Cook, Heinemann.

Edelsky, C., Hudelson, S., Flores, B., Barkin, F., Altweger, B., & Kristina, J. (1983). Semilingualism and language deficit. *Applied Linguistics, 4*(1), 3-22.

Edwards, V., & Sienkewicz, T.J. (1990). *Oral cultures past and present: Rappin' and Homer.* Oxford, England: Blackwell.

Erickson, F. (1984). School literacy, reasoning, and civility: An anthropologist's perspective. *Review of Educational Research, 54,* 525-546.

Ernst, G., Statzner, E., & Trueba, H.T. (Eds.). (1994). Alternative visions of schooling: Success stories in minority settings. *Anthropology & Education Quarterly, 25* (3).

Farr, M. (1994). Biliteracy in the home: Practices among Mexicano families. In D. Spener (Ed.), *Adult biliteracy in the United States* (pp. 89-110). Washington, DC and McHenry IL: Center for Applied Linguistics and Delta Systems.

Ferreiro, E., & Teberosky, A. (1982). *Literacy before schooling* (K.G. Castro, Trans.). Portsmouth, NH: Heinemann.

Field, M.L. (1992). Reading for cross-cultural literacy. In F. Dubin & N.A. Kuhlman (Eds.), *Cross-cultural literacy: Global perspectives on reading and writing* (pp. 163-173). Englewood Cliffs, NJ: Regents/Prentice-Hall.

Fillmore, L.W., & Valadez, C. (1986). Teaching bilingual learners. In M.C. Wittrock (Ed.), *Handbook of research on teaching* (3rd ed.) (pp. 648-685). New York: MacMillan.

Fishman, A. (1988). *Amish literacy: What and how it means.* Portsmouth, NH: Heinemann.

Fishman, J.A. (1966). *Language loyalty in the United States: The maintenance and perpetuation of non-English mother tongues by American ethnic and religious groups.* Berlin: Mouton.

Fishman, J.A. (1967). Bilingualism with and without diglossia: Diglossia with and without bilingualism. *Journal of Social Issues, 23*(2), 29-38.

Fishman, J.A. (1980a). Ethnocultural dimensions in the acquisition and retention of biliteracy. *Basic Writing, 3*(1), 48-61.

Fishman, J.A. (1980b). Language maintenance. In S.T. Thernstrom et al. (Eds.), *Harvard encyclopedia of American ethnic groups* (pp. 629-638). Cambridge, England: Cambridge University Press.

Fishman, J.A. (1991). *Reversing language shift: Theoretical and empirical foundations of assistance to threatened languages.* Philadelphia: Multilingual Matters.

Freebody, P., & Welch, A.R. (Eds.). (1993). *Knowledge, culture, and power: International perspectives on literacy as policy and practice.* Pittsburgh: University of Pittsburgh Press.

Freire, P. (1970a). *Pedagogy of the oppressed* (M.B. Ramos, Trans.). New York: Herder & Herder.

Freire, P. (1970b). *Cultural action for freedom.* Cambridge, MA: Harvard Educational Review.

Freire, P., & Macedo, D. (1987). *Literacy: Reading the word and the world.* New York: Seabury Press.

Fullan, M. (1994). *Change forces: Probing the depths of educational reform?* Bristol, PA: Falmer Press, Taylor & Francis.

Galbraith, J.K. (1992). *The culture of contentment.* Boston: Houghton Mifflin.

Gardner, R.C. (1985). *Social psychology and second language learning.* London: Edward Arnold.

Gee, J.P. (1986). Orality and literacy: From the savage mind to ways with words. *TESOL Quarterly, 20,* 719-746.

Gee, J.P. (1990). *Social linguistics and literacies: Ideologies in discourses.* New York: Falmer Press.

Genesee, F. (1979). Acquisition of reading skill in immersion programs. *Foreign Language Annals, 12,* 71-77.

Gibson, M.A., & Ogbu, J.U. (Eds.). (1991). *Minority status and schooling: A comparative study of immigrant and involuntary minorities.* New York: Garland.

Giroux, H.A. (1983a). *Theory and resistance in education: A pedagogy for the opposition.* South Hadley, MA: Bergin & Garvey.

Giroux, H.A. (1983b). Theories of reproduction and resistance in the new sociology of education: A critical analysis. *Harvard Educational Review, 53,* 257-293.

Giroux, H.A. (1988). *Teachers as intellectuals.* New York: Bergin & Garvey.

Goldman, A. (1994, Sept. 6). Schools tackling job training needs. *Los Angeles Times* (Orange County Ed.), p. B1.

Goodman, K., Goodman, Y., & Flores, G. (1979). *Reading in the bilingual classroom: Literacy, biliteracy.* Rosslyn, VA: National Clearinghouse for Bilingual Education.

Goody, J. (1987). *The interface between the written and the oral.* Cambridge, England: Cambridge University Press.

Goody, J.R., & Watt, I. (1963). The consequences of literacy. *Comparative Studies in Society and History, 5,* 304-26.

Gould, S.J. (1981). *The mismeasure of man.* New York: Norton.

Graff, H.J. (1979). *The literacy myth: Literacy and social structure in the 19th century city.* New York: Academic Press.

Graff, H.J. (1987). *The labyrinths of literacy: Reflections on literacy past and present.* New York: Falmer Press.

Greenfield, P. (1972). Oral or written language: The cognitive consequences of literacy development in Africa, U.S., and England. *Language and Speech, 15*(1), 169-178.

Grillo, R.D. (1989). *Dominant languages.* Cambridge, England: Cambridge University Press.

Hakuta, K. (1986). *Mirror of language: The debate on bilingualism.* New York: Basic Books.

Hall, E.T. (1959). *The silent language.* Garden City, NY: Anchor Books.

Harste, J.C., & Mikulecky, L.J. (1984). The context of literacy in our society. In A.C. Purves & O. Niles (Eds.), *Becoming readers in a complex society* (pp. 47-78). Chicago: University of Chicago Press.

Hatch, E.M. (1983). *Psycholinguistics: A second language perspective.* Rowley, MA: Newbury House.

Havelock, E.A. (1963). *Preface to Plato.* Cambridge, MA: Belknap Press of Harvard University Press.

Heath, S.B. (1980). The functions and uses of literacy. *Journal of Communication, 30*(1), 123-133.

Heath, S.B. (1983). *Ways with words: Language, life and work in communities and classrooms.* Cambridge, England: Cambridge University Press.

Heath, S.B. (1986). Social contexts of language development. In California State Department of Education (Ed.), *Beyond language: Social and cultural factors in schooling* (pp. 143-186). Los Angeles: California State University, Evaluation, Dissemination, and Assessment Center.

Heath, S.B. (1988a). Protean shapes in literacy events: Ever-shifting oral and literate traditions. In E.R. Kintgen, B.M. Kroll, & M. Rose (Eds.), *Perspectives on literacy* (348-370). Carbondale, IL: Southern Illinois University Press.

Heath, S.B. (1988b). What no bedtime story means. In J.S. Wurzel (Ed.), *Toward multiculturalism: A reader in multiculturalism* (pp. 162-184). Yarmouth, MA: Intercultural Press.

Hewitt, R., & Inghilleri, M. (1993). Oracy in the classroom: Policy, pedagogy, and group oral work. *Anthropology & Education Quarterly, 24*, 308-317.

Hirsch, E.D., Jr. (1987). *Cultural literacy: What every American needs to know.* Boston: Houghton Mifflin.

Hirsch, E.D., Jr., Kett, J.F., & Trefil, J. (1988). *The dictionary of cultural literacy. What every American needs to know*. Boston: Houghton Mifflin.

Hornberger, N.H. (1989). Continua of biliteracy. *Review of Educational Research, 59*(3), 271-296.

Hornberger, N.H. (1990). Creating successful learning contexts for biliteracy. *Penn Working Papers in Educational Linguistics, 6*(1), 1-21. (ERIC Document Reproduction Service No. ED 335 930)

Hornberger, N.H., & Hardman, J. (1994). Literacy as cultural practice and cognitive skill: Biliteracy in an ESL class and a GED program. In D. Spener (Ed.), *Adult biliteracy in the United States* (pp. 147-169). Washington, DC and McHenry, IL: Center for Applied Linguistics and Delta Systems.

Hudson, T. (1981). The effects of induced schemata on the "short circuit" in L2 reading: Non-decoding factors in L2 reading performance. *Language Learning, 32*, 1-31.

Hunter, C., & Harman, D. (1979). *Adult illiteracy in the United States*. NY: McGraw-Hill.

Illich, I. (1979). Vernacular values and education. *Teacher's College Record, 81*(1), 31-75.

Kalmar, T.M. (1994). ¿Guariyusei?: Adult biliteracy in its natural habitat. In D. Spener (Ed.), *Adult biliteracy in the United States* (pp. 123-146). Washington, DC and McHenry, IL: Center for Applied Linguistics and Delta Systems.

Kaplan, D.A. (1993, September 20). Dumber than we thought. *Newsweek*, pp. 44-45.

Kaplan, R.B. (1966). Cultural thought patterns in intercultural education. *Language Learning, 16*, 1-20.

Kaplan, R.B. (1986). Cultural thought patterns revisited. In U. Connor & R.B. Kaplan (Eds.), *Writing across languages. Analysis of L2 text* (pp. 9-21). Reading, MA: Addison-Wesley.

Kaplan, R.B., et al. (Eds.). (1984). Introduction. *Annual Review of Applied Linguistics, 1983* (pp. vii-xv). Rowley, MA: Newbury House.

Karier, C. (1973). Testing for order and control in the corporate liberal state. In C.J. Karier, P. Violas, & J. Spring (Eds.), *Roots of crisis: American education in the twentieth century* (pp. 108-137). Chicago: Rand McNally College Publishing.

Kirsch, I., & Guthrie, J.T. (1977-1978). The concept and measurement of functional illiteracy. *Journal of Education, 13*(4), 486-507.

Kirsch, I.S., & Jungeblut, A. (1986). *Literacy: Profiles of America's young adults.* (ETS Report No. 16-PL-02). Princeton, NJ: Educational Testing Service. (ERIC Document Reproduction Service No. ED 275 701)

Kirsch, I.S., Jungeblut, A., Jenkins, L., and Kolstad, A. (1993). *Adult literacy in America: A first look at the results of the National Adult Literacy Survey.* Washington, DC: U.S. Department of Education, Office of Educational Research and Improvement.

Klassen, C., & Burnaby, B. (1993). "Those who know": Views on literacy among adult immigrants in Canada. *TESOL Quarterly, 27*, 377-397.

Kliebard, H.M. (1986). *The struggle for the American curriculum: 1893-1958.* New York: Routledge.

Kloss, H. (1971). Language rights of immigrant groups. *International Migration Review, 5*, 250-268.

Kloss, H. (1977). *The American bilingual tradition.* Rowley, MA: Newbury House.

Kozol, J. (1991). *Savage inequalities: Children in America's schools.* New York: Crown.

Krashen, S. (1981). Bilingual education and second language acquisition theory. In California State Department of Education, Office of Bilingual Education (Ed.), *Schooling and language minority students: A theoretical framework* (pp. 51-116). Los Angeles: California State University, Evaluation, Dissemination and Assessment Center.

Krashen, S., & Biber, D. (1988). *On course: Bilingual education's success in California.* Sacramento, CA: California Association for Bilingual Education.

Krashen, S.D., & Terrell, T.D. (1983). *The natural approach: Language acquisition in the classroom.* Oxford and San Francisco: Pergamon and Alemany.

Kuhn, T.S. (1970). *The structures of scientific revolutions* (2nd ed.). Chicago: University of Chicago Press.

Labov, W. (1970). The study of language in social context. *Studium Generale, 23*, 66-84.

Labov, W. (1973). The logic of non-standard English. In N. Keddie (Ed.), *Tinker, tailor...the myth of cultural deprivation* (pp. 21-66). Harmondsworth, England: Penguin.

Labov, W. (1982). Objectivity and commitment in linguistic science: The case of the Black English trial in Ann Arbor. *Language and Society, 11,* 165-201.

Lambert, W.E. (1974). Culture and language as factors in learning and education. In F.E. Aboud & R.D. Meade (Eds.), *Cultural factors in learning and education.* Bellingham, WA: Fifth Western Washington Symposium on Learning.

Lambert, W.E., & Tucker, G.R. (1972). *Bilingual education of children: The St. Lambert experiment.* Rowley, MA: Newbury House

Landry, R., Allard, R., & Théberge, R. (1991). School and family: French ambiance and the bilingual development of Francophone Western Canadians. *Canadian Modern Language Review, 47,* 878-915.

Langer, J.A. (Ed.). (1987). *Language, literacy, and culture: Issues of society and schooling.* Norwood, NJ: Ablex.

Lankshear, C., & Lawler, M. (1987). *Literacy, schooling and revolution.* New York: Falmer.

Leacock, E.B. (1972). Abstract versus concrete speech: A false dichotomy. In C.B. Cazden, V.P. John, & D. Hymes (Eds.), *Functions of language in the classroom* (pp. 111-134). Prospect Heights, IL: Waveland Press.

LeBlanc, R., & Painchaud, G. (1986). Self-assessment as a second language placement instrument. *TESOL Quarterly, 19,* 673-687.

Leibowitz, A.H. (1969). English literacy: Legal sanction for discrimination. *Notre Dame Lawyer, 25*(1), 7-66.

Leibowitz, A.H. (1971). *Educational policy and political acceptance: The imposition of English as the language of instruction in American schools.* Washington, DC: Center for Applied Linguistics, ERIC Clearinghouse for Linguistics. (ERIC Document Reproduction Service No. ED 047 321)

Leibowitz, A.H. (1974, August). *Language as a means of social control. The United States experience.* Paper presented at the VIII World Congress of Sociology, University of Toronto, Canada. (ERIC Document Reproduction Service No. ED 093 168)

Leibowitz, A.H. (1982). *Federal recognition of the rights of minority language groups.* Rosslyn, VA: National Clearinghouse on Bilingual Education.

Lévi-Strauss, C. (1966). *The savage mind.* Chicago: University of Chicago Press.

Levine, K. (1982). Functional literacy: Fond illusions and false economies. *Harvard Educational Review, 52*(3), 249-267.

Lewis, M. (1978). *The culture of inequality.* Amherst, MA: University of Massachusetts Press.

Linnarud, M. (1978). Cohesion and communication in the target language. *Interlanguage Studies Bulletin, 3,* 23-34.

Luebke, F.C. (1980). Legal restrictions on foreign languages in the Great Plains states, 1917-1923. In P. Schach (Ed.), *Languages in conflict: Linguistic acculturation on the Great Plains* (pp. 1-19). Lincoln, NE: University of Nebraska Press.

Luria, A.R. (1976). *Cognitive development: Its cultural and social foundations.* Cambridge, MA: Harvard University Press.

Lyons, J.J. (1990). The past and future directions of federal bilingual education policy. *Annals of the American Academy of Political and Social Science, 508,* 66-80.

Macías, R.F. (1979). Choice of language as a human right: Public policy implications. In R.V. Padilla (Ed.), *Ethnoperspectices in bilingual education research: Bilingual education and public policy in the United States* (pp. 39-57). Ypsilanti, MI: Eastern Michigan University.

Macías, R.F. (1984). *"Cauldron—boil & bubble": United States language policy towards indigenous language groups in the nineteenth century.* Los Angeles: University of Southern California, Center for Multilingual and Multicultural Research.

Macías, R.F. (1988). *Latino illiteracy in the United States.* Claremont, CA: Tomás Rivera Center. (ERIC Document Reproduction Service No. ED 321 608)

Macías, R.F. (1990). Definitions of literacy: A response. In R.L. Venezky, D.A. Wagner, & B.S. Ciliberti (Eds.), *Toward defining literacy* (pp. 17-23). Newark, DE: International Reading Association.

Macías, R.F. (1993). Language and ethnic classification of language minorities: Chicano and Latino students in the 1990s. *Hispanic Journal of Behavioral Sciences, 15*(2), 230-257.

Macías, R.F. (1994). Inheriting sins while seeking absolution: Language diversity and national statistical data sets. In D. Spener (Ed.), *Adult biliteracy in the United States* (pp. 15-45). Washington, DC and McHenry, IL: Center for Applied Linguistics and Delta Systems.

Macías, R.F., & Spencer, M. (1984). *Estimating the number of language minority and limited English proficient persons in the U.S.: A comparative analysis of the studies.* Los Alamitos, CA: National Center for Bilingual Research.

Majority of Non-English speakers speak Spanish but others have more difficulty with English. (1993, September). *Numbers and Needs*, p. 4.

Martin-Jones, M., & Romaine, S. (1986). Semilingualism: A half-baked theory of communicative competence. *Applied Linguistics, 7*(1), 26-38.

McArthur, E.K. (1993). *Language characteristics and schooling in the United States, a changing picture: 1979 and 1989.* Washington, DC: U.S. Department of Education, Office of Educational Research and Improvement, National Center for Educational Statistics. (NCES Report 93-699).

McClymer, J.F. (1982). The Americanization movement and the education of the foreign-born adult, 1914-25. In B.J. Weiss (Ed.), *American education and the European immigrant: 1840-1940* (pp. 96-116). Urbana, IL: University of Illinois Press.

McDermott, R. (1987a). Achieving school failure: An anthropological approach to illiteracy and social stratification. In G. Spindler (Ed.), *Education and cultural process: Anthropological approaches* (2nd ed.). (pp. 173-209). Prospect Heights, IL: Waveland Press.

McDermott, R. (1987b). The explanation of minority school failure, again. *Anthropology and Education Review, 56*(4), 355-378.

McDonnell, L.M., & Hill, P.T. (1993). *Newcomers in American schools: Meeting the educational needs of immigrant youth.* Santa Monica, CA: Rand.

McKay, S. (1993). *Agendas for second language literacy.* Cambridge, England: Cambridge University Press.

McKay, S.L., & Weinstein-Shr, G. (1993). English literacy in the United States: National policies, consequences. *TESOL Quarterly, 27,* 399-419.

McLaren, P. (1989). *Life in schools: An introduction to critical pedagogy in the foundations of education.* New York: Longman.

Meléndez, W.A. (1990). *Native language instruction: An approach to combat illiteracy among language minority communities.* Research report. Sacramento, CA: California Literacy Task Force.

Mensh, E., & Mensh, H. (1991). *The IQ mythology: Class, race, and gender inequality.* Carbondale, IL: Southern Illinois University Press

Merino, B.J., & Lyons, J. (1990). The effectiveness of a model bilingual program: A longitudinal analysis. *CPS Brief, 2*(3), 1-5.

Mikulecky, L.J. (1990). Literacy for what purpose? In R.L. Venezky, D.A. Wagner, & D.S. Ciliberi (Eds.), *Toward defining literacy* (pp. 24-34). Newark, DE: International Reading Association. (ERIC Document Reproduction Service No. ED 313 677)

Miles, R. (1989). *Racism.* London: Routledge.

Miller, C. (1991). *Some contextual problems relative to the acquisition of literacy by Hmong refugees.* Unpublished masters thesis, California State University, Long Beach.

Milroy, J., & Milroy, L. (1985). *Authority in language: Investigating language prescription and standardization.* London: Routledge and Kegan Paul.

Molesky, J. (1988). Understanding the American linguistic mosaic: A historical overview of language maintenance and language shift. In S.L. McKay & S.C. Wong (Eds.), *Language diversity: Problem or resource* (pp. 29-68). Cambridge, MA: Newbury House.

Morrow, L.M. (1983). Home and school correlates of early interest in literature. *Journal of Educational Research, 76,* 221-230.

Nash, A., Cason, A., Rhum, M., McGrail, L., & Gomez-Sanford, R. (1992). *Talking shop: A curriculum sourcebook for participatory adult ESL.* Washington, DC and McHenry, IL: Center for Applied Linguistics and Delta Systems.

Norgren, J., & Nanda, S. (1988). *American cultural pluralism and the law.* New York: Praeger.

Nunan, D. (1988). *The learner-centered curriculum.* Cambridge, England: Cambridge University Press.

O'Connor, P. (1993). Workplace literacy in Australia: Competing agendas. In P. Freebody & A.R. Welch (Eds.), *Knowledge, culture, and power: International perspectives on literacy as policy and practice* (pp. 187-208). Pittsburgh: University of Pittsburgh Press.

Odlin, T. (1989). *Language transfer: Cross-linguistic influence in language learning.* Cambridge, England: Cambridge University Press.

Ogbu, J.U. (1991). Immigrant and involuntary minorities in comparative perspective. In M.A. Gibson & J.U. Ogbu (Eds.), *Minority status and schooling: A comparative study of immigrant and involuntary minorities* (pp. 3-33). New York: Garland.

Ogbu, J.U., & Matute-Bianchi, M.E. (1986). Understanding sociocultural factors: Knowledge, identity, and school adjustment. In California State Department of Education (Ed.), *Beyond language: Social and cultural factors in schooling for language minority students.* Los Angeles: California State University, Evaluation, Dissemination and Assessment Center.

Oller, J., & Perkins, K. (1980). *Research in language testing.* Rowley, MA: Newbury House.

Olson, D.R. (1977). From utterance to text: The bias of language in speech and writing. *Harvard Educational Review, 47,* 257-281.

Olson, D.R. (1984). See! Jumping! Some oral language antecedents of literacy. In H. Goelman, A.A. Oberg, & F. Smith (Eds.), *Awakening to literacy* (pp. 185-192). Portsmouth, NH: Heinemann.

Olson, D.R. (1994). *The world on paper: The conceptual and cognitive implications of reading and writing.* Cambridge, England: Cambridge University Press.

O'Malley, J.M., & Chamot, A.U. (1990). *Learning strategies in second language acquisition.* Cambridge, England: Cambridge University Press.

O'Neil, W. (1973). The politics of bidialectism. In R.H. Bentley & S.D. Crawford (Eds.), *Black language reader* (pp. 184-191). Glenview, IL: Scott Foresman.

O'Neill, W.F. (1983). *Rethinking education: Selected readings in educational ideologies.* Dubuque, IA: Kendall/Hunt.

Ong, W.J. (1982). *Orality and literacy: The technologizing of the word.* London: Methuen.

Penfield, J. (1982). *Chicano English: Implications for assessment and Literacy development.* (Bilingual Education Paper Series). Los Angeles: California State University, Evaluation, Dissemination and Assessment Center. (ERIC Document Reproduction Service No. ED 255 050)

Perdue, C. (Ed.). (1984). *Second language acquisition by adult immigrants: A field manual.* Rowley, MA: Newbury House.

Philips, S.U. (1972). Participant structures and communicative competence: Warm Springs children in community and classroom. In C. Cazden, V. John, & D. Hymes (Eds.), *Functions of language in the classroom* (pp. 370-394). Prospect Heights, IL: Waveland Press.

Philips, S.U. (1983). *The invisible culture: Communication and community on the Warm Springs Indian Reservation.* (Research on Teaching Monograph Series). New York: Longman.

Phillips, K. (1993). *Boiling point: Republicans, Democrats, and the decline of middle-class prosperity.* New York: Random House.

Phillipson, R. (1988). Linguicism: Structures and ideologies in linguistic imperialism. In T. Skutnabb-Kangas & J. Cummins (Eds.), *Minority education: From shame to struggle* (pp. 339-358). London: Multilingual Matters.

Pitt, L. (1976). *We Americans. Vol I. Colonial Times to 1877.* Glenview, IL: Scott Foresman.

Ramírez, J.D. (1992). Executive summary. *Bilingual Research Journal, 16*(1-2), 1-62.

Reder, S., & Wikelund, K.R. (1993). Literacy development and ethnicity: An Alaskan example. In B. Street (Ed.), *Cross-cultural approaches to literacy* (pp. 176-197). Cambridge, England: Cambridge University Press.

Resnick, D.P., & Resnick, L.B. (1977). The nature of literacy: An historical exploration. *Harvard Educational Review, 47,* 370-385.

Risen, J. (1994, August 29). Fed ties decisions to natural 6% jobless rate. *Los Angeles Times,* (Orange County Ed.), p. A1.

Rivera, C. (Ed.). (1984). *Language proficiency and academic achievement.* Avon, England: Multilingual Matters.

Robson, B. (1982). Hmong literacy, formal education, and their effects on performance in an ESL class. In B.T. Downing & D.P. Olney (Eds.), *The Hmong in the west* (pp. 201-225). Minneapolis: University of Minnesota, Center for Urban and Regional Affairs.

Rodby, J. (1992). *Appropriating literacy: Writing and reading in English as a second language.* Portsmouth, NH: Boynton/Cook, Heinemann.

Romaine, S. (1989). *Bilingualism.* Oxford, England: Blackwell.

Rosen, H. (1985). The voices of communities and language in classrooms. *Harvard Educational Review, 55,* 448-456.

Roy, J.D. (1987). The linguistic and sociolinguistic position of Black English and the issue of bidialectism in education. In P. Homel, M. Palij, & D. Aaronson (Eds.), *Childhood bilingualism: Aspects of linguistic, cognitive, and social development* (pp. 231-242). Hillsdale, NJ: Lawrence Erlbaum Associates.

Ruíz, R. (1984). Orientations in language planning. *NABE Journal 8*(2), 15-32.

Ryan, W. (1972). *Blaming the victim.* New York: Random House.

Santos, R.L. (1985). *A methodological report on the sampling design of the 1979 National Chicano Survey.* (SCCR Working Paper No. 11). Stanford, CA: Stanford Center for Chicano Research.

Schieffelin, B.B., & Cochran-Smith, M. (1984). Learning to read culturally: Literacy before schooling. In H. Goelman, A.A. Oberg, & F. Smith (Eds.), *Awakening to literacy* (pp. 3-23). Portsmouth, NH: Heinemann.

Schieffelin, B.B., & Gilmore, P. (Eds.). (1986*). The acquisition of literacy: Ethnographic perspectives.* Norwood, NJ: Ablex.

Schumann, J. (1978). *The pidginization process: A model for second language acquisition.* Rowley, MA: Newbury House.

Scollon, R., & Scollon, S. (1981). *Narrative, literacy and face in interethnic communication.* Norwood, NJ: Ablex.

Scribner, S. (1988). Literacy in three metaphors. In E.R. Kintgen, B.M. Kroll, & M. Rose (Eds.), *Perspectives on literacy* (pp. 71-81). Carbondale, IL: Southern Illinois University Press.

Scribner, S., & Cole, M. (1978). Literacy without schooling: Testing for intellectual effects. *Harvard Educational Review, 48,* 448-461.

Scribner, S., & Cole, M. (1981). *The psychology of literacy*. Cambridge, MA: Harvard University Press.

Scribner, S., & Cole, M. (1988). Unpacking literacy. In E.R. Kintgen, B.M. Kroll, & M. Rose (Eds.), *Perspectives on literacy* (pp. 57-70). Carbondale, IL: Southern Illinois University Press.

Shannon, P. (1989). *Broken promises: Reading instruction in twentieth-century America*. South Hadley, MA: Bergin & Garvey.

Shannon, P. (1990). *The struggle to continue*. Portsmouth, NH: Heinemann.

Shor, I. (1987). *Freire for the classroom: A sourcebook for liberatory teaching*. Portsmouth, NH. Heinemann.

Shuman, A. (1993). Collaborative writing. In B. Street (Ed.), *Cross-cultural approaches to literacy* (pp. 247-271). Cambridge, England: Cambridge University Press.

Shuy, R. (1980). Vernacular Black English: Setting the issues in time. In M. Farr Whiteman (Ed.), *Reactions to Ann Arbor: Vernacular Black English and education* (pp. 1-9). Arlington, VA: Center for Applied Linguistics.

Simon, P. (1988). *The tongue-tied American*. New York: Continuum.

Simpkins, G.C., Simpkins, G., & Holt, G. (1977). *Bridge: A cross-cultural reading program*. Boston: Houghton Mifflin.

Simpson, D. (1986). *The politics of American English, 1776-1850*. New York: Oxford University Press.

Singleton, D. (1989). *Language acquisition: The age factor*. Philadelphia: Multilingual Matters.

Skutnabb-Kangas, T. (1981). *Bilingualism or not: The education of minorities*. (L. Malmberg & D. Crane, Trans.). Clevedon, England: Multilingual Matters.

Skutnabb-Kangas, T., & Cummins, J. (Eds.). (1988). *Minority education: From shame to struggle*. Philadelphia: Multilingual Matters.

Skutnabb-Kangas, T., & Phillipson, R. (1989). *Wanted! Linguistic human rights*. (Rolig-Papir, No. 44). Denmark: Roskilde University Center.

Sledd, J. (1969). Bi-dialectism: The linguistics of white supremacy. *English Journal, 58*, 1307-1315, 1329.

Sledd, J. (1973). Doublespeak: Dialectology in the service of Big Brother. In R.H. Bentley & S.D. Crawford (Eds.), *Black language reader* (pp. 191-214). Glenview, IL: Scott Foresman.

Smith, E.A. (1993). The black child in the schools: Ebonics and its implications for the transformation of American education. In A. Darder (Ed.), *Bicultural studies in education: The struggle for educational justice* (pp. 58-76). Claremont, CA: Claremont Graduate School, Institute for Education in Transformation.

Spener, D. (Ed). (1994). *Adult biliteracy in the United States*. Washington, DC and McHenry, IL: Center for Applied Linguistics and Delta Systems.

Spolsky, B. (1984). A note on the dangers of terminological innovation. In C. Rivera (Ed.), *Language proficiency and academic achievement* (pp. 41-43). Avon, England: Multilingual Matters.

Spring, J. (1994). *Deculturalization and the struggle for equality: A brief history of the education of dominated cultures in the United States.* New York: McGraw-Hill.

Stewart, D. (1993). *Immigration and education: The crisis and the opportunities.* New York: Lexington Books.

Stewart, W. (1964). Foreign language teaching methods in quasi-foreign language situations. In W. Stewart (Ed.), *Non-standard speech and the teaching of English.* Washington, DC: Center for Applied Linguistics.

Street, B.V. (1984). *Literacy in theory and practice.* Cambridge, England: Cambridge University Press.

Street, B.V. (Ed.). (1993). *Cross-cultural approaches to literacy.* Cambridge, England: Cambridge University Press.

Street, J.C., & Street, B.V. (1991). The schooling of literacy. In D. Barton & R. Ivanic (Eds.), *Writing in the community* (pp. 143-166). London: Sage.

Stubbs, M. (1980). *Language and literacy: The sociolinguistics of reading and writing.* London: Routledge and Kegan Paul.

Stuckey, J.E. (1991). *The violence of literacy.* Portsmouth, NH: Heinemann.

Szwed, J. (1981). The ethnography of literacy. In M.F. Whiteman (Ed.), *Writing: The nature, development and teaching of written commu-*

nication, Vol. 1: Variation in writing (pp. 13-23). Hillsdale, NJ: Erlbaum.

Tannen, D. (1982). The myth of orality and literacy. In W. Frawley (Ed.), *Linguistics and literacy. Proceedings of the Delaware Symposium on Language Studies.* (pp. 37-50). New York: Plenum.

Tannen, D. (1987). The orality of literature and literary conversation. In J.A. Langer (Ed.), *Language, literacy and culture: Issues of society and schooling* (pp. 67-88). Norwood, NJ: Ablex.

Taylor, D.M. (1983). *Family literacy: Young children learning to read and write.* Portsmouth, NH: Heinemann.

Taylor, D.M. (1987). Social psychological barriers to effective childhood bilingualism. In P. Homel, M. Palij, & D. Aaronson. *Childhood bilingualism: Aspects of linguistic, cognitive, and social development* (pp. 183-196). Hillsdale, NJ: Lawrence, Erlbaum Associates.

Taylor, D.M., & Dorsey-Gaines, C. (1988). *Growing up literate: Learning from inner-city families.* Portsmouth, NH: Heinemann.

Terrell, T.D. (1981). The natural approach in bilingual education. In California State Department of Education, Office of Bilingual Education (Ed.), *Schooling and language minority students: A theoretical framework* (pp. 117-146). Los Angeles: California State University, Evaluation, Dissemination and Assessment Center.

Tollefson, J. (1991). *Planning language, planning inequality: Language policy in the community.* New York: Longman.

Toukomaa, P., & Skutnabb-Kangas, T. (1977). *The intensive teaching of the mother tongue to migrant children of preschool age and children in the lower level of comprehensive school.* (Research Report No. 26). Tampere, Finland: University of Tampere, Department of Sociology and Social Psychology.

Troike, R.C. (1978). Research evidence for the effectiveness of bilingual education. *NABE Journal, 3*(1), 13-24.

Troike, R.C. (1984). SCALP: Social and cultural aspects of language proficiency. In C. Rivera (Ed.), *Language proficiency and academic achievement* (pp. 44-54). Avon, England: Multilingual Matters.

Trueba, H.T. (1984). The forms, functions, and values of literacy: Reading for survival in a barrio as a student. *NABE Journal, 9*(1), 41-51.

Trueba, H.T. (1989). *Raising silent voices: Educating the linguistic minorities for the 21st century.* Rowley, MA: Newbury House.

Trueba, H.T., Jacobs, L., & Kirton, E. (1990). *Cultural conflict and adaptation: The case of Hmong children in American society.* New York: Falmer.

Valadez, C.M. (1981). Identity, power, and writing skills: The case of the Hispanic bilingual student. In M.F. Whiteman (Ed.), *Writing: The nature, development and teaching of written communication, Vol. 1.* (pp. 167-178). Hillsdale, NJ: Erlbaum.

Vargas, A. (1986). *Illiteracy in the Hispanic community.* Washington, DC: National Council of La Raza.

Veltman, F. (1983). *Language shift in the United States.* Berlin: Mouton.

Venezky, R.L., Kaestle, C., & Sum, A. (1987). *The subtle danger: Reflections on the literacy abilities of America's young adults.* (Report No. 16-CAEP-01). Princeton, NJ: Educational Testing Service, Center for the Assessment of Educational Progress.

Venezky, R.L., Wagner, D.A., & Ciliberti, B.S. (Eds.). (1990). *Toward defining literacy.* Newark, DE: International Reading Association.

Vygotsky, L.S. (1978). *Mind in society: The development of higher psychological processes.* (M. Cole, V. John-Steiner, S. Scribner, & E. Souberman, Trans.). Cambridge, MA: Harvard University Press.

Waggoner, D. (1993). Majority of non-English speakers speak Spanish but others have more difficulty. *Numbers and Needs, 3*(5), 1-3.

Wald, B. (1984). A sociolinguistic perspective on Cummins' current framework for relating language proficiency to academic achievement. In C. Rivera (Ed.), *Language proficiency and academic achievement* (pp. 55-70). Avon, England: Multilingual Matters.

Walsh, C.E. (Ed.). (1991). *Literacy as praxis: Culture, language, and pedagogy.* Norwood, NJ: Ablex.

Walters, K. (1992). Whose culture? Whose literacy? In D.E. Murray (Ed.), *Diversity as resource: Redefining cultural literacy* (pp. 3-29). Alexandria, VA: Teachers of English to Speakers of Other Languages.

Weinberg, M. (1983). *The search for quality integrated education: Policy and research on minority students in school and college.* Westport, CT: Greenwood.

Weinberg, M. (1995). *A chance to learn: A history of race and education in the United States* (2nd. ed.). Long Beach, CA: California State University Press.

Weinberg, M. (Comp.). (1991). *Racism in the United States: A comprehensive classified bibliography.* New York: Greenwood.

Weinstein, G. (1984). Literacy and second language acquisition: Issues and perspectives. *TESOL Quarterly, 18,* 471-484.

Weinstein-Shr, G. (1990). From problem solving to celebration: Discovering and creating meanings through literacy. In J. Bell (Ed.), ESL literacy [Special issue]. *TESL Talk, 20*(1), 68-88.

Weinstein-Shr, G. (1993a). Literacy and social process: A community in transition. In B. Street (Ed.), *Cross-cultural approaches to literacy* (pp. 272-293). Cambridge, England: Cambridge University Press.

Weinstein-Shr, G. (1993b). Directions in adult ESL literacy—An invitation to dialogue. *TESOL Quarterly, 27,* 517-533.

Weinstein-Shr, G. (1995). *Literacy and older adults in the United States.* Philadelphia: National Center for Adult Literacy.

Weinstein-Shr, G., & Quintero, E. (Eds.). (1995). *Immigrant learners and their families: Literacy to connect the generations.* Washington, DC and McHenry, IL: Center for Applied Linguistics and Delta Systems.

Weiss, B.J. (Ed.). (1982). *Education and the European immigrant: 1840-1940.* Champaign/Urbana, IL: University of Illinois Press.

Welch, A.R., & Freebody, P. (1993). Introduction: Explanations of current international "literacy crises." In P. Freebody & A.R. Welch (Eds.), *Knowledge, culture, and power: International perspectives on literacy as policy and practice* (pp. 6-22). Pittsburgh: University of Pittsburgh Press.

Wells, G. (1986). *The meaning makers: Children learning language and using language to learn.* Portsmouth, NH: Heinemann.

Wiley, T.G. (1986). The significance of language and cultural barriers for the Euro-American elderly. In C. Hayes, R.A. Kalish, & D. Guttman (Eds.), *The Euro-American elderly: A guide to practice* (pp. 35-50). New York: Springer.

Wiley, T.G. (1988). *Literacy, biliteracy, and educational achievement among the Mexican-origin population in the United States.*

Unpublished doctoral dissertation, University of Southern California, Los Angeles.

Wiley, T.G. (1990). Literacy, biliteracy and educational achievement among the Mexican-origin population in the United States. *NABE Journal, 14*(1-3), 109-127.

Wiley, T.G. (1990-1991). Literacy among the Mexican-origin population: What a biliteracy analysis can tell us. *AMAE, Journal of the Association of Mexican American Educators,* 17-38.

Wiley, T.G. (1991). *Measuring the nation's literacy: Important considerations.* ERIC Digest. Washington, DC: National Clearinghouse on Literacy Education. (ERIC Document Reproduction Service No. ED 334 870)

Wiley, T.G. (1993a). Discussion of Klassen & Burnaby and McKay & Weinstein-Shr: Beyond assimilationist literacy policies and practices. *TESOL Quarterly, 27,* 421-430.

Wiley, T.G. (1993b). *Issues of access, participation and transition in adult ESL. Working paper.* Washington, DC: Southport Institute for Policy Analysis.

Williams, S.W. (1991). Classroom use of African American language: Educational tool or social weapon? In C.E. Sleeter (Ed.), *Empowerment through multicultural education* (pp. 199-215). New York: State University of New York Press.

Wink, J. (1993). Labels often reflect educators' beliefs and practices. *Bilingual Education Office Outreach, 4*(2), 28-29.

Wolfram, W. (1994). Bidialectal literacy in the United States. In D. Spener (Ed.), *Adult biliteracy in the United States* (pp. 71-88). Washington, DC and McHenry, IL: Center for Applied Linguistics and Delta Systems.

Wolfram, W., & Christian, D. (1980). On the application of sociolinguistic information: Test evaluation and dialect differences in Appalacian English. In T. Shopen & J.M. Williams (Eds.), *Standards and dialects in English* (pp. 177-204). Cambridge, MA: Winthrop.

Wolfram, W., & Fasold, R.W. (1973). Toward reading materials for speakers of Black English: Three linguistically appropriate passages. In R.H. Bentley, & S.D. Crawford (Eds.), *Black language reader* (pp. 172-184). Glenview, IL: Scott Foresman.

Wright, E. (1980). School English and public policy. *College English, 42,* 327-342.

Wrigley, H.S. (1993). One size does not fit all: Educational perspectives and program practices in the U.S. *TESOL Quarterly, 27,* 449-465.

Wrigley, H.S., Chisman, F.P., & Ewen, D.T. (1993). *Sparks of excellence: Program realities and promising practices in adult ESL.* Washington, DC: Southport Institute for Policy Analysis.

Wrigley, H.S., & Guth, J.A. (1992). *Bringing literacy to life: Issues and options in adult ESL.* San Mateo, CA: Aguirre International. (Now available from San Diego, CA: Dominie Press.)

Wyman, M. (1993*). Round-trip to America: The immigrants return to Europe, 1880-1930.* Ithaca, NY: Cornell University Press.

Zanger, V.V. (1991). Social and cultural dimensions of the education of language minority students. In A.M. Ambert (Ed.), *Bilingual education and English as a second language: A research handbook, 1988-1990* (pp. 3-54). New York: Garland.

INDEX

A

abstraction, 37-39, 159, 171

accommodation, 127, 148

accountability of schools, 194

adaptation, 147-48

Adult Basic Education (ABE) programs, 73, 113

Adult Performance Level, 72-73

adults
  bilingual education for, 153
  ethnographic studies of, 141
  literacy instruction for, 180-82
  as second-language users, 189

African American Language (AAL), 6n3, 125-30

African Americans, 54n4, 142-43
  bilingual education and, 128-30
  children, 126-27
  educational gains of, 108
  educational policy and, 126-30
  intelligence testing and, 64
  as language minority, 6n3, 85
  literacy practices of, 144-46
  and literacy requirements, 59, 65, 126
  and NALS, 80-81
  stigmatization of, 125-27

working-class communities, 144-45

youth, 193

aging, and second-language learning, 180

ambiguity, in ethnic identification, 79-80

Americanization programs, 99

amnesty program, 190-91

Arabic, 41

Arce, C. H., quoted, 92

Asian, use of term, 120

assimilation, linguistic, 187n6

Athabaskan Alaskan Natives, 49

attitudes, and language acquisition, 24-25

Auerbach, E. R., quoted, 145, 195-96

autonomous approach, 31, 33-38, 49-50, 154, 189

B

Bailey, R. W., quoted, 119

Baker, C., quoted, 128, 155-57

Basic Interpersonal Communication Skills (BICS), 158-61, 164, 170-73

Bernstein, B., 187n7

Bhatia, T. K., quoted, 22, 124

bias
  class, 45
  cultural, 45
  in intelligence testing, 63
  reflected in schools, 143
  in standardized tests, 74

Bible, 59, 67, 138

BICS. *See* Basic Interpersonal Communication Skills

bidialect education, 129-30

bilingual education, 12, 100, 121, 140
  AAL and, 131
  for African Americans, 128-30
  availability of, 113
  effectiveness of, 21-22
  policy issues in, 182-85
  transitional, 121, 166, 183-84, 187n6
  See also educational policy; schooling

bilingual education theory, 153-55
  critiques of, 167-77
  influential constructs in, 155-62
  operationalizing of, 177-78

bilingualism
  additive, 155, 157, 170
  benefits of, 18-19

of immigrant children, 139-40
and intelligence, 57
and language shift, 23
limited, 156
partial, 156
proficient, 156
subtractive, 156-57, 164, 170
views of, 155-62

biliteracy, 3, 14, 18, 25
  cognitive effects of, 42
  English-Spanish, 105
  and National Chicano Survey, 92-94

biliterates, 19

Binet, Alfred, 60-61

Black English. *See* African American Language (AAL)

blame, ideology of, 99-100, 154

Bond, Horace Mann, quoted, 64

Bridge: A Cross-cultural Reading Program, 128

Brigham, Carl, *A Study in American Intelligence,* 63

Brodkey, L., quoted, 99

Burnaby, B., 190

C

California
  bilingual education in, 186n2
  educational system in, 194
  immigrants in, 169, 192

immigrant students in, 112, 120

Office of Bilingual Education, 163-66

CALP. *See* Cognitive Academic Language Proficiency (CALP)

Canada
  literacy crisis in, 98
  mass literacy campaigns in, 101-2
  study of bilingualism in, 163
  study of transfer in, 176

categorization, tests of, 41-42

Chermayeff, I., quoted, 61-62

Cherokee, and English-only policies, 21

Chicanos. *See* Latinos

children
  African American, 126-27
  bilingual education for, 153
  bilingualism of, 139-40
  bilingual raising of, 19-20
  individual progress of, 140
  as interpreters for parents, 139
  language-minority, educational progress of, 109-11
  literacy deficiencies of, 143
  literacy development of, 49-51, 139
  literacy instruction for, 179-80
  working-class, 148

Chinese, 46, 139

Christian, D., quoted, 74-75

Clarke, M., 175

class differences, and literacy assessment, 85

class tensions, among immigrant students, 190

Cochran-Smith, M., 137-42
  quoted, 137, 139-40

Cognitive Academic Language Proficiency (CALP), 158-61, 164, 170-73, 176

cognitive demand, 158-59, 164, 171
  language proficiency and, 161-62

cognitive styles, 39

cohesion hypothesis, 175

Cole, M., 30, 33-34, 45, 77-78
  quoted, 31, 38-42, 50, 68

Collins, J., quoted, 100

Collins, R., 46-47, 107

common underlying proficiency, 159, 162, 165, 176

communicative quadrant, 177-78

communities
  African American working-class, 144-45
  literacy events in, 143
  literacy practices of, 51, 136, 142-43
  study of literacy in, 136-44
  working-class, 144

comparisons
cross-group, 1-2, 59, 62, 84, 108-11, 135-36, 174
within-group, 108

compulsory ignorance laws, 125-26, 192

concreteness, 37-38, 171

conservatism, in oral cultures, 37

context, 164, 171
social, 48, 158, 174

Contextual Interaction Model, 163-66

significance of, 166-67

contextual support, language proficiency and, 161-62

control, literacy events and, 146

conversion, religious, 138

Cook-Gumperz, J., 30, 32

Cortés, C. E., quoted, 165-66

Coulmas, F., quoted, 101, 103

Crawford, J., 17, 21

credential inflation, 108

creole, defined, 133n3

creolization, 133n3

cultural identity, 49

culture of inequality, 99-100

Cummins, J., 155, 157-58, 169, 177-78
quoted, 160, 162, 170-71, 173-74

Current Population Survey, 8

curriculum
decisions, 195-96
design, 49-52, 182
hidden, 147

D

Dandy, E. B., quoted, 125

de Castell, S., quoted, 51

decontextualization hypothesis, 173-75, 178, 183

decreolization, 133n3

deculturation of Native Americans, 20

deficiency explanations, 154

deficit view, 140, 148, 154, 168

deschooling
of literacy, 137
of society, 124

devaluation of literacy skills, 107

diglossia, 133n4

discrimination, 54n4

distancing, 54n2

domains of literacy, 76-78
in NALS, 80-85

Donaldson, M., 170

Dorsey-Gains, C., quoted, 141-42

dual language use, 18

Dumont, R. V., Jr., quoted, 182

E

Ebonics. *See* African American Language

eclecticism, 153-54, 167

ecological validity, of direct measures of literacy, 73-74

economic position, 98-99, 103-6

Edelsky, C., 179
quoted, 158

Edelsky, C., et al., 170-71, 184
quoted, 168-69

educational histories of immigrant students, 112

educational policy, 46, 49-52, 121
for African Americans, 126-30
for bilingual education, 182-85
and ESL programs, 113-14
impact of, 190-93
impact on language-majority youth, 193-95
and literacy assessment, 57

educational progress, cross-group data, 109-11

Educational Testing Service, 80

Edwards, V., 39

elites, literacy expectations for, 107

emigration, from United States, 16

employers
and ESL programs, 115

and literacy assessment, 57

empowerment, 146, 195

empowerment approach to bilingualism, 157

encoding/decoding, tests of, 41-42

English
and adult literacy instruction, 182
Appalachian, 131
as language of national assessment, 59
language shift toward, 23
nonstandard, 71, 75, 119
as official language of instruction, 12, 46
as old colonial language, 15
oral, as ESL emphasis, 113
threats to dominance of, 12-14
in West African literacy study, 42

English as a Second Language (ESL) programs, 113
and academic programs, 114-15
and acquisition of oral language, 161-62
and bilingual education, 153
goals and content of, 114-15
stigmatization and, 122

English Language Proficiency Survey, 71

English-only instruction, 19-22, 100

English Only policies, 17-19

eradication of native language, 125

Erickson, F., quoted, 47-49, 51-52

ESL. *See* English as a Second Language (ESL) programs

ethnic diversity, NALS and, 80-81

ethnicity, 84, 88-91

ethnic minorities, educational gains of, 108

ethnographic methods, used by educators, 195

ethnographic studies, 68, 95, 136-44, 181

ethnographic training for teachers, 150

Eurocentrism, 35

F

family literacy programs, 140

federal government, role in immigrant education, 113-14

Ferreiro, E., 130

Fillmore, L. W., 179

Fishman, J. A., quoted, 24

Flores, G., 179

Florida, immigrant students in, 112

foreign language instruction, 121

Freebody, P., quoted, 98

Freire, P., 3, 32

G

Garret, Henry, 60

Gee, J. P., 30, 37, 39, 154
quoted, 44, 73

German, 46

Goddard, H. H., 60-62

Goldman, A., quoted, 117n2

Goodman, K., 179

Goodman, Y., 179

Goody, J., 40

Goody, J. R., 34-36

Graff, H. J., quoted, 101-2

great divide, cognitive, 3, 29
autonomous approach and, 34-38
background of, 34
ideological approach and, 43-45
social practices approach and, 38-43

Greeks, as inventors of logic, 35

Grillo, R. D., 32-33

Guth, J. A., 181

Guthrie, J. T., 72

H

Hakuta, K., 155
  quoted, 19-20, 61, 63, 156

Harman, D., quoted, 74

Havelock, E. A., 34

Heath, S. B., 31, 33, 50-51, 150
  quoted, 51, 135-36, 142-45, 147-49
  Ways with Words, 145

Hill, P. T., quoted, 112-13, 193-94

Hirsch, E. D., 50

Hispanic, use of term, 120

Hispanics. *See* Latinos

Hudson, T., 175

Hunter, C., quoted, 74

I

ideological approach, 32-33, 43-45, 51-52, 138, 141, 143, 196
  applied to social practices studies, 144-47

Illich, I., quoted, 123-24

Illinois, immigrant students in, 112

illiteracy
  concerns about, 1
  as personal failure, 99-100
  as result of socioeconomic problems, 102-3
  as social disease, 1
  social effects of, 52

and stigmatization, 99-100
  U.S. definition of, 65
  use of term, 6n1, 25, 119

illiteracy, English
  as cause of crime and unemployment, 99-100
  perceived causes of, 15-17

immersion programs, 163, 187n5
  dual, 187n6, 197

immigrants, 12
  intelligence tests for, 61-62
  literacy assessment for, 59, 66-67, 82-84
  Mexican, 112-13
  recent, 138-40
  students, 112-14
  See also adults; children; language minorities

immigration, 13-14, 16, 78

immigration policy, 190-93

Immigration Reform and Control Act, 190

immigration restrictionists, 13

incorporation, 148-50

Institute for Social Research, 92

intelligence tests, 57

interaction in schools, 164-65

J

Japanese, 46

Jenkins, L., quoted, 81-85, 101, 114

job competition, 114

Jungeblut, A., 76
quoted, 81-85, 101, 114

K

Kaplan, R. B., et al., quoted, 66

Kirsch, I. S., 72, 76
quoted, 81-85, 101, 114

Klassen, C., 190

Kolstad, A., quoted, 81-85, 101

Kolstad, L., quoted, 114

Krashen, S., 165

L

L1 (first language), 152

L2 (second language), 152

labeling, 119-20, 129, 168-70
bilingualism and, 157-58
educational, 122-23

labor, foreign, importation of, 192-93

Labov, W., 38

Lambert, W. E., 155

language
academic, 36, 170-71

contextualized, 159

decontextualized, 174

equated with literacy, 158

as global cognitive ability, 158

as means of maintaining cultural identity, 129

nonstandard, 36, 123-25

oral vs. written, 130, 173-75

second, reading in, 175

standard, imposition of, 123-25

as status marker, 121-22

language acquisition, psychosocial model of, 155-56

language attitudes of dominant groups, 190

language background, as category for comparison, 84

language choice, 24, 182, 191

language classification, 157-58

language differences, vs. language deficiencies, 169

language diversity, 8, 12, 22, 81, 132

language maintenance, 24

language minorities, 1, 52
attitudes toward dominant language, 24-25
discrimination and, 122
employment prospects for, 106
and English illiteracy, 15-17
English literacy among, 152

and English Only policies, 17-19

"illiteracy" among, 25

literacy crisis and, 98

literacy instruction for, 179-82

patterns of literacy among, 14

and rising literacy standards, 107

and sampling bias in literacy assessment, 79

societal attitudes toward, 189-90

stigmatization of, 100

as students, 50

U.S. definition of, 65

use of term, 6n3

as victims of cultural control, 45-46

language of instruction, 194

choice of, 182, 191

language planning, 22

language proficiency, 125

academic, 173, 183

as basis for classification, 157-58

and cognitive demand, 161-62

and contextual support, 161-62

conversational, 173

determining, 167-68

dimensions of, 164

as gatekeeping mechanism, 173

global, 187n3

levels of, 160

language requirements, 122

language rights, 25

languages, indigenous, 15

language strategies, 178

language styles, 31-32

language suppression, 46

language use, 136, 140

language varieties, 180

Latinos, 105

educational progress of, 108-11

and NALS, 80-81

and restrictive educational policies, 46

and self-reported literacy measures, 71

Leacock, E. B., 39

learning, skill-specific, 41

Leibowitz, A. J., quoted, 46

letter writing, 139

Levine, K., 32, 107

Lewis, Michael, quoted, 99-100

limited-English proficient (LEP), use of term, 122-23

linguicism, 121, 131

literacies

alternative, 45, 184

analogical, 69

and literacy, 29

as social practices, 69

literacy
- and abstract thought, 38
- academic, 162
- acquiring, 135-36
- approaches to, 30-31, 188
- basic, 67
- beliefs about, 2-3
- of children, 51
- cognitive effects of, 29-31, 34, 42-44
- confused with English literacy, 14-15, 25
- as continuum, 76-78
- conventional, 67
- cultural, 50
- defined, 58, 65-66
- development, 49-50
- document, 76
- and economic position, 98-99, 103-6
- elite, 69
- elitist view of, 47
- empowering aspects of, 196
- English, as only literacy worth noting, 14-15, 25, 63, 76, 78
- equated with language, 158
- ethnographic studies of, 136-44
- functional, 67, 72-73, 146
- as goal of bilingual education, 184
- as group resource, 142
- intergenerational transmission of, 138
- and literacies, 29
- minimal, 66-67
- native-language, 3, 14, 26, 79, 113, 139, 191
- non-English, 78-79, 106
- and nonstandard language, 123-25
- *vs.* orality, 34-38, 40-41
- as practice, 32-33
- prior, 82
- prose, 76
- quantitative, 76
- restricted, 68, 138
- rising standards for, 106-8
- and school achievement, 47
- and schooling, 30
- second-language, 14
- significance of, 180
- as social achievement, 33
- social consequences of, 45-49
- social construction of, 32
- and socioeconomic problems, 101-3
- and socioeconomic status, 44
- technicist definition of, 98
- vernacular, 68
- *See also* autonomous approach; ideological approach; social practices approach

literacy assessment, 58-64, 75-76
- approaches to, 69-76
- constructive reasons for, 64-65
- direct measures, 72-75

national measures, 78-80

self-reported measures, 70-71, 75, 105

surrogate measures, 71-72

literacy crisis, 25, 79, 82, 98, 197

perpetual, 100, 115-16

literacy events, 31, 136, 139

in communities, 143

issues of control in, 145-47

literacy expectations, 106-8, 135-36, 143

literacy functions, 136-37, 180

literacy/illiteracy dichotomy, 76-78, 92

literacy instruction

in AAL, 128

adult issues in, 180-82

imposed on society, 51

K-12 issues in, 179-80

as pedagogical skills, 50-51

as skills, 41

literacy network, 142

literacy practices, 32-33, 39-40, 45, 48, 50, 137, 145

of adults, 181

of communities, 136, 142-43

passive, 138

in schools, 135-36, 142-43

and transfer, 176

literacy problems, 33, 197

literacy requirements, 59, 65, 122, 126

literacy stereotypes, 138-40, 143-44

literacy surveys, 2, 57, 80-95

literacy tasks, social contexts of, 48

literate environment, 139

logic, formal, 35

logical reasoning, tests of, 41-42

Luke, A., quoted, 51

Luria, A. R., 38, 45

M

Macías, R. F., 14

quoted, 69, 78-80, 85, 94, 123

mainstream, use of term, 6n4, 143

maintenance bilingual policies, 128

markedness, 133n5

Martin-Jones, M., quoted, 168-69, 172

Martin Luther King Jr. Elementary School Children vs. Ann Arbor Board of Education, 126-27, 148

mass literacy campaigns, nineteenth-century, 101-2

McArthur, T., quoted, 119

McDonnell, L. M., quoted, 112-13, 193-94

media, labeling and, 119-20, 135

memory, 36, 41-42

Mensh, E., quoted, 60

Mensh, H., quoted, 60

metalanguage, 49-50

middle class
  educational advantages of, 187n7
  as teachers, 149

migration, European, 16

Mikulecky, L. J., quoted, 67

Miles, R., quoted, 120

military
  and intelligence testing, 62, 64
  and literacy assessment, 57, 71-72

Miller, C., 190

minorities. *See* language minorities

mismatch, linguistic, 152-53

mobility
  intergenerational, 114
  socioeconomic, 102-3

Monitor Model, 165

monolingualism, English, 7-12, 22-23, 78-80
  ideology of, 25-26

multilingualism, cognitive effects of, 42

N

Nanda, S., quoted, 20

National Adult Literacy Survey (NALS), 80-85, 103-6
  results of, 86-91

National Assessment of Educational Progress, 79

National Chicano Survey (NCS), 17, 85-94, 105-6, 112
  geographic scope of, 96n3

National Commission on Excellence and Education, *A Nation at Risk*, 98

National Literacy Act of 1991, 81

Nation at Risk, A (National Commission on Excellence and Education), 98

Native Americans, 12
  and language suppression, 46
  as non-English speakers, 11

native-language instruction, 12, 113
  and African Americans, 129

native speakers, 2

Natural Approach to English as a second language, 187n4

negotiation skills of bilingual children, 140

New Guinea, study of literacy in, 138

New York, immigrant students in, 112

non-English language back-ground (NELB), use of term, 123

non-English speakers, 10
See also language minorities

nonliteracy, 14

nonliterate, use of term, 119

nonnative speakers, 2, 9
See also language minorities

Norgren, J., quoted, 20

norms
mainstream, 144-47
standardized tests and, 57-58

North Carolina, literacy studies in, 142-43

O

objectivity, 38

Odlin, T., quoted, 176-77

Oller, J., quoted, 159

Olson, D. R., 34-35, 152, 170
quoted, 43, 49-50

Ong, W. J., 34, 36-37, 44
quoted, 36-38

orality *vs.* literacy, 34-38, 40-41, 178

oral language, 145-47
and cognitive demand, 170-71

oral proficiency, 79, 175

P

parents
literacy deficiencies of, 143
as literacy tutors of children, 139
literate, 35, 49

pedagogy, 44-45, 195-96
See also bilingual education theory

Perdue, C., 189

Perkins, K., quoted, 159

Philadelphia, immigrants in, 138-41

Phillipson, R., quoted, 121-22

pidgin, defined, 133n3

Pitt, L., 12

population, U.S., ethnic origins of, 12

poverty and literacy levels, 68, 103-4

practice, use of term, 39-40

practices, biased, 45-49

preliterate, use of term, 119

prestige factor, 47

privilege, surrendering, 149

R

race, 6n2, 84, 88-91

racialization, 120

racial minorities, educational gains of, 108

racism, 121, 145-47
   and intelligence testing, 58-64
   and literacy assessment, 58-59

reading development, 130
   second-language, 175

reductionism, 178

refugee resettlement, 189

religion, 138

reproduction, 149

reproduction theory, 54n3

resistance theory, 54n3

Resnick, D. P., 66, 106-7

Resnick, L. B., 66, 106-7

Romaine, S., quoted, 168-69, 172

Rosen, H., quoted, 145-46

Roy, J. D., quoted, 126

S

Schieffelin, B. B., 137-42
   quoted, 137, 139-40

schismogenesis, 48

school achievement, 47

school culture, 49

school failure, 48-49, 100

schooling, 34, 40-43, 70-71
   and academic language proficiency, 183

alternative approaches to, 184
defective, 45-49
and elite literacy, 69
and employment, 106
lack of, 197
level of, 75
and literacy, 30, 89-91
prior, 84
See also bilingual education; educational policy

school reform, 193-95

schools, 33
   language use in, 140-41
   literacy practices in, 51, 135-36, 142-43
   as only legitimate vehicle for literacy, 124
   and overlooked abilities, 141-42
   and practice of incorporation, 149
   reflection of biases in, 143
      role in maintaining social status quo, 147-50
   as social context, 172-73

Scollon, R., 49

Scollon, S., 49

Scribner, S., 2-3, 30, 33-34, 45, 77-78
   quoted, 31, 38-42, 50, 68

self-assessment, 70-71

semantic integration, tests of, 41-42

semilingualism, 168-70
  double, 156

semiliterate, use of term, 119

separate underlying proficiency (SUP) model, 159

Shapiro, M. J., quoted, 61-62

Shuman, A., quoted, 68, 149

Sienkewicz, T. J., 39

signature, as literacy measure, 70

Simon, Senator Paul, 26
  quoted, 8

simulation, and direct measures of literacy, 73

skepticism, 35

skills, use of term, 39-40

Skutnabb-Kangas, T., quoted, 157

social class, 95, 123

social control, 52, 148
  academic language and, 123

social practices, and cognitive demand, 172

social practices approach, 31-33, 38-40, 135-44
  ideological critique of, 144-47

social stratification, 47, 147-50
  literacy levels and, 102

socioeconomic problems, 101-3

socioeconomic status, 44

sociolinguistics, 131-32

South Carolina, literacy studies in, 142-43

Spain, imposition of literacy in, 123-24

Spanish, 8, 17-18, 46, 79, 130-31

speech, 35-37

Spener, D., quoted, 190-92

Spolsky, B., 171

Spring, J., quoted, 20

standardized tests, 47
  and determination of language proficiency, 167-68

standards, national, 184

Stanford-Binet intelligence test, 60-61

status ascription, 121-22, 157-58

stigmatization
  illiteracy and, 99-100
  of nonnative speakers, 189

Street, B. V., 30, 39, 102, 154
  quoted, 32, 44-45

Street, J. C., quoted, 44-45

students, as ethnographers, 150

Study in American Intelligence, A (Brigham), 63

subject matter instruction, as skills, 41

T

Tannen, D., 31-32, 173-75
  quoted, 174-75

Taylor, D. M., quoted, 141-42

teachers
  and language study, 131-32
  and language use, 140
  as learners, 150
  and literacy practices of students, 148
  role in incorporation, 149
  See also pedagogy

Teberosky, A., 130

Terman, Lewis, 60-62

test data, inauthentic, 167-68

tests, 74
  See also intelligence tests; standardized tests

test-wiseness, 170

Texas, immigrant students in, 112

Thorndike, Edward, 60

threshold, 159, 164, 167, 175-77

time, historical *vs.* mythic, 35

Tollefson, J., 30

transfer, 159, 175-77, 183

trilingualism, 176

Troike, R. C., quoted, 171-72

U

underachievement, 46, 99-100

underclass, growth of, 114

unionism, 102-3

United States
  and English monolingualism, 8-12
  language suppression in, 46

urbanization, cognitive effects of, 42

U.S. Census, 2, 59, 70-71, 79, 112
  1990 data, 8-12
  terminology used by, 119-20

U.S. Department of Education, 80

U.S. Immigration Commission, 12

V

Vai, the, 39-43, 68, 77-78

Valadez, C. M., 3, 179
  quoted, 180

Vargas, A., quoted, 101

variation, within-group, 84

Veltman, F., quoted, 23

verbal explanation, tests of, 41-42

Voting Rights Act of 1965, 65

Vygotsky, L. S., 45

W

Wald, B., 171
  quoted, 178
Washington Post, 82-83
Wasserman, F., quoted, 61-62
Watt, I., 34-36
Ways with Words (Heath), 145
Weinberg, M., 45-46, 121, 133n2
  quoted, 20-21, 46, 60-61, 63-64
Weinstein-Shr, G., quoted, 141
Welch, A. R., quoted, 98
Wells, G., 140
West Africa, literacy in, 39-43, 68, 77-78
Whites, 120
  educational advantages of, 107-8
  and educational disincentives, 114
  literacy advantages of, 141-43, 148
  NALS and, 85
  and rising literacy standards, 107
  as teachers, 149

Wiley, T. G., quoted, 115
Williams, S. W., 128-29
Wolfram, W., 131
  quoted, 74-75, 128-30
work force, literacy levels of, 101
working class, and mainstream norms, 144-47
Wright, E., 38, 148
Wrigley, H. S., 181
writing, 34-37, 179
Wyman, M., 15

X

xenophobia, 58-64

Y

Young Adult Literacy Survey, 80
youth
  African American, 193
  language-majority, 193-95
  Latino, 193
  literacy levels of, 86-87

Note: References to footnotes appear in the index as shown in the following example:

187n7 (refers to page 187, note 7)

Language in Education: Theory and Practice

The Educational Resources Information Center (ERIC), which is supported by the Office of Educational Research and Improvement of the U.S. Department of Education, is a nationwide system of information centers, each responsible for a given educational level or field of study. ERIC's basic objective is to make developments in educational research, instruction, and teacher training readily accessible to educators and members of related professions.

The ERIC Clearinghouse on Languages and Linguistics (ERIC/CLL), one of the specialized information centers in the ERIC system, is operated by the Center for Applied Linguistics (CAL) and is specifically responsible for the collection and dissemination of information on research in languages and linguistics and on the application of research to language teaching and learning.

In 1989, CAL was awarded a contract to expand the activities of ERIC/CLL through the establishment of an adjunct ERIC clearinghouse, the National Clearinghouse for ESL Literacy Education (NCLE). NCLE's specific focus is literacy education for language minority adults and out-of-school youth.

ERIC/CLL and NCLE commission recognized authorities in languages, linguistics, adult literacy education, and English as a second language (ESL) to write about current issues in these fields. Monographs, intended for educators, researchers, and others interested in language education, are published under the series title, Language in Education: Theory and Practice (LIE). The *LIE* series includes practical guides for teachers, state-of-the-art papers, research reviews, and collected reports.

For further information on the ERIC system, ERIC/CLL, or NCLE, contact either clearinghouse at the Center for Applied Linguistics, 1118 22nd Street, NW, Washington, DC 20037.Internet e-mail: ncle@cal.org.

Joy Kreeft Peyton, Fran Keenan, Series Editors
Vickie Lewelling, ERIC/CLL Publications Coordinator
Miriam J. Burt, NCLE Publications Coordinator

Other *LIE* Titles Available from Delta Systems

The following are other titles in the *Language in Education* series published by the Center for Applied Linguistics and Delta Systems Co., Inc.:

Adult Biliteracy in the United States (ISBN 0-937354-83-X)
edited by David Spener

Approaches to Adult ESL Literacy Instruction
(ISBN 0-937354-82-1)
edited by JoAnn Crandall and Joy Kreeft Peyton

Assessing Success in Family Literacy Projects: Alternative Approaches to Assessment and Evaluation
(ISBN 0-93-7354-85-6)
edited by Daniel D. Holt

Immigrant Learners and Their Families: Literacy to Connect the Generations (ISBN 0-937354-84-8)
edited by Gail Weinstein-Shr and Elizabeth Quintero

Making Meaning, Making Change: Participatory Curriculum Development for Adult ESL Literacy (ISBN 0-937354-79-1)
by Elsa Roberts Auerbach

Talking Shop: A Curriculum Sourcebook for Participatory Adult ESL (ISBN 0-937354-78-3)
by Andrea Nash, Ann Cason, Madeline Rhum, Loren McGrail, and Rosario Gomez-Sanford

Writing Our Lives: Reflections on Dialogue Journal Writing with Adults Learning English(ISBN 0-937354-71-6)
edited by Joy Kreeft Peyton and Jana Staton

To order any of these titles, call Delta Systems, Co., Inc. at (800) 323-8270 or (815) 363-3582 (9-5 EST) or write to them at 1400 Miller Pkwy., McHenry, Illinois 60050 (USA).